DATA STRUCTURES AND ALGORITHMS

Shubham Gupta

Toronto Academic Press

Data Structures and Algorithms

Shubham Gupta

Toronto Academic Press
224 Shoreacres Road
Burlington, ON L7L 2H2
Canada
www.tap-books.com
Email: orders@arclereducation.com

ISBN: 978-1-77469-766-5

ABOUT THE AUTHOR

Shubham Gupta is a highly skilled software engineer with over seven years of experience in the field. He holds a Master's degree in Software Engineering from KIET Group of Institutes, where he gained a deep understanding of software development methodologies and best practices. Throughout his career, Shubham has worked with a variety of clients, from small startups to large corporations. He is dedicated to delivering high-quality software solutions that meet the unique needs of his clients and help them achieve their business goals. Shubham is well-versed in a wide range of programming languages, frameworks, and technologies. He has a particular expertise in web development, and has worked on numerous projects involving the development of web-based applications and services. In addition to his technical skills, Shubham is also a strong communicator and team player. He enjoys collaborating with other professionals to develop solutions that are both technically sound and user-friendly. Shubham is passionate about his work and is always looking for ways to improve his skills and stay up-to-date with the latest industry trends and technologies. His commitment to excellence has earned him a reputation as a trusted and reliable software engineer.

Contents

3 Analysis of Arrays and Sets 53

4 Algorithm Selection 75

5 Stacks and Queues 91

6 Trees 133

List of Figures

List of Tables

List of Abbreviations

B2C	Business-to-Consumer
CSR	Corporate Social Responsibility
DRM	Digital Rights Management
EU	European Union
FIFO	First In, First Out
FQ-tree	Fixed Query tree
GUIs	Graphical User Interfaces
ISP	Internet Service Provider
LIFO	Last-in-First-Out
NP	Nondeterministic Polynomial Time
OOP	Object-Oriented Programming
PETs	Privacy-Enhancing Technologies
RAM	Random-Access Machine
VPNs	Virtual Private Networks

PREFACE

Data structures are specialized formats for organizing, storing, and manipulating data in computer programs. There are several types of data structures, including arrays, linked lists, stacks, queues, and trees. Algorithms are a set of instructions or procedures that are designed to solve a specific computation problem.

In today's fast-paced digital age, efficient data management is more critical than ever before. As the amount of data being generated and processed increases exponentially, the need for powerful algorithms and data structures becomes increasingly pressing. Data structures and algorithms are important concepts in computer science, and their understanding is crucial for building efficient and scalable software systems. A good understanding of data structures and algorithms can help software developers to design efficient programs, optimize code performance and solve complex computational problems.

The discussion of the book starts with the fundamentals of data structures and algorithms, followed by the classification of algorithms used in data structures. Also, the concept of arrays and sets used in data structures and the selection of algorithms are described in detail in this book. The fundamental concept of two very important data structures, stacks, and queues, is also explained in detail. Another important data structure known as a tree, which consists of nodes connected by edges, is described in the book. The fundamental search algorithms that are used to locate an element within the structure are also part of this book. Lastly, the governance of algorithms and limitations of governance options are described in detail at the end of this book.

This book comprises eight chapters; the first chapter discusses the fundamentals of data structures and algorithms with emphasis on the need for data structures, issues addressed by algorithms, and the benefits and drawbacks of data structures. The second chapter deals with the classification of algorithms and provides insight into the differences between them.

The third chapter is about the analysis of two important data structures, arrays, and sets, and describes the temporal complexity of various arrays and set operations. The fourth chapter discusses the process or flows for the selection of a suitable algorithm.

The fifth chapter describes the concept of stacks and queues in data structures, along with the implementation of these concepts using arrays and linked lists. The sixth chapter deals with the concepts of trees, basic binary operations, and the efficiency of binary trees. The seventh chapter is about search algorithms that are used in the data structure to find an element inside the structure, and the eighth chapter is about the governance of algorithms and the limitations of governance options.

This book has been written specifically for students and scholars to meet their needs in terms of knowledge and to provide them with a broad understanding of data structures and algorithms. We aim for this book to be a resource for academics in many subjects since we believe it will provide clarity and insight for its readers.

—Author

CHAPTER 1

FUNDAMENTALS OF DATA STRUCTURES AND ALGORITHMS

UNIT INTRODUCTION

An algorithm is a well-described computational process that accepts every value, or set of values, as input and outputs any value or set of values. As a result, an algorithm is a set of computing procedures that changes any input into an output. A further way to think about an algorithm is as a tool for solving a well-defined computing issue (Aggarwal & Vitter, 1988; Agrawal et al., 2004). Generally, the issue description presupposes the intended relationship between outputs and inputs, but the algorithm specifies a specific computing procedure for attaining that relationship.

Sorting is considered a basic step in computer science since it is helpful as an intermediary step in many applications. As a result, access to a huge variety of effective sorting algorithms is available (Ahuja & Orlin, 1989; Ahuja et al., 1989). The best algorithm for any specific application is determined by various factors, including the different items to be organized, the degree whereby the items are slightly organized, the computer architecture, potential item value limitations, and the kind of storage devices to be utilized: disks, main memory, or tapes.

When an algorithm halts with the appropriate output for each input example, it is thought to be appropriate. A proper algorithm solves the stated computing issue. An erroneous algorithm, on either side, cannot halt at all on certain input examples, or it can halt with an inaccurate response (Ahuja et al., 1989; Courcoubetis et al., 1992). In contrast to assumptions, erroneous algorithms may occasionally be advantageous if the rate of mistake may be controlled. Therefore, only accurate algorithms will be of concern (Szymanski & Van Wyk, 1983; King, 1995; Didier, 2009) (Figure 1.1).

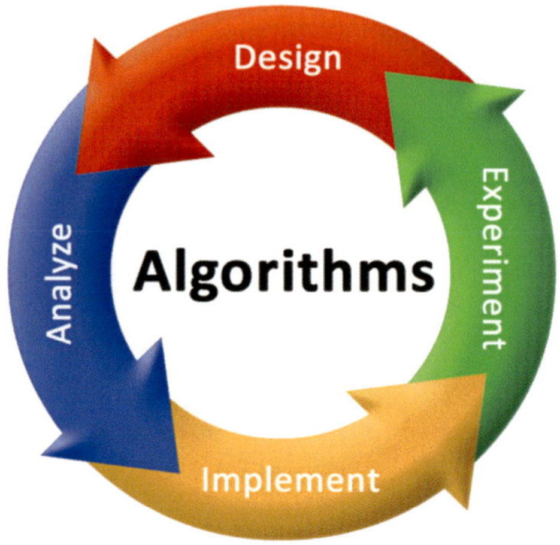

Figure 1.1. Illustration of algorithms' basic structure and overview (Source: Tim Roughgarden, Creative Commons License).

An algorithm may be written in English, in the format of a computer program, or even as a hardware design. The only criterion is that the problem definition must include a clear description of the computational procedure to be used (Snyder, 1984). The following are the features of an algorithm:

- Each instruction should take an indefinite amount of time to complete.
- Almost every instruction should be explicit and accurate, that is, each instruction must have just one meaning.
- The consumer must get the expected outcomes after following the directions.
- There must be no unlimited repeating of a single or several instructions, implying that the algorithm must eventually finish.

Did you Know?

The origins of algorithms can be traced back to ancient Babylonians, who used mathematical algorithms to solve problems related to commerce, trade and taxation.

Data structure is how data is organized in a computer's memory. (or sometimes on a disk). Data structures include hash tables, binary trees, linked lists, and stacks. Structures' data are manipulated by algorithms in a variety of ways, for as, by adding new data items, looking for certain items, and sorting the items. An algorithm is similar to a recipe in that it contains a thorough set of directions for performing a task.

What kinds of issues can be resolved with this knowledge? Roughly categorize the instances in which they are helpful into three categories:

- Storage of real-world data
- Tools for programmers
- Modeling

The structure of data is a methodical strategy to arrange data so that it can be used effectively. Fundamental terms of the data structure are as follows.

Interface: Each data structure has a respective interface. An interface shows the set of operations a data structure can perform, and the data structure is capable of performing. An interface specifies the supported operations, parameter types, and return types for each supported operation.

Implementation: The implementation provides the inner representation of a data structure. The implementation also describes the algorithms used for the data structure operations.

Learning Objectives

Readers will have the chance to understand the following by the chapter's conclusion:

- Understand the fundamental concepts of data structures and algorithms.
- Learn about the issues solved by algorithms and the need for data structures.
- Advantages and disadvantages of different data structures.
- Learn about analyzing algorithms and data structures

Key Terms

1. Algorithms
2. Array
3. Data structures
4. Data Item
5. Entity
6. Field
7. File
8. Group Item
9. Linked list
10. Queues
11. Stacks
12. Trees

1.1. ISSUES SOLVED BY ALGORITHMS

KEYWORD

Database is an organized collection of structured information, or data, typically stored electronically in a computer system.

Scientists have developed algorithms for a variety of computer problems, including sorting. Algorithms have a broad range of practical usage across the world. The following are certain such instances:

i. The Human Genome Project are made tremendous progress in recent years toward the goal of classifying all one hundred thousand genes found in the DNA of humans, specifying the sequences of the 3 billion chemical base pairs that make up human DNA, storing this massive amount of information in databases, and developing data analysis techniques. Each procedure necessitates the use of complex algorithms. Several strategies for solving such biological challenges use various principles, allowing scientists to complete jobs while maximizing resource use (Aki, 1989; Akra & Bazzi, 1998). We may obtain more data from laboratory procedures, which saves us time, both machine and human, and money (Regli, 1992; Ajtai et al., 2001).

ii. The Internet allows individuals worldwide to swiftly access and recover vast amounts of data. Various websites on the Internet handle and utilize this massive amount of data with the help of intelligent algorithms. Identifying effective paths for data to go and utilizing a search engine that may rapidly identify sites with our exact necessary information are two instances of challenges that fundamentally make utilization of various algorithms (Alon, 1990).

iii. It allows to negotiate and electronically trade services and things, which is a major advantage of electronic commerce. It is reliant upon the confidentiality of personal data such as details of credit card, keywords, and statements of bank to function properly. Public-key cryptography and digital signs are two of the essential technologies which are used in electronic commerce, and they are both important. Numerical algorithms and numeral theory are the foundations of such technologies (Andersson & Thorup, 2000; Bakker et al., 2012).

iv. Manufacturing and a variety of other commercial activities occasionally demand the allocation of scarce sources in the most advantageous manner. For example, an oil firm would want to determine where it must locate its wells to maximize the amount of profit it expects to make. Assigning crews to flights in the most cost-effective way feasible while ensuring that every trip is covered and that all applicable government laws regarding the scheduling of the crew are met is something an airline would aspire to do (Ramadge & Wonham, 1989; Amir et al., 2006). Certain political candidates may be faced with the decision of where to spend their money when purchasing campaign advertising to increase their chances of winning the election. An ISP (internet service provider) may be interested in knowing where they might put extra resources to better satisfy their customers' needs. All of the issues are instances of problems that may be handled by applying linear programming techniques (Dengiz et al., 1997; Berger & Barkaoui, 2004) (Figure 1.2).

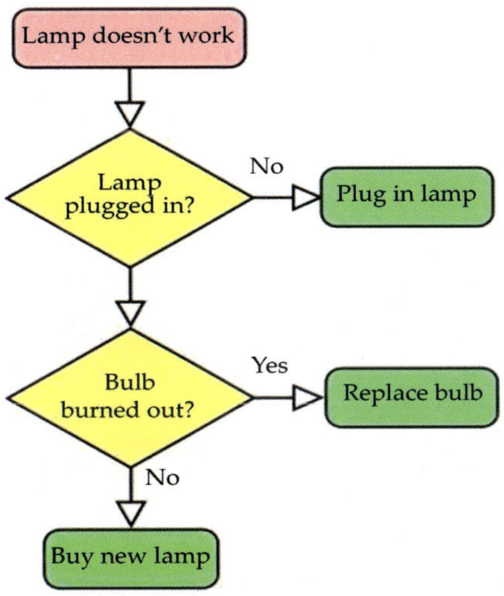

Figure 1.2. Flowchart of algorithm application (Source: JT Newsome, Creative Commons.

The basic approaches that imply to such difficulties and problem regions will be discussed. We'll look at ways to tackle a variety of specific issues, such as the ones listed below:

i. Assume there exists a detailed plan with the distance among each set of two intersections noted, and the quickest path from one intersection to the next needs to be discovered. Even if we ban routes from crossing over themselves, there might be a tremendous number of viable paths (Festa & Resende, 2002; Zhu & Wilhelm, 2006). How do you pick the fastest of all the available paths in this scenario? In this case, the plan will be described as a graph and then seek the shortest path between the graph's vertex points.

ii. Suppose that there are two systematic orders of symbols,

$X = (x_1, x_2 \ldots, x_m)$ and $Y = (y_1, y_2, \ldots, y_n)$ as well as the largest communal subsequence of Y and X is to be discovered. A subsequence of X would comprise X minus with some (or all) of its components removed. One subsequence of (A, B, C, D, E, F, G, H, I) is, for example (B, C, E, G). The length of shared subsequence of X and Y determines the degree of similarity between the two sequences. For instance, if the two orders under consideration are basic pairs in the strands of DNA, they can be choosen to consider the same because a lengthy ordinary subsequence is shared. If X has m symbols and Y has n symbols, then there are 2^m and 2^n possible subsequences for X and Y, correspondingly. Unless both m and n are very tiny, choosing all probable subsequences of X and Y and then by matching it can take an excessive amount of time (Wallace et al., 2004; Wang, 2008).

KEYWORD

Exponential function is a mathematical function used to calculate the exponential growth or decay of a given set of data.

iii. We are presented with a mechanical design for a library of components. Every component may include examples of other components, and we are obligated to mention the components in the order in which they are used so that every component appears before any other component that includes that component (Maurer, 1985; Smith, 1986). Assuming that the design has n pieces, then there would be nS alternative ordering, where the number nS represents the factorial function of the design. Since the factorial function increases more quickly as compared to an exponential function, this is not viable for us to produce every potential order and afterwards carry out its validation inside that order in such a way that every component comes before the components that are utilizing it. A problem of this nature is an example of topological sorting (Herr, 1980; Stock & Watson, 2001).

iv. In this case, let us suppose we have been given n points in the plane, and we want to discover the convex hull of such points, which is the small convex polygon encompassing the points in the plane. Immediately, we may believe of every point as being distinguished by the presence of a nail penetrating through a piece of cardboard. The convex hull will be indicated through a tight rubber band that surrounds all of the nails at this point. In the convex hull, every nail about which the rubber band makes a turn is represented by one of its vertices. As a result, every of the 2n subsets of the points may be used as the vertices of the convex hull. Knowing the points that are vertices of the convex hull is not sufficient in this case; we also require to be familiar with the sequence in which they occur on the convex hull. Because of this, a variety of options for the convex hull vertices are accessible to the user (Price, 1973; Berry & Howls, 2012).

These lists have two characteristics with a wide range of exciting algorithmic problems:

i. They have many potential solutions, a large percentage of which fail to fix the problem. Identifying the "best" solution or the one that addresses the problem might be difficult (Arora, 1994).
ii. The majority of them have real-world applicability. Finding the shortest route was the simplest of the issues described above. Any transport organization, including a shipping company or a railroad, has a financial incentive to locate the shortest route via a road or a rail network because shorter routes result in cheaper labor and fuel costs (Bellare & Sudan, 1994; Friedl & Sudan, 1995). A routing node on the Internet, for example, could want to find the quickest way by the network so that a message can be routed quickly. Alternatively, someone going from Washington to Chicago may choose to get driving directions from a reliable website or use his or her GPS while driving (Sudan, 1992; Arora & Lund, 1996).
iii. It isn't required for every issue to be addressed by algorithms because a collection of contender solutions may be easily discovered. Consider the case when we are given a set of numerical figures that show signal specimens. We'd want to calculate the discrete DFT of such data right now (Fredman & Willard, 1993; Raman, 1996). The DFT translates the domain of time into the domain of frequency by creating a set of numeric coefficients, allowing us to specify the intensity of distinct frequencies in the sampled signal. Apart from being at the heart of signal processing, DFT has extensive applications in the compression of data, and multiplication of huge integers and polynomials (Polishchuk & Spielman, 1994; Thorup, 1997).

KEYWORD

Algorithm is a procedure used for solving a problem or performing a computation.

1.2. DATA STRUCTURES

A data structure is a method of storing and arranging information to make it easier to modify and access. No one data structure generally works fine for all applications, therefore it's significant to understand the benefits and drawbacks of some of them (Brodnik et al., 1997). The following are the features of data structures:

i. **Correctness:** A data structure must implement its interface correctly.
ii. **Time Complexity**: The execution of data structure operations must be as brief as possible.
iii. **Space Complexity:** A data structure action should use the least memory available.

Did you Know?

The concept of data structures can be traced back to the 1940s, when John von Neumann introduced the concept of a stored program computer.

1.2.1. Data Structure's Need

As applications become increasingly complex and data-rich, they frequently encounter three problems.

i. Consider a store's inventory that contains 1 million (10^6) items. The application has to browse over 1 million (10^6) items each time an item has to be searched, thus slowing the process of searching. As the data amount increases, the search will get slower.
ii. Processor Speed −Although the CPU can handle billions of data records, its speed is restricted.
iii. Multiple Requests − Due to numerous data queries of tens of thousands of users on a web server, even a speedy server will occasionally fail.

Data structures come to the rescue to address the issues mentioned above. Searching through every item in the data structure may not be necessary because the necessary data can be found fairly immediately.

1.2.2. Execution Time Cases

Three scenarios are typically used to compare the relative execution times of different data structures.

i. Worst Case − A data structure action uses all its available processing power. An operation requires no more compared to (n) time if the worst-case duration is (n), in which (n) is a function of n.
ii. Average Case: This illustrates how long the data structure operation usually takes. If an operation requires n seconds to complete, then m operations will require mxn seconds.

iii. Best Case: This is when an operation on a data structure is executed quickly. When an operation takes n seconds to complete, the total time required for the procedure could be as high as n(n).

1.2.3. Basic Terminologies

Following are definition of some of the terminologies used in data structures:

- **Data:** Data is a value and collection of values.
- **Data Item:** "data item" refers to a distinct element of values.
- **Group Items:** The data object is broken down into smaller things.
- **Elementary Items:** Non-splitable data elements are elementary objects.
- **Entity & Attribute:** Entity has specific properties or characteristics that can have values applied to them.
- **Entity Set:** An entity set comprises entities with related attributes.
- **Field:** A single basic informational unit that represents a property of an entity.
- **Record:** A record groups a particular entity's field values.
- **File:** A file is a collection of documents for entities in a particular entity set.

KEYWORD

Data structure is a specialized format for organizing, processing, retrieving and storing data.

1.2.4. Overview of Data Structures

Considering data structures in terms of their advantages and disadvantages is another perspective. The key data storage structures covered are summarized in Table 1.1. This is a birds-eye perspective of a terrain that will be explored later from the ground. The benefits and drawbacks of all of the data structures discussed in this book are shown in Table 1.1.

Table 1.1. Benefits and drawbacks of different data structures (Source: Robert Lafore, Creative Commons License)

Data Structure	Advantages	Disadvantages
Array	Quick insertion and access if the index is known.	Slow deletion, slow search, and fixed size.

Ordered array	Quicker than an unsorted array for searching.	Fixed-size, slow deletion, an insertion.
Stack	Access is last-in, first-out.	Accessing other objects slowly.
Queue	Gives access on a first-in, first-out basis.	Accessing other objects slowly.
Linked list	Quick addition and deletion.	Search slowly.
Binary tree	Quick insertion, search, and deletion (if the tree remains balanced).	Complex deletion algorithm.
Hash table	Fast access if the key is known. Speedy insertion.	Slow deletion, sluggish access if the key is unknown, and inefficient memory consumption.
Heap	Access to the largest item and quick insertion and deletion.	Accessing other objects slowly.

1.2.5. Hard Problems

Talking when it comes to efficient algorithms, the most commonly used metric for efficiency is speed, which is defined as the amount of time it takes for an algorithm to output its consequence. Furthermore, there have been a few situations for which there is ineffective solution at any given point in time. It is considered worthwhile to study problems with NP (nondeterministic polynomial time) solutions for two main reasons (Phillips & Westbrook, 1993; Ciurea & Ciupala, 2001). Firstly, even if there has not yet been discovered an efficient algorithm for an NP-complete issue, no single individual has ever demonstrated that an efficient algorithm for this problem can't be discovered. Nobody knows whether or whether not there are any effective algorithms available for NP-complete problems, which is a true statement. As a second point, there is an interesting feature of a collection of NP-complete problems in that if an efficient algorithm emerges for any one of them, then such an effective algorithm would exist for all of them as well (Cheriyan & Hagerup, 1989; 1995). Because of the link among NP-complete issues and the absence of effective solutions, the lack of effective solutions becomes even more frustrating. Third, multiple NP-complete problems are comparable to each other, but they are not similar to the issues for which we already have effective algorithms. Computer professionals are fascinated by the fact that a slight modification in the issue description may result in a significant difference in the competency of the most well-known algorithm in the world (Cheriyan et al., 1990; 1996). It is important to be conversant with NP-complete issues since certain of them emerge unexpectedly frequently in real-world applications. Given

KEYWORD

Non-deterministic polynomial time (NP) is actually a marker used to point to a set of problems and bounds of the capability of certain types of computing.

the fact that you have been tasked with developing an effective algorithm for any NP-complete issue, it is likely that you would waste a significant amount of time in a unproductive pursuit. If on either side, you may demonstrate that the issue is NP-complete, you may devote your attention instead to inventing an proficient algorithm that delivers a decent, but the inefficient solution (Leighton, 1996; Roura, 2001; Drmota & Szpankowski, 2013).

Consider the case of a delivery company with a main depot, which is already in existence. Throughout the day, its delivery vehicles are loaded at the depot and then dispatched to different locations to deliver items to customers. Every truck is expected to return to the depot before the end of the day so that it may be prepared for loading the following day's loads (Bentley et al., 1980; Chan, 2000; Yap, 2011). Specifically, the corporation desires to pick a series of delivery stops that results in the shortest total distance traveled by every vehicle to reduce prices. In this issue, which is known as the "traveling-salesman problem," the NP-completeness of the solution has been established. It doesn't have a fast algorithm to work with. Furthermore, given some specific assumptions, we may identify effective algorithms that provide an average distance that is not more than the shortest feasible distance (Shen & Marston, 1995; Verma, 1997).

KEYWORD

Traveling salesman problem (TSP) is an algorithmic problem tasked with finding the shortest route between a set of points and locations that must be visited.

1.2.6. Parallelism

Over many years, we had been able to depend upon the speed of processor clock increasing at a consistent pace. Even though physical restrictions provide an eventual impediment to ever-increasing clock speeds, the following is true: as with the clock's speed, power density increases super-linearly; as a result, chips are at risk of melting once their clock speeds reach a certain threshold (Meijer & Akl, 1987, 1988). We build circuits with many processing cores to conduct more computations per second and so achieve higher throughput. Such multicore computers may be compared to a large number of sequential computers on a single chip, or we may refer to them as a form of "parallel computer," depending upon your perspective. To get the maximum potential performance out of multicore machines, we should design algorithms with parallelism in mind while developing them. Algorithms that use several cores, like "multithreaded" algorithms, are particularly advantageous. From a theoretical standpoint, this sort of model has significant advantages, and as a result, it serves as the foundation for a large number of successful computer systems (Wilf, 1984).

1.3. ALGORITHMS LIKE A TECHNOLOGY

Assume that computers had been significantly faster than they were now and their memory had been completely free. May you imagine every other cause to be interested in algorithms at this point? We will still like to explain that our solution ends and does so with a accurate result, therefore the answer remains affirmative. Given the high speed with which computers operate, any exact approach of problem-solving would be rendered ineffective (Igarashi et al., 1987; Park & Oldfield, 1993). You most likely will want your software execution to fall inside the limits of good software engineering practice (for instance, your execution must be well recorded and well designed), although, you are more than likely going to use whatever method is the quickest and most straightforward to put into action (Glasser & Austin Barron, 1983).

KEYWORD

Software engineering is an engineering-based approach to software development.

Computers can be extremely fast, but they are not capable of becoming indefinitely fast. Similar to that, while their memory can be cheap, it's not completely free. Time for computation is, thus, a finite source, just as memory is a finite resource. It is important to make effective use of such resources, and algorithms that are effective in terms of space or time may assist us in doing so (Wilson, 1991; Buchbinder et al., 2010).

Efficiencies of different algorithms that are created for the solution of the same issue frequently differ significantly in terms of their effectiveness. When compared to the variations resulting from hardware and software, such changes might be far more noticeable (Vanderbei, 1980; Babaioff et al., 2007; Bateni et al., 2010).

For greater understanding, consider two alternate sorting methods. The 1st is known as insertion sort, and it takes about equivalent to c_1n^2 to sort n items; where c_1 is a constant that is independent of n; this implies that it takes roughly proportionate to n^2. The 2nd technique is known as merge sort, and it takes roughly the same amount of time as $c_2n\lg n$, wherein lgn represents $\log_2 n$ and c_2 is another constant that is independent of n. Insertion sort often is a small constant variable as compared to merge sort, like c_1 is smaller than c_2. We'll see that constant variables have a far less influence on the running duration than the reliance upon the input size n (Aslam, 2001; Du & Atallah, 2001; Eppstein et al., 2005). If we represent the running time of insertion sort as c1n n and the running time of the merge sort algorithm as $c_2n\lg n$, we can see that although insertion sort has a factor of n in its running time, merge sort has a factor of lgn, which is significantly less. Even though insertion sort is normally quicker than merge sort for smaller input sizes, once the size of input n grows large enough, merge sort's benefit of lgn versus n would greater than compensate for the dissimilarity in constant variables. There would always be a crossover point outside of which merge sort is quicker, irrespective of how much smaller c_1 is relative to c_2 (Sardelis &Valahas, 1999; Dickerson et al., 2003).

Did you Know?

The world's first computer algorithm was written by Ada Lovelace, a mathematician and computer programmer who is widely regarded as the world's first computer programmer.

Consider the following scenario: a faster computer (designated as computer A) is conducting insertion sort besides a slower computer (designated as computer B) that is doing merge sort. Every one of them should sort a ten-million-number array that has been given to them. (Although ten million digits can sound high, given that the numbers are 8-byte integers, the input would only take up around eighty megabytes, which is more than enough space for even a low-cost laptop computer's memory to be filled several times over.) Take, for example, the assumption that computer A is capable of processing ten billion instructions for one second, while computer B is capable of processing just ten million instructions per second; this makes computer A one thousand times more powerful than computer B in terms of raw computing capacity (Goodrich et al., 2005). Let us assume that the world's most cunning programmer writes insertion sort for computer A in machine language, and the resultant code needs $2n^2$ instructions to arrange n integers, to emphasize the drastic difference. Furthermore, consider the following scenario: an average programmer applies merge sort by utilizing a higher-level language and an ineffective compiler, and the resultant code requires 50nlgn instructions. Thus, computer A would require the following resources to sort ten million numbers:

$$\frac{2\cdot(10^7)^2 \text{ instructions}}{10^{10} \text{ instructions / se cond}} = 20{,}000 \text{ sec onds (more than 5.5 hours)}$$

On the other hand, computer B would take:

$$\frac{50\cdot 10^7 \lg 10^7 \text{ instructions}}{10^7 \text{ instructions / se cond}} \approx 1163 \text{ sec onds (less than 20 min utes)}$$

Yet with a poor compiler, computer B would be greater than seventeenth times quicker than computer Through utilizing an algorithm that running time increases more gradually. When sorting one hundred million values, the benefit of merge sort becomes even more apparent: insertion sort would take more than twenty-three days, but merge sort would take less than 4 hours. Generally, the relative advantage of merge sorting decreases as the size of the problem grows (Eppstein et al., 2008; Acar, 2009).

1.4. ALGORITHMS AND OTHER TECHNOLOGIES

The preceding case demonstrates that algorithms, such as the hardware of computer, must be considered technology. The system's overall performance is determined by both the use of effective algorithms and the use of fast hardware. Algorithms are making fast development in the same way that other computer technologies are (Amtoft et al., 2002; Ausiello et al., 2012). You could wonder if algorithms are genuinely that is significant on modern computers when other sophisticated technologies are taken into account, such as:

i. Intuitive, simple graphical user interfaces (GUIs),
ii. Advanced computer architectures and production technologies,
iii. Object-oriented systems and object-oriented programming,
iv. Wireless and wired networking that is quick,
v. Web technologies which are integrated.

Yes, it is correct. Although some programs (such as simple web-based apps) may not need algorithmic content at the utilization level, many others do. Suppose a web-based service that explains how to go from one area to another (Szymanski, 1975; Aslam, 2001). Such service's implementation will be reliant on a graphical user interface, wide-area networking, fast hardware, and, most likely, object orientation. However, algorithms will be required for specific activities like identifying routes (most likely utilizing a shortest-path method), interpolating addresses, and displaying maps (Bach, 1990; Avidan & Shamir, 2007).

Furthermore, even an application that doesn't need algorithmic data at the application level is heavily reliant on algorithms. Because the application requires fast hardware and the design hardware utilize algorithms. Moreover, the program makes utilize graphical user interfaces, which are created using algorithms (Winograd, 1970; Bach & Shallit, 1996). Furthermore, the application might depend on networking, and routing in networks is mostly based on algorithms. If the program is written in a language apart from machine language, it should be processed through a compiler, assembler, or interpreter, each of which employs a variety of algorithms. As a result, we may determine that algorithms are at

KEYWORD

Graphical user interface is a form of user interface that allows users to interact with electronic devices through graphical icons and audio indicator such as primary notation, instead of text-based UIs, typed command labels or text navigation.

the heart of nearly all computer technology today (Bailey et al., 1991; Baswana et al., 2002).

Furthermore, with computers' ever-increasing capabilities, we are using them to solve more complicated issues than ever before. As may be observed from the comparison of insertion sort and merge sort, the variations in performance among algorithms become more noticeable in the bigger problem (Bayer, 1972; Arge, 2001; Graefe, 2011). One identifying characteristic that distinguishes professional programmers from newbies is having a firm foundation of algorithmic knowledge and technique. Since we may do a few things with the aid of contemporary computer technologies without knowing anything about algorithms, we may accomplish a lot more with a solid understanding of algorithms (Blasgen et al., 1977).

KEYWORD

Computation time is the length of time required to perform a computational process.

1.5. ANALYZING DATA STRUCTURES AND ALGORITHMS

We must forecast the resources required by an algorithm during evaluating it. We are often concerned with sources like computer hardware or communication bandwidth, memory, because most of the time, we want to quantify computational time (Frigo et al., 1998; Blumofe & Leiserson, 1999). Identifying the most effective contestant algorithm for a topic is usually done by analyzing multiple contestant algorithms. This form of assessment may reveal more than one feasible candidate; although, we may typically eliminate weaker algorithms throughout the process (Blelloch & Gibbons, 2004).

We need to have an implementation technology model in place before we may perform an algorithm analysis. This model should take into account the technology's resources and its costs. Regarding the implementation technique, we'll use a generic one-processor or the random-access machine (RAM) model of computing. Furthermore, our algorithms would be implemented as computer programs. Every instruction in the RAM model is performed once a time, with no concurrent operations (Brent, 1974; Buhler et al., 1993; Brassard & Bratley, 1996).

The RAM model's instructions, and their charges, should be precisely defined. This effort would not only be arduous but would also provide limited insight into the algorithm's analysis and design. However, extreme caution must be exercised to avoid misusing the RAM model. For instance, if a RAM has a sort instruction, we may arrange with just one instruction. Moreover, such a RAM is impractical as practical computers lack these instructions (Chen & Davis, 1990; Prechelt, 1993). As a result, we shall concentrate on the design of actual computers. The RAM model incorporates data transfer (store, copy, load,), arithmetic (such as division, multiplication, addition, subtraction, remainder, floor, ceiling, and so on), and control instructions that are commonly found in actual computers (subroutine call and return conditional and unconditional branch). Every instruction requires a set amount of time to complete.

KEYWORD

Random-access machine (RAM) is an abstract machine in the general class of register machines.

1.5.1. Order of Growth

We may improve our study of the INSERTION-SORT easier by using a few simplifying assumptions. The real cost of every statement may be ignored as a 1st step by utilizing the constants c_i to denote such costs. Afterwards, we'll see that even such constants supply us with more information than we require. The worst-case running time was defined in the preceding sections as an^2 = b n+ C for certain constants a, b, and c that is based on the statement costs c_i. As a result, we may disregard both the abstract costs c_i and the real statement costs.

The sequence or rate of increase of the running time, which we are interested in, is another simplifying assumption that may be created. As a result, we only analyze the leading component of the formula (which is an^2), because the lower-order terms are fairly irrelevant for high values of n. In addition, the constant coefficient of the leading term is ignored since it is less relevant as compared to the rate of increase in finding computing effectiveness for large inputs. In the situation of insertion sort, we only have the n^2 factor from the leading word after discarding the constant coefficient of the leading term and the lower-order terms.

1.5.2. Insertion Sort Analysis

The time needed by the INSERTION-SORT method is mostly dependent on the input: sorting 1,000 numbers, for example, would take significantly longer than sorting three numbers. Furthermore, based upon how much each input sequence has been sorted, INSERTION-SORT might take a varied amount of time to arrange two input sequences of the similar size. Usually, the time needed by an algorithm grows in proportion to the size of the input, thus it is common to express program execution time as a function of input size. To do so, we need to be more careful in our definitions of "size of input" and "runtime."

The optimum estimate for the amount of the input is based upon the problem under analysis. The most common measure for a variety of issues, like sorting or calculating DFT, is the number of items in the input, for instance, n is the size of the array for arrangement. The whole number of bits necessary to indicate the input in conventional binary notation is the most ideal measure of the size of the input for various additional issues, such as the multiplication of two numbers. Sometimes, it is more appropriate to use two integers rather than one to express the input size. For instance, if an algorithm's input is a graph, the number of vertices and edges in the graph may be used to define the size of the input. For each of the difficulties we've looked at, we'll note to you which input size measures are being used.

KEYWORD

Insertion sort is a simple sorting algorithm that builds the final sorted array one item at a time by comparisons.

The primitive operations or the number of executed steps determines an algorithm's *running time* for a given input. It is necessary to define the step idea in such a way that it is machine-independent. Let us adopt the following viewpoint for the time being. A fixed sum of time is needed to implement every line of our pseudocode. Even though the time necessary to execute one line can vary from the time needed to execute another, we would suppose that every implementation of the ith line takes a constant amount of time equivalent to c_i. Such viewpoint is consistent with the RAM model, and it also illustrates how pseudo is implemented on the vast majority of real computers.

The next demonstration looks at the progression of the equation that is utilized to calculate the INSERTION-SORT running time. From a complicated formula that makes usage of all of the statement costs (that is, c_i) to a simplified representation that is brief and easier to manipulate, the expression progresses through the stages. This straightforward language makes it easier to measure the effectiveness of a specific algorithm in comparison to other algorithms. The demonstration of the INSERTION-SORT method in terms of the "cost" associated with every statement time and the number of times it is attempted to execute the statement.

For every j= 2, 3, 4, . . ., n, wherein n = *length*. A denotes the number of tries the 'while loop' experiment in line 5 is performed for that specific value of j. A 'for' or 'while' statement that exits conventionally (that is, because of a test in a looping header) has its execution performed once more than the body of the loop that exited conventionally. It is considered that comments are non-executable statements that don't spend any time when they are executed (Table 1.2).

Table 1.2. Illustration of insertion sort for different times and cost (Source: Tim Roughgarden, Creative Commons License).

Sr. No.	Times	Cost	INSERTION SORT (A)
1	n-1	0	//Insetion of A[j] into a arranged sequence a[1 . . . j-1]
2	n-1	0	\\feeding addition of value in A[i]
3	n	c1	for j=2 to length.A
4	n-1	c2	key=A[j]
5	n-1	c4	i = j-1
6	$\sum_{i=2}^{n} t_j$	c5	while A[i]>key and i>0
7	$\sum_{j=2}^{n} (t_j - 1)$	c6	A[i+1]=A[i]
8	$\sum_{j=2}^{n} (t_j - 1)$	c7	i =i-1
9	n-1	c8	A[i+1]=key

The phenomenon has several complexities. In most cases, computational steps defined in English are versions of a technique that takes longer than the expected (set) amount of time. For example, " the sorting of the points by x-coordinates" usually takes longer than the time allocated. It's also worth noting that a statement that invokes a subroutine spends the same amount of time, even if the function takes longer. As a result, for this sort of phenomenon, we identify the calling process.

The overall running time of an algorithm is the addition of the running times of all the statements that have been performed. Every statement which is executed in c_i steps and is executed n times in total will contribute $c_i n$ to the overall running time. We add the multiplication of the times and cost columns to get the overall running time of INSERTION-SORT on an input consisting n values, indicated by T(n), and we get

$$T(n) = c_1 n + c_2(n-1) + c_4(n-1) + c_5 \sum_{j=2}^{n} t_j + c_6 \sum_{j=2}^{n} (t_j - 1) + c_7 \sum_{j=2}^{n} (t_j - 1) + c_8(n-1)$$

Although when dealing with known-size inputs, an algorithm's execution time can be influenced through which input of that size is specified. The best-case situation in INSERTION-SORT, for example, is when the arrangement is already ordered. Whenever the initial value of i is j-1, we receive A[i]≤key in line 5 for the values of j= 2, 3... n. Consequently, t_j=1 for j= 2, 3. . . n and the running time of the best-case is

$$T_n = c_1 n + c_2(n-1) + c_4(n-1) + c_5(n-1) + c_8(n-1)$$
$$= (c_1 + c_2 + c_4 + c_5 + c_8)n - (c_2 + c_4 + c_5 + c_8)$$

For constants a and b, this running time may be represented as +b. Because a and b are both based upon the statement costs ci, n is a *linear function.*

The worst-case situation happens when the array is sorted in reverse order, that is, in decreasing order. Then, every element A[j] should be compared to each element in the entire sorted sub-array A[1... j-1], and consequently tj=j for j=2, 3,..., n. Remember that

$$\sum_{j=2}^{n} j = \frac{n(n+1)}{2} - 1$$

and

$$\sum_{j=2}^{n} (j-1) = \frac{n(n-1)}{2}$$

KEYWORD

Linear function is defined as a function that has either one or two variables without exponents.

The running time of INSERTION-SORT in the situation of worst-case is:

$$T(n) = c_1 n + c_2(n-1) + c_4(n-1) + c_5\left(\frac{n(n+1)}{2} - 1\right) + c_6\left(\frac{n(n-1)}{2}\right) + c_7\left(\frac{n(n-1)}{2}\right) + c_8(n-1)$$
$$= \left(\frac{c_5}{2} + \frac{c_6}{2} + \frac{c_7}{2}\right)n^2 + \left(c_1 + c_2 + c_4 + \frac{c_5}{2} - \frac{c_6}{2} + c_8\right) - (c_2 + c_4 + c_5 + c_8)$$

For constants a, b, and c, the running time of such worst-case may be represented as an^2=bn+c. Because these constants are dependent on the statement costs c_i, it is a quadratic function of n.

In the Insertion sort scenario, an algorithm's running time is usually set for every specific input; while there have been some "randomized" algorithms whose behavior varies even for a fixed input.

1.5.3. Analysis of Worst-Case and Average-Case

To better understand the insertion sort, we have studied both cases: the best scenario, in which the input arrangement has already been categorized, and the worst situation, in which the arrangement has already been categorized in the opposite direction. All of our attention is focused solely on the worst-case, which is the longest possible running time for every input of size n. The following are the 3 most important causes for this perspective:

a). By calculating the running time for the worst-case of an algorithm, we may obtain an upper bound on the running time of every input. Understanding the upper bound assures that the algorithm would not take much longer than it has been estimated to take. As a result, it removes the need for us to make an informed judgment, and we may safely trust that things would not become much worse.

b). The worst-case scenario occurs fairly frequently for certain algorithms. Whenever we check any database to discover certain particular data, we would frequently come into the worst-case scenario of the searching algorithm, which occurs when the data we seek is not there in the information.

c). The "average case" is almost always just as dreadful like the "worst-case" scenario. Consider the following scenario: we randomly select n integers and then apply insertion sort on them. Is it possible to estimate the amount of time necessary for identifying where to put element A[j] in sub-array A[1... j-1] using a timer? Usually, 50% of the items included in A[1... j-1] are more than A[j], and 50% are less than A[j]. As a result, we would be inspecting around 50% of the sub-array A[1... j-1], and as a result, tj is approximately j=2. The running time of the average case is found to be a quadratic function of the amount of the input as the running time of the worst case is shown to be in the same way.

ACTIVITY 1.1

Read lastest case studies and research papers on data structures and algorithms in order to understand the real-world applications of data structures and algoritums.

When dealing with a given situation, the capability of average-case evaluation is controlled since it is not always evident what constitutes an "average" input. Most of the time, we want to suppose that almost all inputs of a particular size are equally probable. In actuality, such an supposition can be broken; yet, at times, we can utilize a *randomized algorithm*, which produces arbitrary selections to permit for probabilistic evaluation and to provide results in a predicted running time by using a randomized method.

SUMMARY

Data structures are used to organize and store data in a computer program, allowing for efficient retrieval and manipulation of the data. Common data structures include arrays, linked lists, stacks, queues, trees and graphs. Algorithms on the other hand are step-by-step procedures used to solve a particular problem. Algorithms can be applied to data structures to perform operations such as searching, sorting and traversing the data. Some common algorithms include binary search, bubble sort and quick sort. Choosing the right data structure and algorithm for a particular problem can greatly impact the efficiency and effectiveness of a program. It's important for computer scientists and programmers to have a strong understanding of these fundamental concepts in order to create efficient and effective software solutions.

REVIEW QUESTIONS

1. What is a data structure?
2. What are the common types of data structures?
3. Why is it important to choose the right data structure for a particular problem?
4. What is an algorithm and what are some common algorithms used in programming?
5. How can you implement a data structure or algorithm in a programming language?

MULTIPLE CHOICE QUESTIONS

1. Which of the following is a non-linear data structure?

a. Array
b. Linked list
c. Queue
d. Tree

2. Which of the following is not an algorithm?

a. Bubble sort
b. Quick sort
c. Binary tree
d. Linear search

3. What is the space complexity of an algorithm?

a. The amount of memory needed to store the input data
b. The amount of memory needed to store the output data
c. The amount of memory needed to store the program code
d. The amount of memory needed to execute the algorithm

4. **Which of the following is not a common algorithm?**
   a. Array
   b. Tree
   c. Function
   d. Graph
5. **Which of the following is a linear data structure?**
   a. Array
   b. AVL trees
   c. Binary trees
   d. Graphs

Answers to Multiple Choice Questions

1. (d) 2. (c) 3. (d) 4. (c) 5. (a)

REFERENCES

1. Abramowitz, M., & Stegun, I. A., (1965). *Handbook of Mathematical Functions with Formulas, Graphs, and Mathematical Table* (Vol. 2172, pp. 1–23). New York: Dover.
2. Acar, U. A., (2009). Self-adjusting computation:(an overview). In: *Proceedings of the 2009 ACM SIGPLAN Workshop on Partial Evaluation and Program Manipulation* (pp. 1–6). ACM.
3. Ahuja, R. K., & Orlin, J. B., (1989). A fast and simple algorithm for the maximum flow problem. *Operations Research, 37*(5), 748–759.
4. Ahuja, R. K., Orlin, J. B., & Tarjan, R. E., (1989). Improved time bounds for the maximum flow problem. *SIAM Journal on Computing, 18*(5), 939–954.
5. Ajtai, M., Megiddo, N., & Waarts, O., (2001). Improved algorithms and analysis for secretary problems and generalizations. *SIAM Journal on Discrete Mathematics, 14*(1), 1–27.
6. Aki, S. G., (1989). *The Design and Analysis of Parallel Algorithms, 1*, 10.
7. Akra, M., & Bazzi, L., (1998). On the solution of linear recurrence equations. *Computational Optimization and Applications, 10*(2), 195–210.
8. Alon, N., (1990). Generating pseudo-random permutations and maximum flow algorithms. *Information Processing Letters, 35*(4), 201–204.
9. Amir, A., Aumann, Y., Benson, G., Levy, A., Lipsky, O., Porat, E., & Vishne, U., (2006). Pattern matching with address errors: Rearrangement distances. In: *Proceedings of the Seventeenth Annual ACM-SIAM Symposium on Discrete Algorithm* (Vol. 1, pp. 1221–1229). Society for Industrial and Applied Mathematics.

10. Amtoft, T., Consel, C., Danvy, O., & Malmkjær, K., (2002). The abstraction and instantiation of string-matching programs. In: *The Essence of Computation* (pp. 332–357). Springer, Berlin, Heidelberg.
11. Andersson, A. A., & Thorup, M., (2000). Tight(er) worst-case bounds on dynamic searching and priority queues. In: *Proceedings of the Thirty-Second Annual ACM Symposium on Theory of Computing* (Vol. 1, pp. 335–342). ACM.
12. Arge, L., (2001). External memory data structures. In: *European Symposium on Algorithms* (pp. 1–29). Springer, Berlin, Heidelberg.
13. Arora, S., & Lund, C., (1996). Hardness of approximations. In*: Approximation Algorithms for NP-Hard Problems* (pp. 399–446). PWS Publishing Co.
14. Arora, S., (1994). *Probabilistic Checking of Proofs and Hardness of Approximation Problems.* Doctoral dissertation, Princeton University, Department of Computer Science.
15. Arora, S., Lund, C., Motwani, R., Sudan, M., & Szegedy, M., (1998). Proof verification and the hardness of approximation problems. *Journal of the ACM (JACM), 45*(3), 501–555.
16. Aslam, J. A., (2001). *A Simple Bound on the Expected Height of a Randomly Built Binary Search Tree*,1, 20-35.
17. Ausiello, G., Crescenzi, P., Gambosi, G., Kann, V., Marchetti-Spaccamela, A., & Protasi, M., (2012). *Complexity and Approximation: Combinatorial Optimization Problems and Their Approximability Properties.* Springer Science & Business Media.
18. Avidan, S., & Shamir, A., (2007). Seam carving for content-aware image resizing. In: *ACM Transactions on Graphics (TOG)* (Vol. 26, No. 3, p. 10). ACM.
19. Babaioff, M., Immorlica, N., Kempe, D., & Kleinberg, R., (2007). A knapsack secretary problem with applications. In: *Approximation, Randomization, and Combinatorial Optimization: Algorithms and Techniques* (pp. 16–28). Springer, Berlin, Heidelberg.
20. Bach, E., & Shallit, J. O., (1996). *Algorithmic Number Theory: Efficient Algorithms* (Vol. 1). MIT press.
21. Bach, E., (1990). Number-theoretic algorithms. *Annual Review of Computer Science, 4*(1), 119–172.
22. Bailey, D. H., Lee, K., & Simon, H. D., (1991). Using Strassen's algorithm to accelerate the solution of linear systems. *The Journal of Supercomputing, 4*(4), 357–371.
23. Bakker, M., Riezebos, J., & Teunter, R. H., (2012). Review of inventory systems with deterioration since 2001. *European Journal of Operational Research, 221*(2), 275–284.
24. Baswana, S., Hariharan, R., & Sen, S., (2002). Improved decremental algorithms for maintaining transitive closure and all-pairs shortest paths. In: *Proceedings of the 34th Annual ACM Symposium on Theory of Computing* (pp. 117–123). ACM.
25. Bateni, M., Hajiaghayi, M., & Zadimoghaddam, M., (2010). Submodular secretary problem and extensions. In: *Approximation, Randomization, and Combinatorial*

Optimization: Algorithms and Techniques (pp. 39–52). Springer, Berlin, Heidelberg.

26. Bayer, R., (1972). Symmetric binary B-trees: Data structure and maintenance algorithms. *Acta Informatica, 1*(4), 290–306.
27. Beauchemin, P., Brassard, G., Crépeau, C., Goutier, C., & Pomerance, C., (1988). The generation of random numbers that are probably prime. *Journal of Cryptology, 1*(1), 53–64.
28. Bellare, M., & Sudan, M., (1994). Improved non-approximability results. In: *Proceedings of the Twenty-Sixth Annual ACM Symposium on Theory of Computing* (pp. 184–193). ACM.
29. Bender, M. A., Demaine, E. D., & Farach-Colton, M., (2000). Cache-oblivious B-trees. In: *Foundations of Computer Science, 2000; Proceedings. 41st Annual Symposium* (pp. 399–409). IEEE.
30. Ben-Or, M., (1983). Lower bounds for algebraic computation trees. In: *Proceedings of the Fifteenth Annual ACM Symposium on Theory of Computing* (pp. 80–86). ACM.
31. Bent, S. W., & John, J. W., (1985). Finding the median requires 2n comparisons. In: *Proceedings of the Seventeenth Annual ACM Symposium on Theory of Computing* (pp. 213–216). ACM.
32. Bentley, J. L., Haken, D., & Saxe, J. B., (1980). A general method for solving divide-and-conquer recurrences. *ACM SIGACT News, 12*(3), 36–44.
33. Berger, J., & Barkaoui, M., (2004). A parallel hybrid genetic algorithm for the vehicle routing problem with time windows. *Computers & Operations Research, 31*(12), 2037–2053.
34. Berry, M. V., & Howls, C. J., (2012). *Integrals with Coalescing Saddles, 36*, 775–793.
35. Bienstock, D., & McClosky, B., (2012). Tightening simple mixed-integer sets with guaranteed bounds. *Mathematical Programming, 133*(1), 337–363.
36. Bienstock, D., (2008). Approximate formulations for 0-1 knapsack sets. *Operations Research Letters, 36*(3), 317–320.
37. Blasgen, M. W., Casey, R. G., & Eswaran, K. P., (1977). An encoding method for multifield sorting and indexing. *Communications of the ACM, 20*(11), 874–878.
38. Blelloch, G. E., & Gibbons, P. B., (2004). Effectively sharing a cache among threads. In: *Proceedings of the Sixteenth Annual ACM Symposium on Parallelism in Algorithms and Architectures* (pp. 235–244). ACM.
39. Blelloch, G. E., & Greiner, J., (1996). A provable time and space efficient implementation of NESL. In: *ACM SIGPLAN Notices* (Vol. 31, No. 6, pp. 213–225). ACM.
40. Blelloch, G. E., & Maggs, B. M., (1996). Parallel algorithms. *ACM Computing Surveys (CSUR), 28*(1), 51–54.
41. Blelloch, G. E., Hardwick, J. C., Sipelstein, J., Zagha, M., & Chatterjee, S., (1994). Implementation of a portable nested data-parallel language. *Journal of Parallel and Distributed Computing, 21*(1), 4–14.

42. Bloom, N., & Van, R. J., (2002). Patents, real options and firm performance. *The Economic Journal, 112*(478).
43. Blumofe, R. D., & Leiserson, C. E., (1999). Scheduling multithreaded computations by work stealing. *Journal of the ACM (JACM), 46*(5), 720–748.
44. Bollerslev, T., Engle, R. F., & Nelson, D. B., (1994). ARCH models. *Handbook of Econometrics, 4*, 2959–3038.
45. Brassard, G., & Bratley, P., (1996). *Fundamentals of Algorithmics* (Vol. 33). Englewood Cliffs: Prentice Hall.
46. Brent, R. P., (1974). The parallel evaluation of general arithmetic expressions. *Journal of the ACM (JACM), 21*(2), 201–206.
47. Brodnik, A., Miltersen, P. B., & Munro, J. I., (1997). Trans-dichotomous algorithms without multiplication—Some upper and lower bounds. In: *Workshop on Algorithms and Data Structures* (pp. 426–439). Springer, Berlin, Heidelberg.
48. Buchbinder, N., Jain, K., & Singh, M., (2010). Secretary problems via linear programming. In: *International Conference on Integer Programming and Combinatorial Optimization* (pp. 163–176). Springer, Berlin, Heidelberg.
49. Buhler, J. P., Lenstra, H. W., & Pomerance, C., (1993). Factoring integers with the number field sieve. In: *The Development of the Number Field Sieve* (pp. 50–94). Springer, Berlin, Heidelberg.
50. Chan, T. H., (2000). Homfly polynomials of some generalized Hopf links. *Journal of Knot Theory and Its Ramifications, 9*(07), 865–883.
51. Chen, L. T., & Davis, L. S., (1990). A parallel algorithm for list ranking image curves in O (log N) time. In: *DARPA Image Understanding Workshop* (pp. 805–815).
52. Cheriyan, J., & Hagerup, T., (1989). A randomized maximum-flow algorithm. In: *Foundations of Computer Science, 1989, 30th Annual Symposium* (pp. 118–123). IEEE.
53. Cheriyan, J., & Hagerup, T., (1995). A randomized maximum-flow algorithm. *SIAM Journal on Computing, 24*(2), 203–226.
54. Cheriyan, J., Hagerup, T., & Mehlhorn, K., (1990). Can a maximum flow be computed in o (nm) time? In: *International Colloquium on Automata, Languages, and Programming* (pp. 235–248). Springer, Berlin, Heidelberg.
55. Cheriyan, J., Hagerup, T., & Mehlhorn, K., (1996). An o(n^3)-time maximum-flow algorithm. *SIAM Journal on Computing, 25*(6), 1144–1170.
56. Ciurea, E., & Ciupala, L., (2001). Algorithms for minimum flows. *Computer Science Journal of Moldova, 9*(3), 27.
57. Conforti, M., Wolsey, L. A., & Zambelli, G., (2010). Projecting an extended formulation for mixed-integer covers on bipartite graphs. *Mathematics of Operations Research, 35*(3), 603–623.
58. Courcoubetis, C., Vardi, M., Wolper, P., & Yannakakis, M., (1992). Memory-efficient algorithms for the verification of temporal properties. *Formal Methods in System Design, 1*(2, 3), 275–288.

59. D'Aristotile, A., Diaconis, P., & Newman, C. M., (2003). Brownian motion and the classical groups. *Lecture Notes-Monograph Series*, 97–116.
60. Damgård, I., Landrock, P., & Pomerance, C., (1993). Average case error estimates for the strong probable prime test. *Mathematics of Computation, 61*(203), 177–194.
61. Dehling, H., & Philipp, W., (2002). Empirical process techniques for dependent data. In: *Empirical Process Techniques for Dependent Data* (pp. 3–113). Birkhäuser, Boston, MA.
62. Dengiz, B., Altiparmak, F., & Smith, A. E., (1997). Efficient optimization of all-terminal reliable networks, using an evolutionary approach. *IEEE Transactions on Reliability, 46*(1), 18–26.
63. Dickerson, M., Eppstein, D., Goodrich, M. T., & Meng, J. Y., (2003). Confluent drawings: Visualizing non-planar diagrams in a planar way. In: *International Symposium on Graph Drawing* (pp. 1–12). Springer, Berlin, Heidelberg.
64. Didier, F., (2009). *Efficient Erasure Decoding of Reed-solomon Codes* (Vol. 1, pp. 1–22). arXiv preprint arXiv:0901.1886.
65. Drmota, M., & Szpankowski, W., (2013). A master theorem for discrete divide and conquer recurrences. *Journal of the ACM (JACM), 60*(3), 16.
66. Du, W., & Atallah, M. J., (2001). Protocols for secure remote database access with approximate matching. In: *E-Commerce Security and Privacy* (pp. 87–111). Springer, Boston, MA.
67. Duda, R. O., Hart, P. E., & Stork, D. G., (1973). *Pattern Classification* (Vol. 2). New York: Wiley.
68. Eppstein, D., Goodrich, M. T., & Sun, J. Z., (2005). The skip quadtree: A simple dynamic data structure for multidimensional data. In: *Proceedings of the Twenty-First Annual Symposium on Computational Geometry* (pp. 296–305). ACM.
69. Eppstein, D., Goodrich, M. T., & Sun, J. Z., (2008). Skip quadtrees: Dynamic data structures for multidimensional point sets. *International Journal of Computational Geometry & Applications, 18*(1, 2), 131–160.
70. Faenza, Y., & Sanità, L., (2015). On the existence of compact ε-approximated formulations for knapsack in the original space. *Operations Research Letters, 43*(3), 339–342.
71. Festa, P., & Resende, M. G., (2002). GRASP: An annotated bibliography. In: *Essays and Surveys in Metaheuristics* (Vol. 1, pp. 325–367). Springer, Boston, MA.
72. Fourier, J. B. J., (1890).Second extrait: *Oeuvres de Fourier, 1(2), 38–42.*
73. Fourier, J. B. J., (1973). Second extrait: Oeuvres de Fourier, Paris 1890, *1*, 50-72.
74. Fredman, M. L., & Willard, D. E., (1993). Surpassing the information theoretic bound with fusion trees. *Journal of Computer and System Sciences, 47*(3), 424–436.
75. Friedl, K., & Sudan, M., (1995). Some improvements to total degree tests. In: *Theory of Computing and Systems, 1995; Proceedings, Third Israel Symposium* (pp. 190–198). IEEE.

76. Frigo, M., Leiserson, C. E., & Randall, K. H., (1998). The implementation of the cilk-5 multithreaded language. *ACM Sigplan Notices, 33*(5), 212–223.
77. Fussenegger, F., & Gabow, H. N., (1979). A counting approach to lower bounds for selection problems. *Journal of the ACM (JACM), 26*(2), 227–238.
78. Glasser, K. S., & Austin, B. R. H., (1983). The d choice secretary problem. *Sequential Analysis, 2*(3), 177–199.
79. Goodrich, M. T., Atallah, M. J., & Tamassia, R., (2005). Indexing information for data forensics. In: *International Conference on Applied Cryptography and Network Security* (pp. 206–221). Springer, Berlin, Heidelberg.
80. Graefe, G., (2011). Modern B-tree techniques. *Foundations and Trends® in Databases, 3*(4), 203–402.
81. Hall, M., Frank, E., Holmes, G., Pfahringer, Badel'son-Vel'skii, G. M., & Landis, E. M., (1962). *Partial Differential Equations of Elliptic Type* (Vol. 1, pp. 1–22). Springer, Berlin.
82. Herr, D. G., (1980). On the history of the use of geometry in the general linear model. *The American Statistician, 34*(1), 43–47.
83. Icking, C., Klein, R., & Ottmann, T., (1987). Priority search trees in secondary memory. In: *International Workshop on Graph-Theoretic Concepts in Computer Science* (pp. 84–93). Springer, Berlin, Heidelberg.
84. Igarashi, Y., Sado, K., & Saga, K., (1987). Fast parallel sorts on a practical sized mesh-connected processor array. *IEICE Transactions (1976–1990), 70*(1), 56–64.
85. John, J. W., (1988). A new lower bound for the set-partitioning problem. *SIAM Journal on Computing, 17*(4), 640–647.
86. Kim, S. H., & Pomerance, C., (1989). The probability that a random probable prime is composite. *Mathematics of Computation, 53*(188), 721–741.
87. King, D. J., (1995). Functional binomial queues. In: *Functional Programming, Glasgow 1994* (Vol. 1, pp. 141–150). Springer, London.
88. Kirkpatrick, D. G., (1981). A unified lower bound for selection and set partitioning problems. *Journal of the ACM (JACM), 28*(1), 150–165.
89. Kwong, Y. S., & Wood, D., (1982). A new method for concurrency in B-trees. *IEEE Transactions on Software Engineering*, (3), 211–222.
90. Leighton, T., (1996). *Notes on Better Master Theorems for Divide-and-Conquer Recurrences.* Manuscript. Massachusetts Institute of Technology.
91. Maurer, S. B., (1985). The lessons of Williamstown. In: *New Directions in Two-Year College Mathematics* (Vol. 1, pp. 255–270). Springer, New York, NY.
92. Meijer, H., & Akl, S. G., (1987). Optimal computation of prefix sums on a binary tree of processors. *International Journal of Parallel Programming, 16*(2), 127–136.
93. Meijer, H., & Akl, S. G., (1988). Bit serial addition trees and their applications. *Computing, 40*(1), 9–17.

94. Monier, L., (1980). Evaluation and comparison of two efficient probabilistic primality testing algorithms. *Theoretical Computer Science, 12*(1), 97–108.
95. Morain, F., (1988). *Implementation of the Atkin-Goldwasser-Kilian Primality Testing Algorithm*. Doctoral dissertation, INRIA.
96. Munro, J. I., & Poblete, P. V., (1982). *A Lower Bound for Determining the Median*. Faculty of Mathematics, University of Waterloo.
97. Nelson, D. B., & Foster, D. P., (1992). *Filtering and Forecasting with Misspecified ARCH Models II: Making the Right Forecast with the Wrong Model*, 67(2), 303-335.
98. Nievergelt, J., (1974). Binary search trees and file organization. *ACM Computing Surveys (CSUR), 6*(3), 195–207.
99. Park, T. G., & Oldfield, J. V., (1993). Minimum spanning tree generation with content-addressable memory. *Electronics Letters, 29*(11), 1037–1039.
100. Phillips, S., & Westbrook, J., (1993). Online load balancing and network flow. In: *Proceedings of the Twenty-Fifth Annual ACM Symposium on Theory of Computing* (pp. 402–411). ACM.
101. Polishchuk, A., & Spielman, D. A., (1994). Nearly-linear size holographic proofs. In: *Proceedings of the Twenty-Sixth Annual ACM Symposium on Theory of Computing* (pp. 194–203). ACM.
102. Prechelt, L., (1993). *Measurements of MasPar MP-1216A Communication Operations*. Univ., Fak. für Informatik.
103. Price, G. B., (1973). Telescoping sums and the summation of sequences. *The Two-Year College Mathematics Journal, 4*(2), 16–29.
104. Ramadge, P. J., & Wonham, W. M., (1989). The control of discrete event systems. *Proceedings of the IEEE, 77*(1), 81–98.
105. Raman, R., (1996). Priority queues: Small, monotone and trans-dichotomous. In: *European Symposium on Algorithms* (pp. 121–137). Springer, Berlin, Heidelberg.
106. Regli, W. C., (1992). *A Survey of Automated Feature Recognition Techniques, 1*, 1–22.
107. Roura, S., (2001). Improved master theorems for divide-and-conquer recurrences. *Journal of the ACM (JACM), 48*(2), 170–205.
108. Sardelis, D. A., & Valahas, T. M., (1999). Decision making: A golden rule. *The American Mathematical Monthly, 106*(3), 215–226.
109. Schönhage, A., Paterson, M., & Pippenger, N., (1976). Finding the median. *Journal of Computer and System Sciences, 13*(2), 184–199.
110. Shen, Z., & Marston, C. M., (1995). A study of a dice problem. *Applied Mathematics and Computation, 73*(2, 3), 231–247.
111. Smith, R. S., (1986). Rolle over Lagrange—Another shot at the mean value theorem. *The College Mathematics Journal, 17*(5), 403–406.
112. Snyder, L., (1984). *Parallel Programming and the Poker Programming Environment*

(No. TR-84-04-02, pp. 1–30). Washington Univ. Seattle Dept of Computer Science.

113. Stock, J. H., & Watson, M. W., (2001). Vector autoregressions. *Journal of Economic Perspectives, 15*(4), 101–115.
114. Sudan, M., (1992). Efficient checking of polynomials and proofs and the hardness of approximation problems. *Lecture Notes in Computer Science,* 1001.
115. Szymanski, T. G., & Van, W. C. J., (1983). Space efficient algorithms for VLSI artwork analysis. In: *Proceedings of the 20th Design Automation Conference* (pp. 734–739). IEEE Press.
116. Szymanski, T. G., (1975). *A Special Case of the Maximal Common Subsequence Problem*. Technical Report TR-170, Computer Science Laboratory, Princeton University.
117. Thorup, M., (1997). *Faster Deterministic Sorting and Priority Queues in Linear Space* (pp. 550–555). Max-Planck-Institut für Informatik.
118. Vanderbei, R. J., (1980). The optimal choice of a subset of a population. *Mathematics of Operations Research, 5*(4), 481–486.
119. Verma, R. M., (1994). A general method and a master theorem for divide-and-conquer recurrences with applications. *Journal of Algorithms, 16*(1), 67–79.
120. Verma, R. M., (1997). General techniques for analyzing recursive algorithms with applications. *SIAM Journal on Computing, 26*(2), 568–581.
121. Wallace, L., Keil, M., & Rai, A., (2004). Understanding software project risk: A cluster analysis. *Information & Management, 42*(1), 115–125.
122. Wang, Y., (2008). Topology control for wireless sensor networks. In: *Wireless Sensor Networks and Applications* (Vol. 1, pp. 113–147). Springer, Boston, MA.
123. Wilf, H. S., (1984). A bijection in the theory of derangements. *Mathematics Magazine, 57*(1), 37–40.
124. Williamson, J., (2002). Probability logic. In: *Studies in Logic and Practical Reasoning* (Vol. 1, pp. 397–424). Elsevier.
125. Wilson, J. G., (1991). Optimal choice and assignment of the best m of n randomly arriving items. *Stochastic Processes and Their Applications, 39*(2), 325–343.
126. Winograd, S., (1970). On the algebraic complexity of functions. In: *Actes du Congres International Des Mathématiciens* (Vol. 3, pp. 283–288).
127. Wunderlich, M. C., (1983). A performance analysis of a simple prime-testing algorithm. *Mathematics of Computation, 40*(162), 709–714.
128. Xiaodong, W., & Qingxiang, F., (1996). A frame for general divide-and-conquer recurrences. *Information Processing Letters, 59*(1), 45–51.
129. Yap, C., (2011). A real elementary approach to the master recurrence and generalizations. In: *International Conference on Theory and Applications of Models of Computation* (pp. 14–26). Springer, Berlin, Heidelberg.
130. Zhu, X., & Wilhelm, W. E., (2006). Scheduling and lot sizing with sequence-dependent setup: A literature review. *IIE Transactions, 38*(11), 987–1007.

CHAPTER 2

CLASSIFICATION OF ALGORITHMS

UNIT INTRODUCTION

An algorithm is a technique or group of methods for completing a problem-solving activity. The term algorithm, which comes from Medieval Latin, refers to more than only computer programming. There are many different sorts of algorithms for various issues. The belief that there are only a finite number of algorithms and that one must learn all of them is a fallacy that leads many potential programmers to turn to lawn maintenance as a source of revenue to cover their expenses (Rabin, 1977; Cook, 1983; 1987).

When an issue develops throughout the course of developing the complete software, an algorithm is created. A variety of classification schemes for algorithms are discussed in detail in this chapter. There is no single "correct" classification that applies to all situations. When comparing the tasks of classifying algorithms and attributing them, it is important to remember that the former is more difficult (Karp, 1986; Virrer & Simons, 1986). Following a discussion of the labeling procedure for a given algorithm (e.g., the divide-and-conquer algorithm), we will examine the various methods for examining algorithms in greater depth. Frequently, the labels with which the algorithms are classified are quite useful and assist in the selection of the most appropriate type of analysis to perform (Cormen & Leiserson, 1989; Stockmeyer & Meyer, 2002) (Figure 2.1).

The number of fundamental jobs that an algorithm completes is used to determine its speed or efficiency. Consider the case of an algorithm whose input is N and which executes a large number of operations.

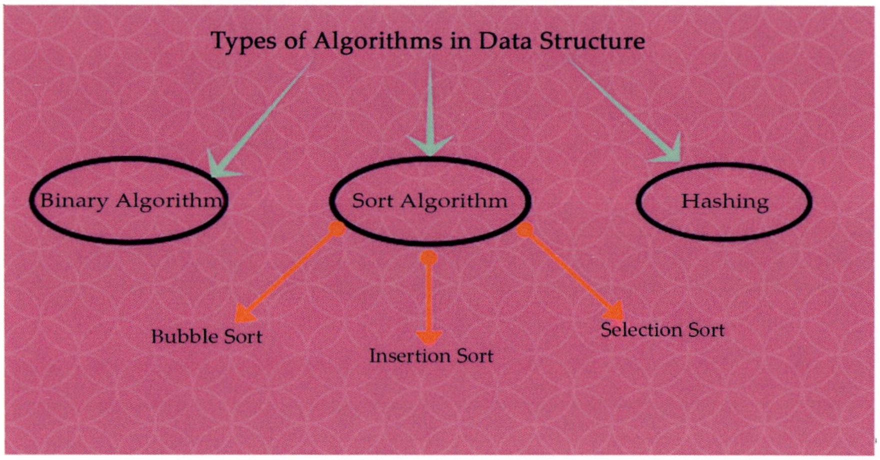

Figure 2.1. Major types of data structure algorithms (Source: Code kul, Creative Commons License).

The characteristics of an algorithm are defined by the connection between the number of tasks completed and the time required to complete each task (Dayde, 1996; Panda et al., 1997; D'Alberto, 2000). Therefore, it must be noted that every algorithm relates to a certain class of algorithms. In the increasing order of their growth, algorithms are classified as:

- Constant time algorithm,
- Logarithmic algorithm,
- Linear time algorithm,
- Polynomial-time algorithm,
- Exponential time algorithm.

Did you Know?

The First computer programmer, Ada Lovelace, worked with Charles Babbage in the 1800s and is credited with writing the first algorithm designed to be processed by a machine.

Learning Objectives

Readers will have the chance to understand the following by the chapter's conclusion:

- Understand the fundamental concepts of algorithms
- Learn about the basics of deterministic and randomized algorithms
- Understand the difference between online and offline algorithms
- Learn about the classification of algorithms based on the main concept

Key Terms

1. Algorithms
2. Approximation Algorithms
3. Dynamic Programming
4. Divide and Conquer
5. Las Vegas
6. Monte Carlo
7. Online
8. Offline

2.1. DETERMINISTIC AND RANDOMIZED ALGORITHMS

KEYWORD

Deterministic algorithm is an algorithm that, given a particular input, will always produce the same output, with the underlying machine always passing through the same sequence of states.

The following is an example of one of the most significant (and unique) differences that may be used to determine if a particular algorithm is deterministic or randomized (Codenotti and Simon, 1998; Kgström and Van Loan, 1998).

On a given input, Deterministic algorithms produce the same outcomes by using the same calculation steps, whereas Randomized algorithms, in contrast to Deterministic algorithms, throw coins during the implementation process. It is possible that the sequence in which the algorithm is implemented or the conclusion of the algorithm will change for each try on a specific input (Flajolet et al., 1990; Nisan & Wigderson, 1995).

For randomized algorithms, there are two more subcategories.

- *Monte Carlo* algorithms
- *Las Vegas* algorithms.

A Las Vegas algorithm will always provide the same output for a given input. Randomization will have no effect on the order of the core implementations.

In the case of Monte Carlo algorithms, the output of these algorithms may vary, if not be incorrect. A Monte Carlo method, on the other hand, produces the right result with a high degree of certainty (Garey, 1979; Kukuk, 1997; Garey & Johnson, 2002).

The issue that arises at this point is: For what purpose are randomized algorithms being developed? The computation/processing may change based on the outcome of the coin toss (Hirschberg & Wong, 1976; Kannan, 1980). However, despite the fact that Monte Carlo algorithms do not produce precise results, they are still sought after for the following reasons:

i. Randomized algorithms typically have the effect of troubling the input, which is why they are used. To put it another way, the input appears to be random, and as a result, undesirable situations are rarely seen.
ii. When it comes to conceptual implementation, randomized algorithms are typically quite stress-free. When compared to their deterministic equivalents, they are typically significantly superior in terms of runtime performance (Figure 2.2).

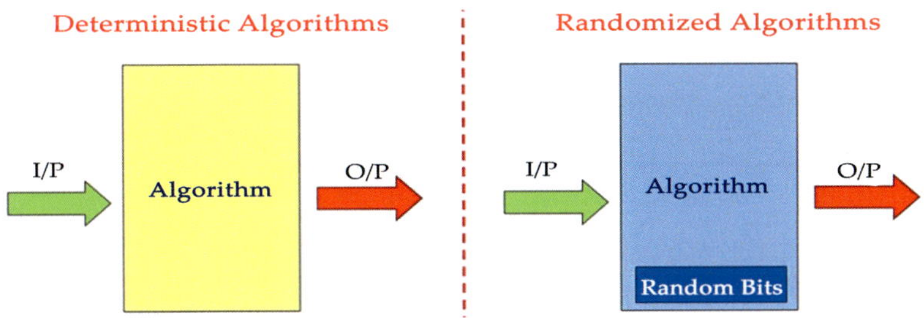

Figure 2.2. Illustration of deterministic and randomized algorithms (Source: Shinta Budiaman, Creative Commons License).

2.2. ONLINE VS. OFFLINE ALGORITHMS

One of the main differences in determining whether a particular algorithm is online or offline is mentioned below.

Online Algorithms are algorithms in which the inputs are unknown at the start. The inputs to algorithms are usually known ahead of time. However, in the case of Online, they are given to them (Chazelle et al., 1989; Roucairol, 1996; Goodman & O'Rourke, 1997) (Figure 2.3).

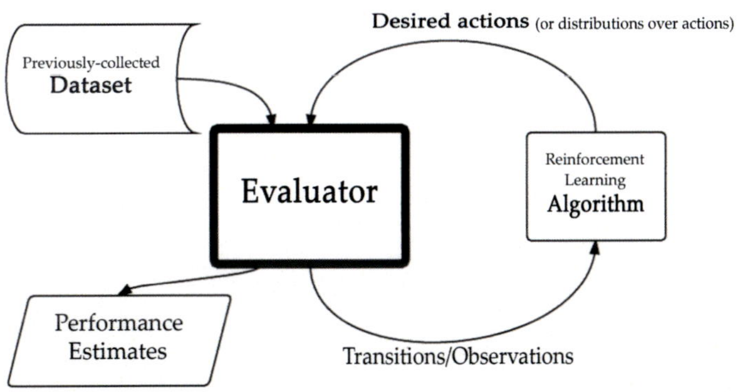

Figure 2.3. Offline Evaluation of Online Reinforcement Learning Algorithms (Source: Travis Mandel, Creative Commons License).

Even though it appears to be a minor issue, its implications for the design and analysis of the algorithms are significant. The competitiveness of these algorithms is typically tested by applying competitiveness knowledge to them. In the worst-case scenario, this examination takes the most time, and when compared to the best algorithm, it normally takes the most time. A ski problem is an example of a problem that may be found on the internet (Wilson & Pawley, 1988; Xiang et al., 2004; Liu et al., 2007).

Every day that a skier goes skiing, he or she must determine whether to purchase or rent skis, at least until the point at which he or she decides to purchase skis is reached. Because of the unpredictable weather, it is impossible to predict how many days a skier will be able to enjoy the sport. Assume that T is the number of days he or she will be skiing. B represents the cost of purchasing skis; 1 unit represents the cost of renting skis (Wierzbicki et al., 2002; Li, 2004; Pereira, 2009).

2.3. EXACT, APPROXIMATE, HEURISTIC, AND OPERATIONAL ALGORITHMS

The majority of algorithms are designed with optimization in mind, such as calculating the direct path, alignment, or marginal edit distance (Aydin & Fogarty, 2004). When a goal is stated, an exact algorithm concentrates on computing the best answer. This is relatively costly in terms of runtime or memory, and it is not practicable for huge inputs (Tran et al., 2004; Thallner & Moser, 2005; Xie et al., 2006). Other approaches are tested at this time. Approximation algorithms are one of the strategies that focus on computing a solution that is just a firm, defined factor poorer than the optimum answer (Ratakonda & Turaga, 2008). This indicates that an algorithm is a c approximation if it can guarantee that the answer it generates is never worse than the factor c when compared to the best solution (Xiang et al., 2003; Aydin & Yigit, 2005).

Remember

The concept of algorithms is not just limited to computer science. It is also used in many other fields including mathematics, physics, and biology

Heuristic algorithms, on the other hand, attempt to provide the best answer without guaranteeing that it will always be the best solution. It is frequently simple to construct a counterexample. A good heuristics algorithm is always at or near the optimal value (Restrepo et al., 2004; Sevkli & Aydin, 2006). Finally, there are algorithms that do not prioritize the optimization of objective functions (Yigit et al., 2004; Sevkli & Guner, 2006). Because they tie a succession of computing tasks controlled by an expert but not in aggregate with a specific goal function, these algorithms are referred to be operational (e.g., ClustalW).

Consider the Traveling Salesman Problem, which has triangle inequality for n cities. This is an example of a problem that is NP-hard. A greedy, deterministic technique is described below that generates two approximations for the traveling salesman problem—the triangle inequality produced in time $O(n^2)$.

- A minimal spanning tree (T) is computed for the whole graph bounded by n cities.

- All edges of the spanning tree *T are duplicated by* producing an Eulerian graph *T'*. The Eulerian path is then found in *T'*
- By using clever shortcuts, the Eulerian cycle is transformed into the Hamiltonian cycle.

2.4. CLASSIFICATION ACCORDING TO MAIN CONCEPT

The algorithms may be classified as follows using the primary algorithmic paradigm that we are familiar with:

- Simple recursive algorithm
- Divide-and-conquer algorithm
- Dynamic programming algorithm
- Backtracking algorithm
- Greedy algorithm
- Brute force algorithm
- Branch-and-bound algorithm

2.4.1. Simple Recursive Algorithm (Figure 2.4)

This kind of algorithm has the following characteristics:

- It fixes the fundamental issues right away.
- It continues to work on the less difficult subproblem.
- It goes through some extra steps to convert the answer to the easier subproblem into the solution to the given problem. Examples are discussed below:

a) Counting how many essentials are in a list:
1. If the specified list is empty, return zero; otherwise,
2. Remove the first item from the equation and add up the remaining requirements in the list.
3. To the result, add one.

b) Checking if a value is present in a list:
1. If the supplied list is empty, return false, otherwise,
2. If the first object in the supplied list is the requested value, return true; otherwise
3. After excluding the first object, see if the value appears elsewhere in the list.

KEYWORD

Greedy algorithm is any algorithm that follows the problem-solving heuristic of making the locally optimal choice at each stage.

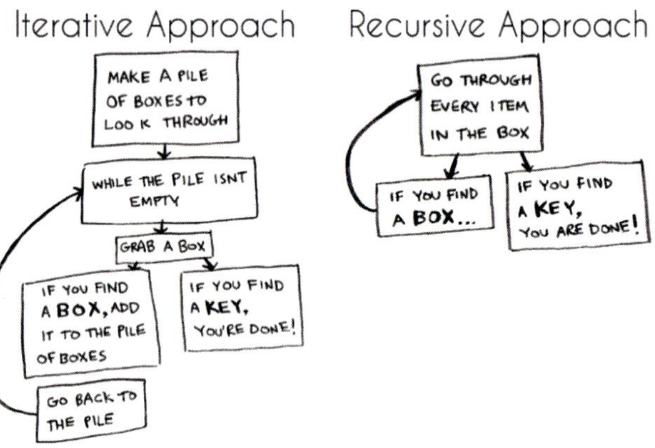

Figure 2.4. Comparison of iterative and recursive approaches (Source: Beau Cranes, Creative Commons License).

2.4.2. Divide-and-Conquer Algorithm

The size of a task is divided by a predetermined factor in this approach. Only a small percentage of the genuine problem is treated in each cycle. This category includes a few of the most efficient and effective algorithms. This type of algorithm has a logarithmic runtime (Battiti & Tecchiolli, 1994; Yigit et al., 2006). This algorithm comprises two parts.

i. The original problem is broken down into smaller, related subproblems, which are then solved in a recursive manner.
ii. The subproblems' solutions are merged to provide the solution to the original problem.

Traditionally, a divide-and-conquer algorithm is defined as one that comprises two or more recursive calls. Consider the following two case studies:

i. Quicksort:
a) Divide the array into two equal pieces, then sort each component quickly.
b) Combining the partitioned portions requires no additional effort.
ii. Merge sort:
a) After slicing the array in half, merge sort each part.
b) By combining the two organized arrays, you may create a single organized array (Figure 2.5).

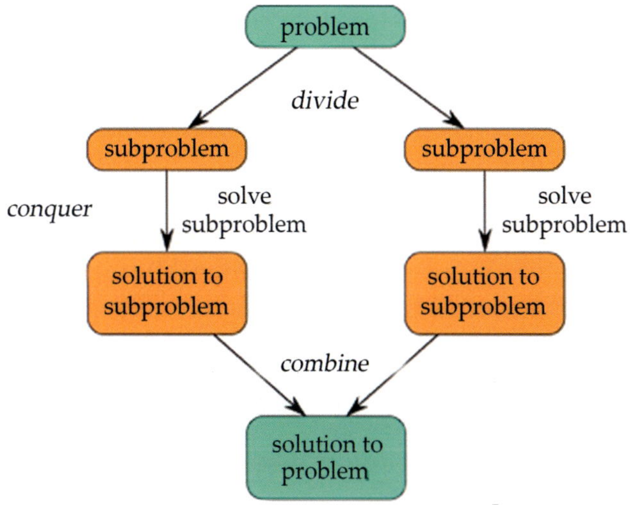

Figure 2.5. Representation of divide and conquer algorithm (Source: Khan Academy, Creative Commons License).

2.4.3. Dynamic Programming Algorithm

The term 'dynamic' refers to the manner through which the algorithm computes the outcome of the computation. A solution to one problem may be contingent on the solution of one or more sub-problems in another situation (Taillard, 1991, 1995). It exemplifies the characteristic of coinciding sub-problems in a straightforward manner. As a result, it is possible that we will have to recalculate the same numbers for sub-problems over and over to answer the main problem. As a result, counting cycles is pointless (Fleurent & Ferland, 1994).

A technique or procedure called dynamic programming can be used to alleviate the frustration caused by these useless computer cycles. As a result of this method, the conclusion of each sub-problem is memorized and is utilized the outcome anytime is required, rather than having to recalculate the result again and over (Glover, 1989; Skorin-Kapov, 1990).

In this case, space is exchanged for time. As an example, more space is employed to grab the computed numbers, allowing the execution speed to be greatly boosted. The connection for the Nth Fibonacci number is the greatest example of a problem that involves several sub-problems that are related to each other. The Fibonacci number is expressed by the equation F (n) = F (n-1) + F (n-2).

The statement above demonstrates that the Nth Fibonacci number is reliant on the two numbers that came before it. To compute F(n) in a predictable manner, the computations must be carried out in the manner outlined below. The colored values that are similar in appearance are those that will be computed repeatedly. Take note that F(n-2) is computed twice, F(n-3) is computed three times, and so on. As a result, we are wasting a significant amount of time. As it turns out, this recursion will do $$2N$$ operations for every given N, and it is completely insoluble on a current PC for any N more than 40 within one to two years on the most recent generation of computers (Shi, 2001; Hu et al., 2003) (Figure 2.6).

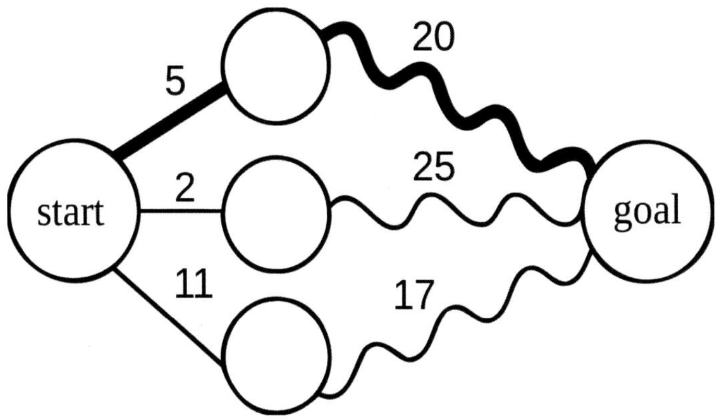

Figure 2.6. Depiction of dynamic programming algorithm (Source: Khan Academy, Creative Commons License).

The greatest potential answer to this problem is to save every value when computing it and retrieve it instead of having to compute it all over again. Because of this, the exponential time method is changed into the linear time algorithm and vice versa (Kennedy et al., 2001). The use of dynamic programming techniques is extremely important to accelerate the solutions to issues that have concurrent subproblems (Kennedy & Mendes, 2002, 2006). This dynamic algorithm memorizes the previous outcomes and then makes use of them to find the new future outcomes (He et al., 2004). The dynamic programming approach is typically used to solve optimization issues in situations where:

- The optimal option must be discovered amid a plethora of other possibilities.
- Coinciding sub-problem and optimum substructure are needed.
- Optimum substructure: an Optimum solution that is composed of optimum solutions to the constituent issues.
- Coinciding sub-problems: Bottom-up methods allow you to preserve and reuse the solutions you find for sub-problems you encounter.

This method differs from the Divide-and-Conquer method, in which the sub-problems seldom overlap. In bioinformatics, there are several instances of this method. For example:

i. Obtaining the best pairwise alignment possible.

a) Optimum substructure: The answers for the most optimal designs of smaller prefixes are incorporated into the arrangement of two prefixes as well.

b) Coinciding sub-problems: The stored results of the design of three sub-problems are used to get the best arrangement of two prefixes.

ii. In an HMM, we are calculating a Viterbi path.

a) Optimum substructure: A Viterbi route for an input prefix that ends in a condition of HMM is composed of shorter Viterbi routes for minor sections of the input and the other HMM conditions, as shown in the figure.

b) Coinciding sub-problems: To find a solution for a Viterbi route for input prefix that ends in a condition of HMM, the saved outcomes of the Viterbi pathways for smaller input prefix and the HMM requirements must be used in conjunction with the HMM conditions.

KEYWORD

Brute force algorithms are exactly what they sound like – straightforward methods of solving a problem that rely on sheer computing power and trying every possibility rather than advanced techniques to improve efficiency.

2.4.4. Backtracking Algorithm

This method is quite like the Brute Force algorithm mentioned later in this chapter. There are significant differences between the two algorithms. In the brute force technique, each possible solution combination is created and checked to see if it is legitimate (Kröse et al., 1993; Pham & Karaboga, 2012). In contrast to the backtracking method, every time a solution is created, it is tested, and only if it meets all of the requirements are further solutions generated; otherwise, the approach is backtracked, and an alternative path for finding the answer is taken (Wu et al., 2005).

The N Queens issue is a well-known example of this type of problem. An N X N chessboard is given, according to the N Queens. On the chessboard, N queens are arranged in such a way that none of them are attacked by the other queens (Figure 2.7).

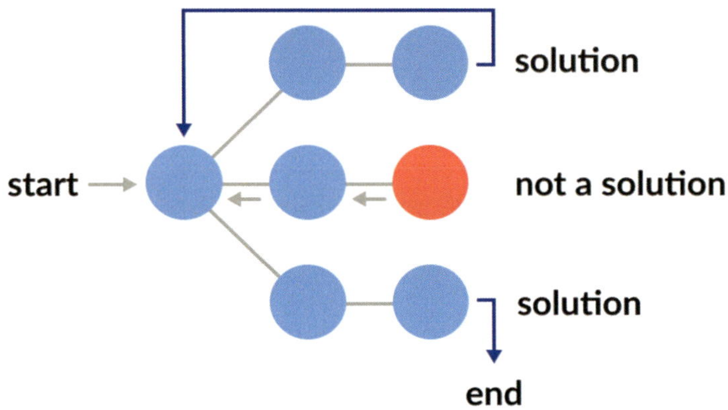

Figure 2.7. Representation of backtracking algorithm (Source: Programiz, Creative Commons License).

This is accomplished by shifting a queen in each column and appropriate row. The status of a queen is verified every time she is moved to ensure that she is not under assault. If this is the case, a different cell inside that column is picked to be the location of the queen. You may think of the process in terms of a tree. Every node in the tree represents a chessboard, each with a unique configuration. If we are unable to move at any point, we can retrace our steps back to the previous node and go on by increasing the number of other nodes.

Did you Know?

Some algorithms are named after the people who developed such as Dijkstra's algorithm for finding the shortest path between two nodes in a graph.

The advantage of this strategy over the Brute force algorithm is that it generates a smaller number of candidates when compared to the Brute force algorithm. With the aid of this strategy, it is possible to isolate the viable answers in a relatively short period of time and with great effectiveness.

Consider the case of an 8 × 8 chessboard; if the Brute Force technique is used, then 4,426,165,368 solutions must be developed, and each one must be checked before a solution is accepted. The quantity of solutions is decreased to around 40,320 in the manner that has been explained.

There are several advantages to using the depth-first recursive hunt outlined above. The following are some of these advantages:

i. Tests to determine whether the solution has been constructed, and if it has, it returns the solution; otherwise.

ii. For each option that can be created at this time, a separate document is required,

a) Make your choice.

b) Recur.

c) If the recursion produces a result, return it.

iii. Return failure if there is no other option.

Consider drawing or painting a map with no more than four colors, i.e., Color (Country *n*).

i. If all of the countries are colored (*n* > no of countries) return success; otherwise,

ii. For each of the four hues, there is n x c.

iii. If the country isn't close to one of the colored countries,

a) Color c is used to color country n.

b) Color country n+1 in a recursive manner.

c) Return success if it was successful.

iv. Return failure (if the loop still exits).

KEYWORD

Recursion is a routine that calls itself again and again directly or indirectly.

2.4.5. Greedy Algorithm

This approach delivers superior results for optimization issues on occasion, and it typically works in phases. At every step:

- You can attain the finest results possible right now without having to worry about future outcomes.
- One can attain a global ideal by picking a local optimal at each stage along the way.

In my issues, using this approach results in the best answer. This approach works well with optimization issues. We will develop a locally optimal solution at each stage of this method, which will lead to a globally optimal solution. We can't back out of a decision once we've made it. Verifying the validity of this method is critical since not all greedy algorithms produce the best answer worldwide (Creput et al., 2005). Consider the scenario in which you are given a specified quantity of coins and asked to make a specific amount of money with those coins (Figure 2.8).

KEYWORD

Optimal solution is a feasible solution where the objective function reaches its maximum (or minimum) value, that means the maximum profit or the least cost.

This method is frequently quite successful and always yields the best solution for certain types of situations. Let's look at another scenario. Let's say a guy wishes to count out a specified amount of money using the fewest possible notes and coins. Here, the greedy algorithm will choose the note or coin with the highest potential value that does not exceed a certain threshold. For example, we have a number of options for earning $6.39 dollars:

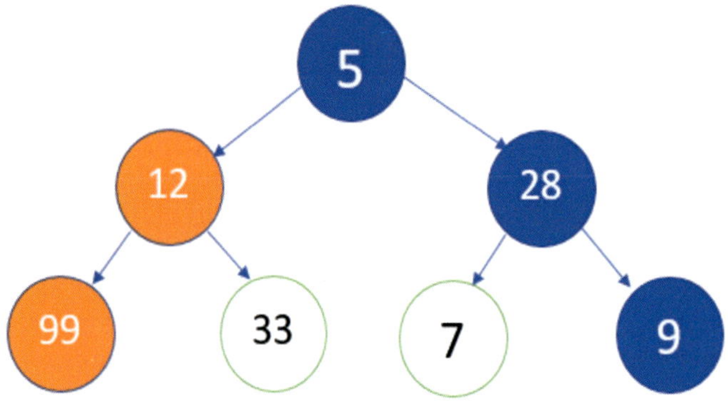

Figure 2.8. Numerical representation of a greedy algorithm (Source: Margaret Rouse, Creative Commons License).

- a bill for $5
- a one-dollar note, for a total of six dollars
- 6.25 dollars with a 25-cent coin
- To make 6.35 dollars, you'll need a ten-cent coin.
- To make $6.39, you'll need four one-cent coins.

The greedy algorithm always finds the best answer for the number of dollars.

2.4.6. Brute Force Algorithm

Using the fundamental specification, this method solves the issue in a straightforward manner. Although this approach is often the simplest to implement, there are several disadvantages to using it to solve a problem. This can only be used to solve issues with small input sizes that are often quite sluggish (Divina & Marchiori, 2005). This algorithm explores all options in search of a good solution to the problem. Brute Force algorithm can be categorized as:

i. Optimizing: This method assists us in identifying the most optimal feasible option. This may involve discovering all of the solutions if the value of the most wonderful option is already known; nevertheless, after the finest potential answer has been identified, it may be necessary to halt searching for other alternatives.

ii. Satisficing: After finding the best potential solution to the problem, this algorithm comes to a complete stop (Figure 2.9).

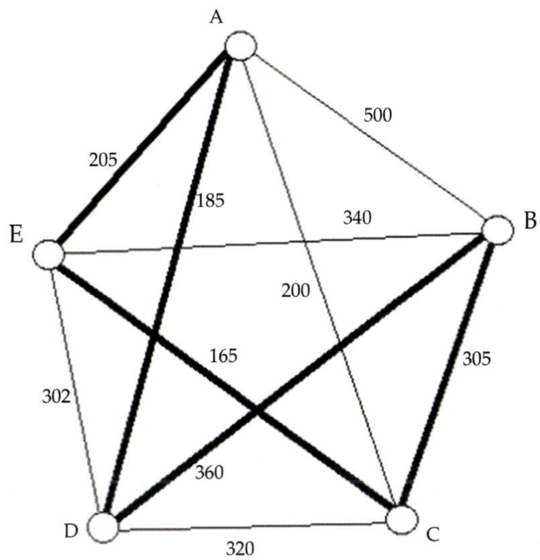

Figure 2.9. Graphical form of brute force algorithm (Source: Margaret Rouse, Creative Commons License).

2.4.7. Branch-and-Bound Algorithm

This type of method is typically employed to assist in the solution of situations when optimization is necessary. An initial tree comprising all the subproblems is formed as soon as the algorithm begins its calculations. The initial problem for which the algorithm is being built is referred to as the root problem. When solving a certain issue, a specific procedure is used to generate the lower and upper jumps (Gunn, 1998; Vapnik, 2013). Each node has its own bonding mechanism, which is implemented.

- If the bounds are comparable, it is possible to estimate a feasible solution to the specific subproblem.
- The issue associated with that specific node should be divided into two subproblems, which should be formed inside the children's nodes if the boundaries are not comparable.

Continue trimming the portions of a tree using the best solution available until all the nodes have been cut (Figure 2.10).

The following is an example of the above-described method in the case of the traveling salesman issue.

i. The salesperson must visit all n cities at least once, and he wishes to reduce the overall distance traveled.
ii. The main issue now is to discover the quickest path through all n cities while visiting each one at least once.
iii. Split the node into two more child issues:

ACTIVITY 2.1

Design and implement a dynamic programming algorithm to solve a specific problem (e.g., the knapsack problem).

a. The quickest way to see the city for a start.
b. The shortest route to avoid visiting the city for a start.

iv. Continue to subdivide the tree in the same manner as it grows.

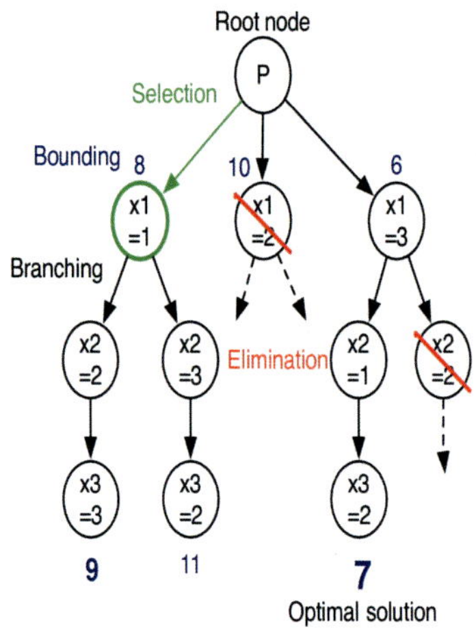

Figure 2.10. Depiction of sequential branch-and-bound method (Source: Malika Mehdi, Creative Commons License).

SUMMARY

In data structures, classification of algorithms refers to categorizing algorithms based on their time and space complexity, as well as their general approach to problem-solving. The time complexity of an algorithm refers to the amount of time it takes to execute, whereas the space complexity refers to the amount of memory required by the algorithm to solve the problem.

Algorithms can be classified based on their approach to problem-solving such as divide and conquer algorithms break a problem down into smaller subproblems and solve each subproblem separately, while dynamic programming algorithms solve a problem by breaking it down into smaller overlapping subproblems and storing the results of each subproblem to avoid redundant computation. Some common classification of algorithms in data structures include dynamic programming algorithms, divide and conquer algorithms, greedy algorithms and sorting algorithms.

REVIEW QUESTIONS

1. How are algorithms classified in data structures based on their approach to problem-solving?
2. What are the differences between deterministic and randomized algorithms?
3. What are online and offline algorithms and how do they differ in their approach to processing data?
4. What are the characteristics of divide and conquer algorithms?
5. What are dynamic programming algorithms and how do they work?

MULTIPLE CHOICE QUESTIONS

1. Which of the following is not a classification of algorithms?

a. Searching algorithms
b. Sorting algorithms
c. Machine learning algorithms
d. Graph algorithms

2. Which of the following is an example of an online algorithm?

a. Bubble sort
b. Quick sort
c. Online and serving algorithm
d. Merge sort

3. **Which of the following is a common searching algorithm used in data structures?**
   a. Merge sort
   b. Quick sort
   c. Breadth-first search
   d. Bubble sort
4. **Which of the following is a characteristic of divide and conquer algorithms?**
   a. They used randomization to achieve a probabilistic solution
   b. They solve problems by breaking them down into smaller subproblems
   c. They make locally optimal choices at each step of the problem-solving process
   d. None of the above
5. **Which of the following is not a backtracking algorithm?**
   a. Knight tour problem
   b. N queen problem
   c. Tower of hanoi
   d. M coloring problem

Answers to Multiple Choice Questions

1. (c) 2. (c) 3. (c) 4. (b) 5. (c)

REFERENCES

1. Aydin, M. E., & Fogarty, T. C., (2004). A distributed evolutionary simulated annealing algorithm for combinatorial optimization problems. *Journal of Heuristics, 10*(3), 269–292.
2. Aydin, M. E., & Fogarty, T. C., (2004). A simulated annealing algorithm for multi-agent systems: A job-shop scheduling application. *Journal of Intelligent Manufacturing, 15*(6), 805–814.
3. Aydin, M. E., & Yigit, V., (2005). 12 parallel simulated annealing. *Parallel Metaheuristics: A New Class of Algorithms, 47*, 267.
4. Battiti, R., & Tecchiolli, G., (1994). The reactive tabu search. *ORSA Journal on Computing, 6*(2), 126–140.
5. Chazelle, B., Edelsbrunner, H., Guibas, L., & Sharir, M., (1989). Lines in space-combinators, algorithms and applications. In: *Proceedings of the Twenty-First Annual ACM Symposium on Theory of Computing* (pp. 382–393). ACM.
6. Codenotti, B., & Simon, J., (1998). *On the Complexity of the Discrete Fourier Transform and Related Linear Transforms Preliminary Version*, 1(2), 22-34.

7. Cook, S. A., (1983). An overview of computational complexity. *Communications of the ACM, 26*(6), 400–408.
8. Cook, S. A., (1987). Prehl'ad teórie výpočtovej složitosti. *Pokroky Matematiky, Fyziky a Astronomie, 32*(1), 12–29.
9. Cormen, T. H., & Leiserson, C. E., (1989). *RL Rivest Introduction to Algorithms*. MIT press. Cambridge, Massachusetts London, England.
10. Creput, J. C., Koukam, A., Lissajoux, T., & Caminada, A., (2005). Automatic mesh generation for mobile network dimensioning using evolutionary approach. *IEEE Transactions on Evolutionary Computation, 9*(1), 18–30.
11. D'Alberto, P., (2000). *Performance Evaluation of Data Locality Exploitation*. University of Bologna, Dept. of Computer Science, Tech. Rep.
12. Dayde, M. J., (1996). *IS Du a Blocked Implementation of Level 3 BLAS for RISC Processors TR_PA_96_06*. Available online: http://www.cerfacs.fr/algor/reports.TR_PA_96_06.ps.gz (accessed on 25 April 2023).
13. Divina, F., & Marchiori, E., (2005). Handling continuous attributes in an evolutionary inductive learner. *IEEE Transactions on Evolutionary Computation, 9*(1), 31–43.
14. Eberhart, R. C., & Shi, Y., (2001). Tracking and optimizing dynamic systems with particle swarms. In: *Evolutionary Computation, 2001; Proceedings of the 2001 Congress* (Vol. 1, pp. 94–100). IEEE.
15. Eberhart, R. C., & Shi, Y., (2004). Guest editorial special issue on particle swarm optimization. *IEEE Transactions on Evolutionary Computation, 8*(3), 201–203.
16. Eberhart, R. C., Shi, Y., & Kennedy, J., (2001). *Swarm Intelligence*. Elsevier.
17. Eberhart, R. C., Shi, Y., & Kennedy, J., (2001). *Swarm Intelligence*. The Morgan Kaufmann series in evolutionary computation.
18. Flajolet, P., Puech, C., Robson, J. M., & Gonnet, G., (1990). *The Analysis of Multidimensional Searching in Quad-Trees*. Doctoral dissertation, INRIA.
19. Fleurent, C., & Ferland, J. A., (1994). Genetic hybrids for the quadratic assignment problem. *Quadratic Assignment and Related Problems, 16*, 173–187.
20. Garey, M. R., & Johnson, D. S., (2002). *Computers and Intractability* (Vol. 29). New York: WH freeman.
21. Garey, M. R., (1979). *DS Johnson Computers and Intractability: A Guide to the Theory of NP-Completeness*, 3(1), 18-24.
22. Glover, F., (1989). Tabu search—Part I. *ORSA Journal on Computing, 1*(3), 190–206.
23. Goodman, J. E., & O'Rourke, J., (1997). *Handbook of Discrete and Computational Geometry* (Vol. 6). CRC Press series on Discrete Mathematics and its Applications.
24. Gunn, S. R., (1998). *Support Vector Machines for Classification and Regression* (Vol. 14, No. 1, pp. 5–16). ISIS Technical Report.
25. He, S., Wu, Q. H., Wen, J. Y., Saunders, J. R., & Paton, R. C., (2004). A particle swarm optimizer with passive congregation. *Biosystems, 78*(1–3), 135–147.

26. Hirschberg, D. S., & Wong, C. K., (1976). A polynomial-time algorithm for the knapsack problem with two variables. *Journal of the ACM (JACM), 23*(1), 147–154.
27. Hu, X., Eberhart, R. C., & Shi, Y., (2003). Particle swarm with extended memory for multiobjective optimization. In: *Swarm Intelligence Symposium, 2003. SIS'03; Proceedings of the 2003 IEEE* (pp. 193–197). IEEE.
28. Kågström, B., & Van, L. C., (1998). Algorithm 784: GEMM-based level 3 BLAS: Portability and optimization issues. *ACM Transactions on Mathematical Software (TOMS), 24*(3), 303–316.
29. Kannan, R., (1980). A polynomial algorithm for the two-variable integer programming problem. *Journal of the ACM (JACM), 27*(1), 118–122.
30. Karp, R. M., (1986). Combinatorics, complexity, and randomness. *Commun. ACM, 29*(2), 97–109.
31. Kennedy, J., & Mendes, R., (2002). Population structure and particle swarm performance. In: *Evolutionary Computation, 2002: CEC'02; Proceedings of the 2002 Congress* (Vol. 2, pp. 1671–1676). IEEE.
32. Kennedy, J., & Mendes, R., (2006). Neighborhood topologies in fully informed and best-of-neighborhood particle swarms. *IEEE Transactions on Systems, Man, and Cybernetics, Part C (Applications and Reviews), 36*(4), 515–519.
33. Kennedy, J., Eberhart, R. C., & Shi, Y., (2001). *Swarm Intelligence*. Morgan Kaufmann Publishers. Inc., San Francisco, CA.
34. Kröse, B., Krose, B., Van, D. S. P., & Smagt, P., (1993). *An Introduction to Neural Networks*, 1, 12-19.
35. Kukuk, M., (1997). *Kompakte Antwortdatenbasen Fiur die LIOSUNG Von Geometrischen Anfrageproblemen Durch Abtastung.* Doctoral dissertation, Diplomarbeit, Informatik VII, universitiat Dortmund.
36. Li, J., (2004). *Peer Streaming: A Practical Receiver-Driven Peer-to-Peer Media Streaming System*. Microsoft Research MSR-TR-2004-101, Tech. Rep.
37. Liu, H., Luo, P., & Zeng, Z., (2007). A structured hierarchical P2P model based on a rigorous binary tree code algorithm. *Future Generation Computer Systems, 23*(2), 201–208.
38. Nisan, N., & Wigderson, A., (1995). On the complexity of bilinear forms: Dedicated to the memory of jacques morgenstern. In: *Proceedings of the Twenty-Seventh Annual ACM Symposium on Theory of Computing* (pp. 723–732). ACM.
39. Panda, P. R., Nakamura, H., & Dutt, N. D., (1997). Tiling and data alignment. *Solving Irregularly Structured Problems in Parallel Lecture Notes in Computer Science.*
40. Pereira, M., (2009). Peer-to-peer computing. In: *Encyclopedia of Information Science and Technology,* (2nd edn., pp. 3047–3052). IGI Global.
41. Pham, D., & Karaboga, D., (2012). *Intelligent Optimization Techniques: Genetic Algorithms, Tabu Search, Simulated Annealing and Neural Networks*. Springer Science & Business Media.

42. Rabin, M. O., (1977). Complexity of computations. *Communications of the ACM, 20*(9), 625–633.
43. Ratakonda, K., & Turaga, D. S., (2008). Quality models for multimedia delivery in a services oriented architecture. *Managing Web Service Quality: Measuring Outcomes and Effectiveness: Measuring Outcomes and Effectiveness.*
44. Restrepo, J. H., Sánchez, J. J., & Mesha, M.H., (2004). Solución al problema de entrega de pedidos utilizando recocido simulado. *Scientia et Technica, 10*(24).
45. Roucairol, C., (1996). Parallel processing for difficult combinatorial optimization problems. *European Journal of Operational Research, 92*(3), 573–590.
46. Sevkli, M., & Aydin, M. E., (2006). A variable neighborhood search algorithm for job shop scheduling problems. In: *European Conference on Evolutionary Computation in Combinatorial Optimization* (pp. 261–271). Springer, Berlin, Heidelberg.
47. Sevkli, M., & Guner, A. R., (2006). A continuous particle swarm optimization algorithm for uncapacitated facility location problem. In: *International Workshop on Ant Colony Optimization and Swarm Intelligence* (pp. 316–323). Springer, Berlin, Heidelberg.
48. Shi, Y., (2001). Particle swarm optimization: Developments, applications and resources. In: *Evolutionary Computation, 2001; Proceedings of the 2001 Congress* (Vol. 1, pp. 81–86). IEEE.
49. Skorin-Kapov, J., (1990). Tabu search applied to the quadratic assignment problem. *ORSA Journal on Computing, 2*(1), 33–45.
50. Stockmeyer, L., & Meyer, A. R., (2002). Cosmological lower bound on the circuit complexity of a small problem in logic. *Journal of the ACM (JACM), 49*(6), 753–784.
51. Stockmeyer, L., (1987). Classifying the computational complexity of problems. *The Journal of Symbolic Logic, 52*(1), 1–43.
52. Taillard, E. D., (1995). Comparison of iterative searches for the quadratic assignment problem. *Location Science, 3*(2), 87–105.
53. Taillard, É., (1991). Robust taboo search for the quadratic assignment problem. *Parallel Computing, 17*(4, 5), 443–455.
54. Thallner, B., & Moser, H., (2005). Topology control for fault-tolerant communication in highly dynamic wireless networks. In: *Intelligent Solutions in Embedded Systems, 2005; Third International Workshop* (pp. 89–100). IEEE.
55. Tran, D. A., Hua, K. A., & Do, T. T., (2004). A peer-to-peer architecture for media streaming. *IEEE Journal on Selected Areas in Communications, 22*(1), 121–133.
56. Vapnik, V., (2013). *The Nature of Statistical Learning Theory*. Springer science & business media.
57. Vitter, J. S., & Simons, R. A., (1986). New classes for parallel complexity: A study of unification and other complete problems for P. *IEEE Transactions on Computers, 35*(5), 403–418.
58. Wierzbicki, A., Strzelecki, R., Swierezewski, D., & Znojek, M., (2002). Rhubarb: A tool for developing scalable and secure peer-to-peer applications. In: *Peer-to-Peer*

Computing, 2002 (P2P 2002); Proceedings Second International Conference (pp. 144–151). IEEE.

59. Wilson, G. V., & Pawley, G. S., (1988). On the stability of the travelling salesman problem algorithm of Hopfield and tank. *Biological Cybernetics, 58*(1), 63–70.
60. Wu, X., Sharif, B. S., & Hinton, O. R., (2005). An improved resource allocation scheme for plane cover multiple access using genetic algorithm. *IEEE Transactions on Evolutionary Computation, 9*(1), 74–81.
61. Xiang, Z., Zhang, Q., Zhu, W., & Zhang, Z., (2003). Replication strategies for peer-to-peer based multimedia distribution service. In: *Multimedia and Expo, 2003: ICME'03; Proceedings 2003 International Conference on* (Vol. 2, pp. II-153). IEEE.
62. Xiang, Z., Zhang, Q., Zhu, W., Zhang, Z., & Zhang, Y. Q., (2004). Peer-to-peer based multimedia distribution service. *IEEE Transactions on Multimedia, 6*(2), 343–355.
63. Xie, Z. P., Zheng, G. S., & He, G. M., (2006). Efficient loss recovery in application overlay stored media streaming. In: *Visual Communications and Image Processing 2005* (Vol. 5960, p. 596008). International Society for Optics and Photonics.
64. Yigit, V., Aydin, M. E., & Turkbey, O., (2004). Evolutionary simulated annealing algorithms for uncapacitated facility location problems. In: *Adaptive Computing in Design and Manufacture VI* (pp. 185–194). Springer, London.
65. Yigit, V., Aydin, M. E., & Turkbey, O., (2006). Solving large-scale uncapacitated facility location problems with evolutionary simulated annealing. *International Journal of Production Research, 44*(22), 4773–4791.

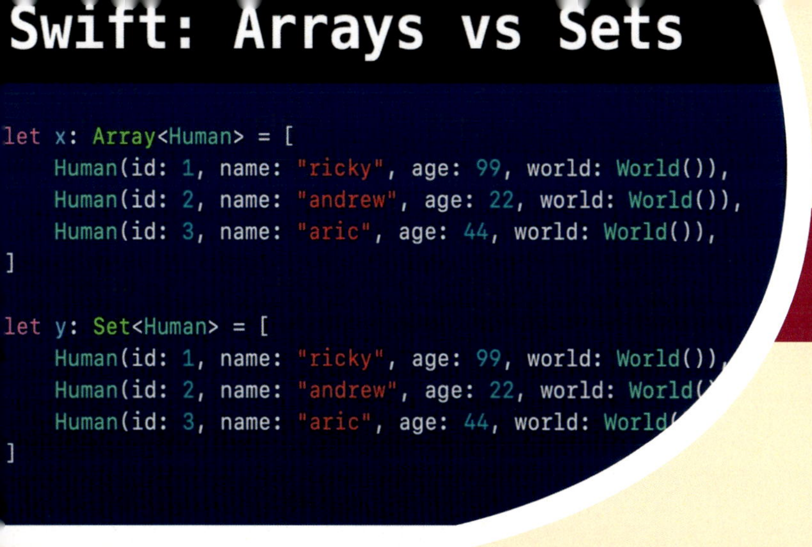

CHAPTER 3

ANALYSIS OF ARRAYS AND SETS

UNIT INTRODUCTION

After writing a few words of computer code, it is realized that data is the heart of programming. All computer programs do is receive, modify, and output data. The software depends on data, whether it's a straightforward application that adds two numbers or enterprise applications that manage entire businesses (Lin et al., 2001).

Data is a general phrase that covers all kinds of information, including the most elementary strings and numbers. The string "Hello World!" seems a data item in the straightforward yet iconic "Hello World!" program (Aho & Hopcroft, 1974). Even the most complex data sets are typically decomposed into a collection of numbers and strings.

Data organization is referred to as data structures. Examine the code below (Gu et al., 1997):

x = "Hello!"

y = "How are you" z = "today?"

Print x + y + z

Three pieces of data are handled by a straightforward program, generating three strings into a single, coherent message. Characterizing the data structure used in a program made it clear that it consists of three separate strings, each referenced by a different variable. This book clarifies that data organization is important for more than just keeping things in order; and how quickly codes are executed. Software may run quite faster or slower depending on how data is arranged (Heintze, 1994). Additionally, the chosen data structures could determine whether the software works or crashes because the load of developing a program cannot be managed and must deal with a lot of data or a web application used mostly by thousands of users at once.

The ability to design swift, elegant code which might guarantee that software runs quickly and without hiccups will substantially improve having a firm understanding of the various datatypes and how each one affects the speed of writing a program (Morris et al., 2008).

The analysis of sets and arrays is made clearer in this chapter. Despite the two data structures' apparent similarity, how to examine each decision's effects on performance is explained.

LEARNING OBJECTIVES

After the chapter, students will be able to understand the following:

- The basic idea and characteristics of arrays as a data structure
- Sets' fundamental concept as a data structure.
- Recognize many operations that may be carried out on sets and arrays.
- Recognize the temporal complexity of various arrays and set operations.

Key Terms

1. Array
2. Data Structure
3. Delete
4. Insert
5. Memory Address
6. Read
7. Search
8. Set
9. Operations
10. Time Complexity

3.1. ARRAY: THE FOUNDATIONAL DATA STRUCTURE

One of the most fundamental data structures in data science is the array. Assuming experience with arrays makes the user aware of why an array is nothing more than a list of data. The array is adaptable and helpful in various circumstances. Let's present one instance for now.

Looking at the software for an application, codes might be encountered that let users make and use grocery store shopping lists (Mitzenmacher, 2001):

Array = ["apples," "bananas," "cucumbers," "dates," "elderberries"]

There are five strings in this array that each represents a possible grocery item. (Must be experimented with elderberries)

An array's index is a number that indicates a piece of data's location inside the array.

Did you Know?

Abacus, a calculating device from the past, is where the idea of arrays originated.

In most programming languages, the index is usually counted from 0. Hence, "apples" is now at index 0 & "elderberries" is at position 4 in the sample array, as shown (Millman & Aivazis, 2011):

"apples"	"bananas"	"cucumbers"	"dates"	"elderberries"
index 0	index 1	index 2	index 3	index 4

The frequent methods that code could interact with a data structure, like an array, to comprehend how well it performs.

Four common uses of data structures as operations are:

i. **Read:** Looking anything up from a specific location inside the data structure is reading. Looking at a value at one specific index in an array is included. For instance, reading from the array would mean searching for the grocery item at index 2.

ii. **Search:** Searching is looking through a data structure for a specific value. Checking an array to determine if a specific value is entailed there and, if so, at what index (Breen et al., 1992). For instance, scanning the array would reveal whether "dates" are on our grocery list and what index it is.

iii. **Insert:** Inserting a new value into our data structure is called insertion. An array entails inserting a fresh value into an extra slot. If "figs" are added to the list of things to buy, a new value to the array must be added.

iv. **Delete:** A value is deleted when taken from the data structure by taking a single value out of an array (Edwards et al., 2014). For instance, removal from the array would occur if the word "bananas" were removed from the grocery list.

This chapter will examine how quickly these operations perform when used on an array.

And this gets to the book's first revolutionary idea: By measuring how "rapid" an operation is, how quickly it goes in terms of just time, but rather how many steps it requires.

Remember

Data structures in computer science can be dynamic or static, having sets being its dynamic data structure and arrays being its static data structure.

Why is this?

No operation can ever be accurately estimated to take 5 seconds. The identical procedure takes a specific machine 5 seconds but takes more time on an outdated piece of hardware or goes much faster on a future supercomputer. Gauging an operation's speed is difficult because it fluctuates based on the hardware used (Fujimoto et al., 1986).

However, the number of steps a process requires allows one to gage how quickly it moves. Operation A is always faster than Operation B across all hardware if Operation A requires five steps & Operation B requires 500 steps. So, counting the stages is essential to figuring out how fast action is.

Measuring an operation's speed is often called determining its temporal complexity. The work will interchangeably use performance, speed, time complexity, and efficiency (Lao et al., 2021). How many steps a particular operation requires is discussed.

Let's examine the four array operations and count the number of steps that each one requires.

3.1.1. Reading

Reading is the first operation to determine the value at a specific array index.

Reading out of an array requires one step. This is due to the computer's ability to jump toward any array index and look inside. Looking up index 2 in the example of ["apples," "bananas," "cucumbers," "dates," and "elderberries,"] the computer would immediately jump to index two and indicate that it has the value "cucumbers" (Verma et al., 2019). How a computer can find an array's index in a single step is explained.

A computer's memory can be considered a massive cluster of cells. The following table shows a mesh of cells, some of which are empty and some of which contain data snippets (Driscoll et al., 1986):

KEYWORD

Snippet is a programming term for a small region of re-usable source code, machine code, or text.

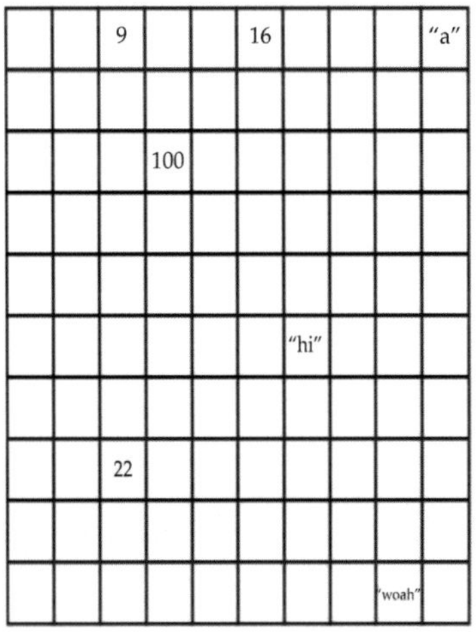

A contiguous collection of empty cells are allocated when a program declares an array for usage by the program. As a result, a computer would choose any row of five empty cells to act as an array if establishing an array was intended to store five elements (Samet, 1984):

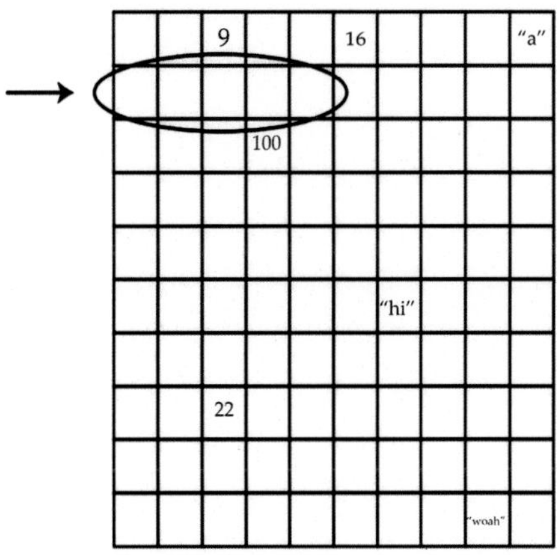

Each memory cell in a computer has a unique address. It resembles a street address in some ways (like 123 Main St.), yet a straightforward number expresses it. The memory address of each cell is one more than the one before it. View the diagram below (Mehlhorn, 2013):

1000	1001	1002	1003	1004	1005	1006	1007	1008	1009
1010	1011	1012	1013	1014	1015	1016	1017	1018	1019
1020	1021	1022	1023	1024	1025	1026	1027	1028	1029
1030	1031	1032	1033	1034	1035	1036	1037	1038	1039
1040	1041	1042	1043	1044	1045	1046	1047	1048	1049
1050	1051	1052	1053	1054	1055	1056	1057	1058	1059
1060	1061	1062	1063	1064	1065	1066	1067	1068	1069
1070	1071	1072	1073	1074	1075	1076	1077	1078	1079
1080	1081	1082	1083	1084	1085	1086	1087	1088	1089
1090	1091	1092	1093	1094	1095	1096	1097	1098	1099

KEYWORD

Memory address is a reference to a specific memory location used at various levels by software and hardware.

The shopping list array, along with its indexes and memory addresses, can be shown in the following diagram (Wiebe et al., 2014):

	"apples"	"bananas"	"cucumbers"	"dates"	"elderberries"
memory address:	1010	1011	1012	1013	1014
index:	0	1	2	3	4

Because of the confluence of the following information, the computer can jump directly to a certain index like an array when reading a value at that position (Wang et al., 2011):

i. A computer can do a one-step jump to almost any memory address. (Consider this as traveling to 123 Main Street; this in a single trip having familiar with the location.)

ii. The memory address that each array starts at is stored in the array. The computer thus conveniently knows this starting address.

iii. The first index of each array is 0 (Charles et al., 2005).

Instructing the computer to retrieve the value on index 3, a computer follows the steps below:

i. At memory address 1010, index 0 of our array is located.
ii. Index 3 will fall precisely three positions after index 0.
iii. Thus, as 1010 + 3 equals 1013, go to memory location 1013 to find index 3 (Amza et al., 1996).

The computer returns the value "dates" after advancing to memory location 1013.

Hence, since reading from such an array only requires one step, it is a very efficient process. The quickest kind of operation is one that only requires one step. The array's ability to quickly search up values at any index is one factor that makes it such a potent data structure.

What if the computer is asked whether "dates" were present in the array rather than asking it what value is present at index 3? The search operation is that, and that is what must be examined.

KEYWORD

Data structure is a specialized format for organizing, processing, retrieving and storing data.

3.1.2. Searching

Searching an array entails determining whether a specific value is present and, if so, at which index. How many steps would be needed to look for "dates" in an array?

The "dates" are immediately visible as the user quickly scans the grocery list and counts, thinking it's at index 3 (Virtanen et al., 2020). On the other hand, a computer lacks sight and must proceed cautiously across the array.

The computer begins at index 0 when looking for a value in an array, checks the value, and moves on to the next index if it doesn't find what it's looking for. It continues doing this until it discovers the value it seeks.

Such illustrations show how the computer search for "dates" within our array of grocery lists:

The machine checks index 0 first (Vigna, 2008):

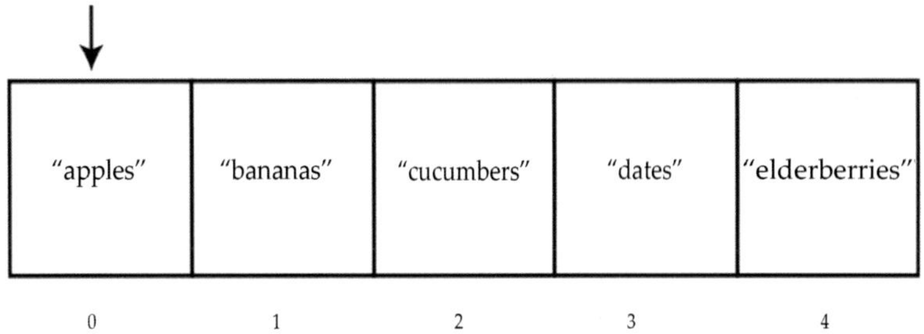

The computer moves to the following index since the item in index 0 is "apples," not just the "dates" that are searched for (Kim et al., 2008):

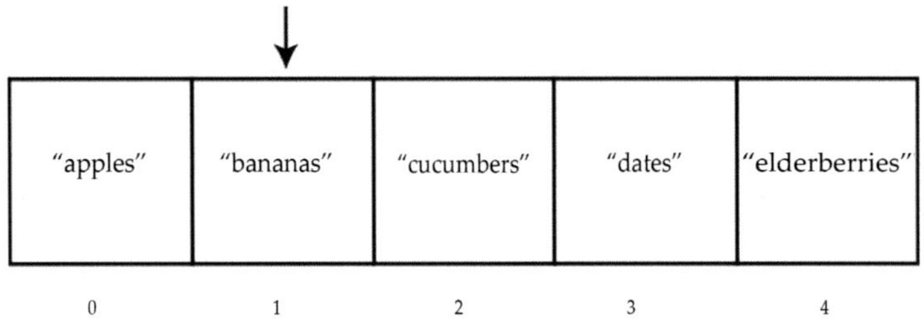

The computer continues onto index 2 because index 1 also lacks the "dates" searched for:

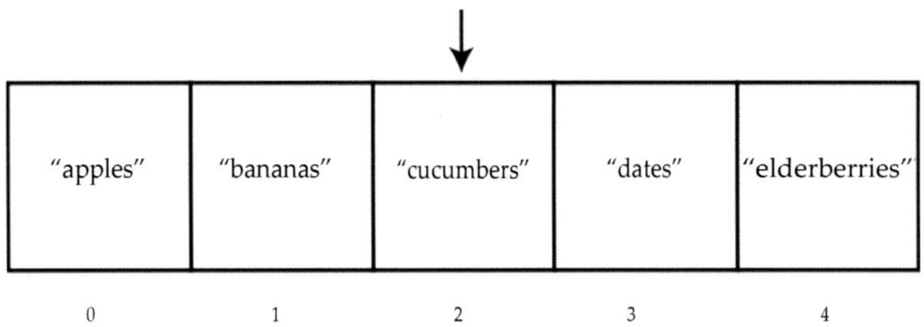

Out of luck once more, so the computer advances to the following cell:

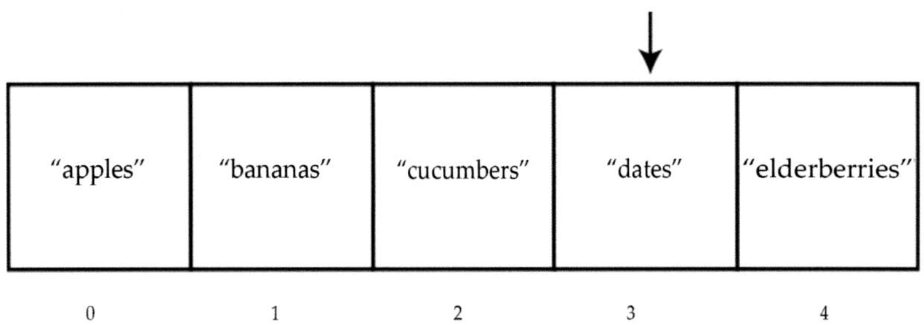

Aha! the strange "dates" are located. Now understand that index 3 contains the "dates" (Van Der Walt et al., 2011). Since what is searched for, the computer doesn't need to continue to the following array cell now.

This case stated that there were a maximum of four steps in the operation because looking into four separate cells before founding the searched value. How many steps would a computer take to complete a search function on an array?

The computer would have to go through each cell of the array until it found the value it was looking for if the value looking for was in the last cell of the array (e.g., "elderberries"). The computer would also need to check every cell to ensure that the searched value doesn't exist in the array if it doesn't appear anywhere (Cormode & Muthukrishnan, 2005). Therefore, five is the greatest number of steps a linear search might take for just an array of five cells. The greatest number of steps a linear search might take for such an array of 500 cells is 500.

Remember

Depending on how they are implemented, operations on arrays & sets can have varying temporal complexity, with certain algorithms being much more efficient than others.

Another way to state is that a linear search will need a max of N steps for an array of N cells. N is a variable that may be changed to any number in this situation (Manber & Myers, 1993). Any event shows that reading is more efficient than searching because reading requires only one step, regardless of the array's size. The insertion operation, or adding a new value to an array, will be examined next.

3.1.3. Insertion

Inserting a new data item into an array determines how efficiently one can do so.

Including "figs" as the final item on a shopping list must be done once because the computer knows the memory address where the array starts. The computer can now determine which memory address to add a new element too because it knows how many items the array currently includes and can do so in a single step. View the diagram below (Aurenhammer, 1991):

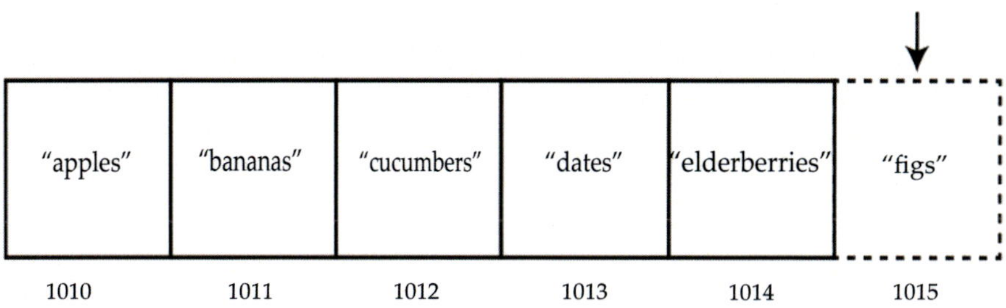

Nevertheless, it is a different situation when adding new data to the beginning or middle of an array. In these circumstances, shifting numerous pieces of data is necessary to make room for putting, necessitating additional procedures.

For illustration, add "figs" to index 2 of the array. View the diagram below (Papazafiropulos et al., 2016):

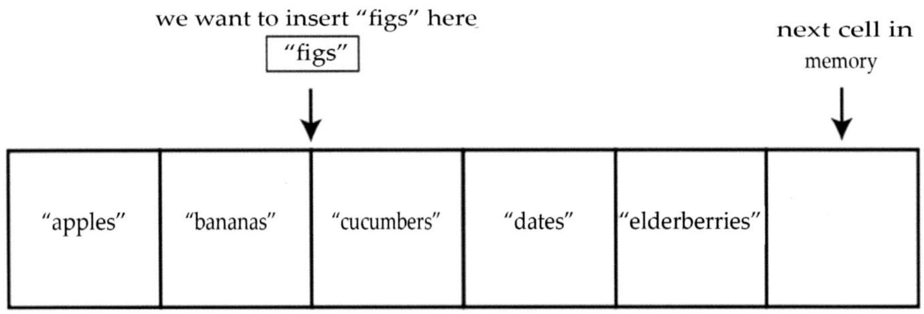

The "figs" must be placed to the right of the "cucumbers," "dates," and "elderberries" to do this. Numerous steps are involved because "dates" must be moved after moving "elderberries" one cell to the right. The "dates" must be moved to make way for the "cucumbers." Go through this procedure together.

Step #1: "Elderberries" is shifted to the right (Harris et al., 2020):

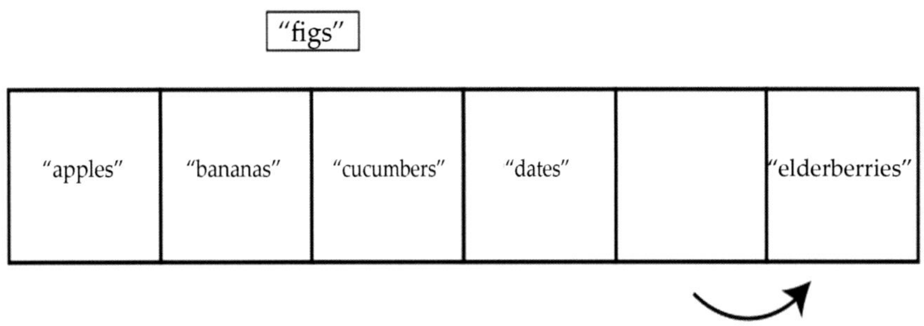

Step #2: "Dates" are shifted to the right:

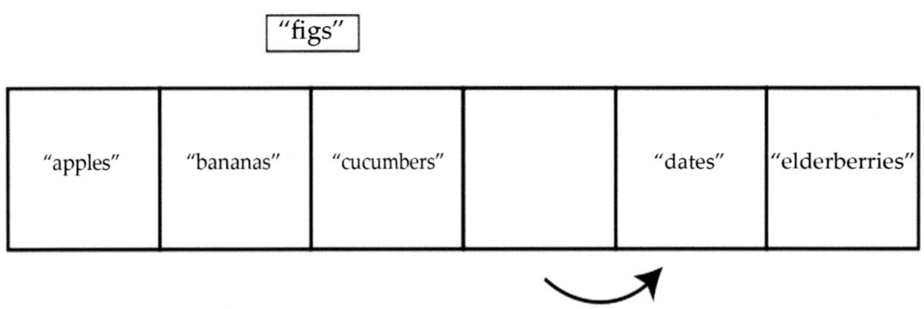

Step #3: We move "cucumbers" to the right (Burlinson et al., 2016):

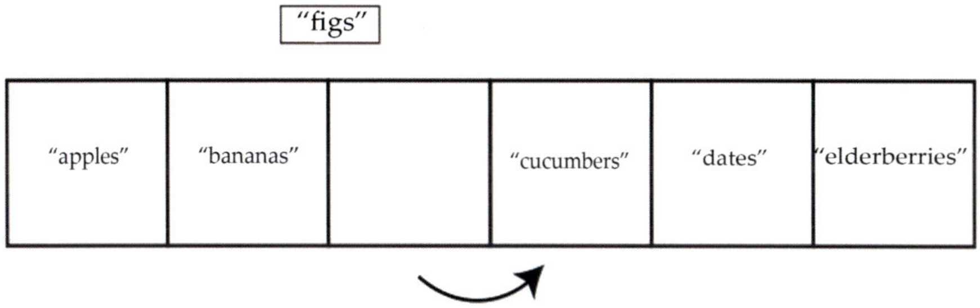

Step #4: Last but not least, we may add "figs" to index 2:

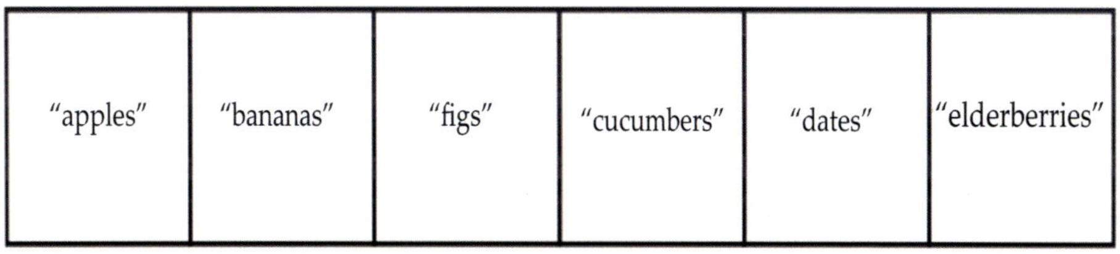

There are four steps in the given case. Three stages involved moving data to the right, and step four involved adding the new value.

Inserting data at the top of the array is the worst-case scenario and the circumstance where insertion requires the most steps (Reynolds, 2002). This is because all other values in one cell move to the right when inserted at the start of the array.

Hence, in the worst case, an array with N elements insertion could require close to N + 1 steps. The worst situation involves adding a value at the start of the array, which involves N shifts (per array data element) and 1 insertion.

The last operation is deletion, which is essentially just insertion done backward.

3.1.4. Deletion

Deleting is removing the values at a specific index out of an array.

Recalling the example array started, remove the values at index 2. which are "cucumbers" in the existing scenario.

Step #1: "Cucumbers" are eliminated from the array (McKinney, 2010):

KEYWORD

Array is a data structure consisting of a collection of elements (values or variables), of same memory size, each identified by at least one array index or key.

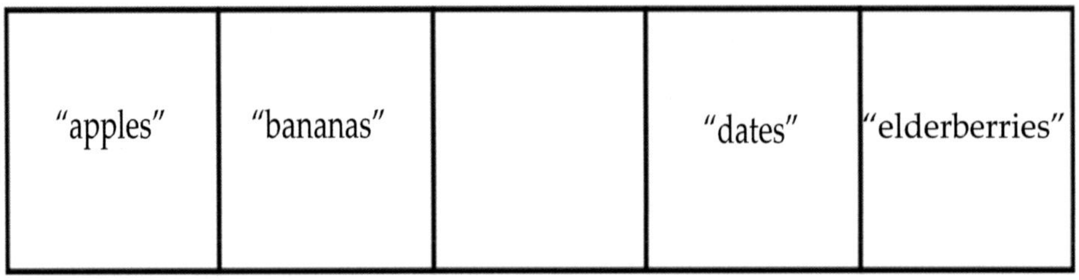

Although theoretically only one step is required to remove "cucumbers," but now a challenge is faced because the array has an empty cell right in the middle. "Dates" and "elderberries" must be moved to the left to address this problem because gaps in the middle of an array are not permitted.

Step #2: "Dates" are moved to the left:

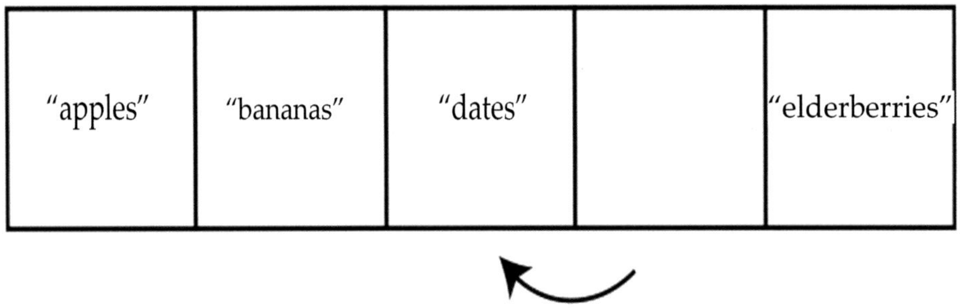

Step #3: "Elderberries" are moved to the left (Goodrich et al., 2014):

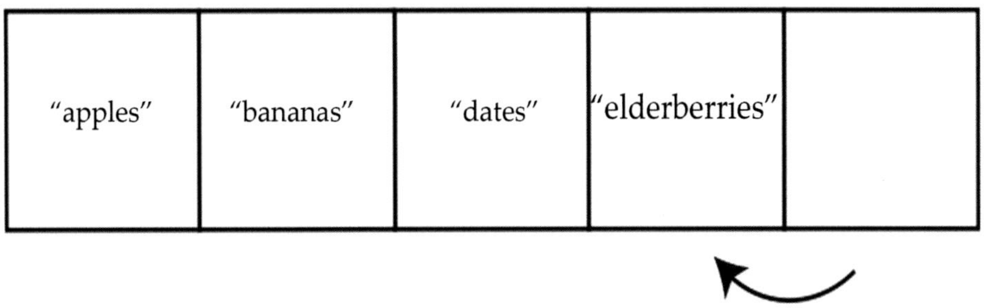

Thus it comes out that three processes are involved in this deletion. The first phase involved deleting the data, while the following two involved shifting data to fill in the gaps.

To fill the gap left by deletion, extra steps are taken to move data towards the left after the first deletion, which is only one stage in the deletion process (Goodrich et al., 2011). The worst-case situation for removing an element is to delete the initial element of the array, similar to insertion. This is because index 0 will be empty and not permitted for arrays, and all of the other elements would need to be shifted to the left to fill the void (Goodrich et al., 2013).

One step is taken to remove the first element from a five-element array, and another four steps to shift the other four elements. One step is taken to delete the first element from an array of 500 elements, and 499 steps to relocate the remaining data (McKinney, 2011). Hence, the maximum number of steps required for deletion for an array with N elements is N.

Though knowing the evaluation of data structure's time complexity, how various data structures perform in different ways is determined. This is crucial because picking the proper data structure for the program can significantly impact how efficient and accurate the code will be.

The next data structure, the set, is so close to the array that they may appear identical at first glance. Yet, the efficiency of operations done on arrays and sets differs.

Did you Know?

Sets are a mathematical idea that has been investigated for centuries; the ancient Greeks were the first to investigate its properties.

3.2. EFFICIENCY AFFECTED IN SETS BY SINGLE RULE

Now let's study another data structure known as Set. A set is a data model that prohibits the inclusion of duplicate values.

There are various sorts of sets, yet array-based sets are focused on the purposes of the article. This set is a simple value list, similar to an array. The only difference between such a set and a traditional array is that duplicate values cannot be added to this set (Belady, 1966).

For instance, if the set ["a," "b," "c"] attempted to add another "b," the computer would not allow it because a "b" currently exists in the set.

Sets are beneficial when avoiding duplicate data is a priority.

In developing an online phonebook, for instance, the same phone number is not required to appear twice. In reality, this issue is seen in the local phonebook: The home phone number is published not only for one person but also incorrectly as the mobile number for a family named Zirkind. Receiving phone calls and voicemails from individuals asking for the Zirkinds is annoying. Likewise, Zirkinds might wonder why nobody ever phones them. And when the user contacts the Zirkinds to inform them of the mistake, the user's wife answers the phone since the user accidentally dialed his number. (Ok, that last part doesn't ever occur.) If only the computer that generated the telephone directory had employed a set.

In any scenario, a set is just an array with the restriction of duplicates not permitted. Yet, this restriction alters the efficiency of one of the four basic operations for the set. Let's examine reading, searching, insertion, and deletion within the framework of an array-based set.

Reading from one set is identical to reading from an array; the computer needs only one step to determine what is needed within a certain index. The system may jump to almost any index between the sets (Vaidya & Clifton, 2005). After all, it knows where the set begins in memory.

It takes almost N steps to determine whether a value exists inside a set, the same as the number of steps required to determine if a value appears within an array. And deletion is equivalent between a set or an array; it requires up to N steps to remove a value and shift data to the left to fill in the gap (Urban & Quilter, 2005). Arrays and sets differ, however, with respect to insertion. Putting a number at the end of a set was the ideal example for an array. While using an array, the computer can insert a value at the end of an array in a single step computer can add a value at the end of an array in one step while using an array.

Although this is exactly what sets are intended to achieve, the computer must first confirm that this value doesn't yet exist within the set: They prevent data duplication. Thus, each insert requires an initial search. No one wants to purchase the same item twice, so having a defined grocery list would be a good idea. If the current set is ["apples," "bananas," "cucumbers," "dates," and "elderberries"] and "figs," needs to add to this listing search is required and follow the procedures below:

Step #1: Index 0 search for "figs" (Kulik et al., 1985):

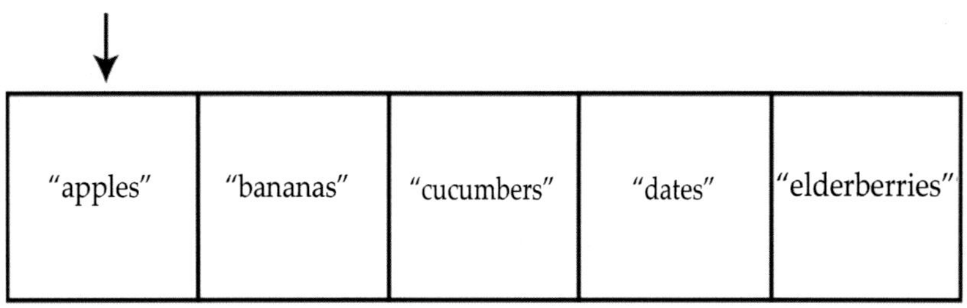

There is a possibility that it exists somewhere in the set. Before introducing "figs," ensure it does not appear anywhere else (ElGamal, 2013).

Step #2: Lookup index 1:

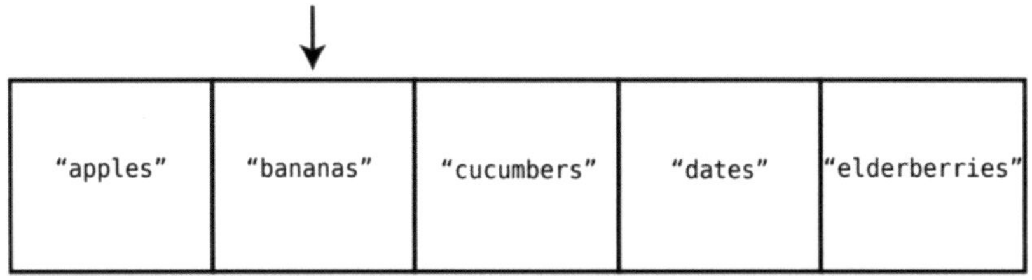

Step #3: Lookup index 2:

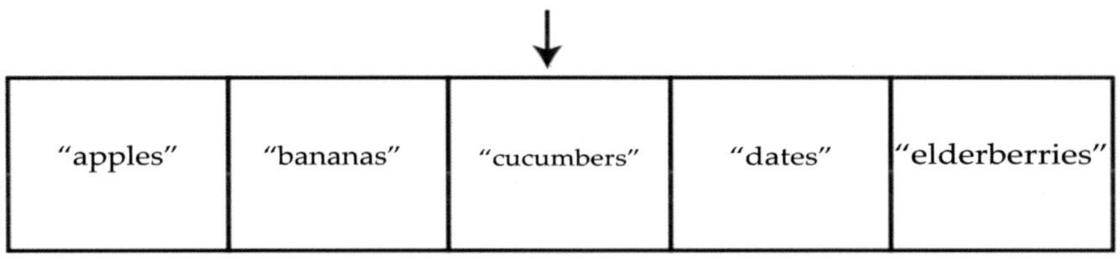

Step #4: Lookup index 3:

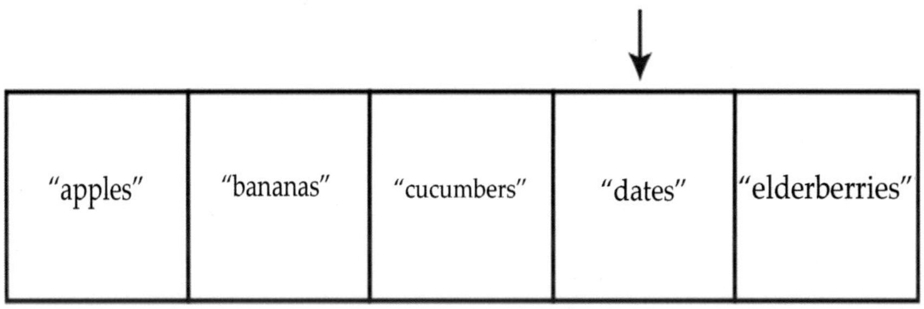

Step #5: Lookup index 4:

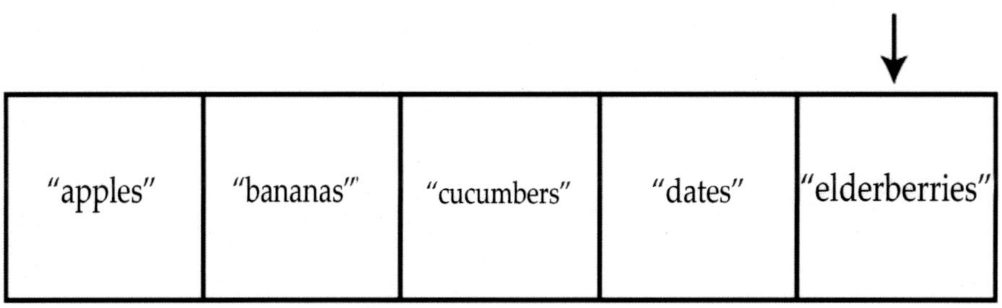

It's okay to input "figs" now since the set is thoroughly investigated. This brings the last action.

Step #6: At the end of the set, add "figs." (Bernard et al., 2012).

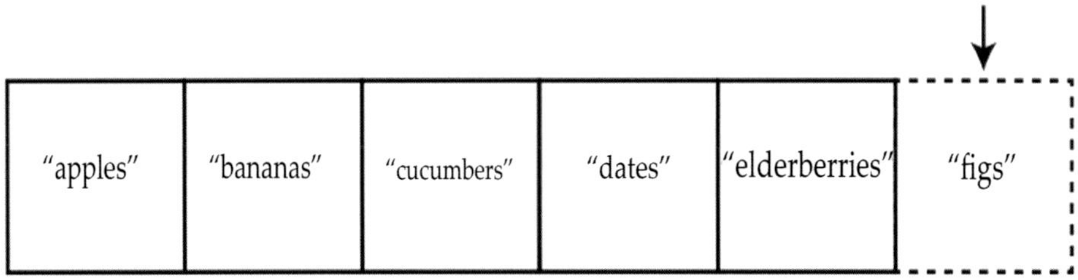

ACTIVITY 3.1

Examine the effectiveness of various operations on arrays & sets, including adding, removing, looking for, and iterating through the elements.

Adding a value at the end of a set is the best case, but still had to go through 6 stages for a set with five items at first. This means a search through all five items is needed before the last insertion step.

In other words: In the best situation, N elements will require N + 1 steps for insertion into a set. This is so that the value can be inserted in one step after N searching steps to ensure it doesn't already exist in the set (Rosenschein & Zlotkin, 1994).

In the worst case, the computer would have to check N cells to ensure the set doesn't already include the value entered at the beginning, take a further N step to move all of the data toward the right, and then take a final step to add the new value. The total steps are 2N plus 1.

Does this imply that sets should be avoided since insertion is slower than normal arrays? Without a doubt, ensure there are no duplicate pieces of data. Sets are crucial. If this is not required, an array might be better because insertions of arrays are quicker than insertions of sets. The best data format for the application will depend on analyzing its requirements.

SUMMARY

Understanding the efficiency of data structures starts with looking at how many steps an operation requires. The proper data structure for software will determine whether it can carry the load or break beneath it. How to apply this analysis and to determine if an array or set could be the better option for a particular application is described in this chapter. Use the same evaluation to assess competing algorithms (even those operating on the same data structure), ensuring the final speed and performance of code now consider the computation time of data structures.

REVIEW QUESTIONS

1. What are data structures, and why are they important in computer programming?
2. What is an array, and what are its characteristics?
3. How is a set different from other data structures?
4. How does the time complexity of operations differ between arrays and sets?
5. Give examples of algorithms or applications where arrays or sets are used.

MULTIPLE CHOICE QUESTIONS

1. Which data structure is used for storing a fixed-size sequential collection of elements of the same type?

a. Arrays
b. Sets
c. Lists
d. Trees

2. Which data structure is used for storing a collection of unique elements?

a. Arrays
b. Sets
c. Lists
d. Trees

3. Which of the following data structures is efficient for random access of elements?

a. Arrays
b. Sets
c. Lists
d. Trees

4. Which of the following data structures allows duplicates

a. Trees
b. Lists
c. Sets
d. Arrays

5. Which of the following operations is faster in a set?

a. Accessing an element by index
b. Removing an element from the middle
c. Testing for membership of an element
d. Sorting of the elements

Answers to Multiple Choice Questions

1. (a) 2. (b) 3. (a) 4. (d) 5. (c)

REFERENCES

1. Aho, A. V., & Hopcroft, J. E., (1974). The design and analysis of computer algorithms (Vol. 1, pp. 2–5). Pearson Education India.
2. Amza, C., Cox, A. L., Dwarkadas, S., Keleher, P., Lu, H., Rajamony, R., & Zwaenepoel, W., (1996). Treadmarks: Shared memory computing on networks of workstations. *Computer, 29*(2), 18–28.
3. Aurenhammer, F., (1991). Voronoi diagrams—A survey of a fundamental geometric data structure. *ACM Computing Surveys (CSUR), 23*(3), 345–405.
4. Belady, L. A., (1966). A study of replacement algorithms for a virtual-storage computer. *IBM Systems Journal, 5*(2), 78–101.
5. Bernard, P. E., Moës, N., & Chevaugeon, N., (2012). Damage growth modeling using the thick level set (TLS) approach: Efficient discretization for quasi-static loadings. *Computer Methods in Applied Mechanics and Engineering, 233*(1), 11–27.
6. Breen, E. J., Joss, G. H., & Williams, K. L., (1992). Dynamic arrays for fast, efficient, data manipulation during image analysis: A new software tool for exploratory data analysis. *Computer Methods and Programs in Biomedicine, 37*(2), 85–92.
7. Burlinson, D., Mehedint, M., Grafer, C., Subramanian, K., Payton, J., Goolkasian, P., & Kosara, R., (2016). BRIDGES: A system to enable creation of engaging data structures assignments with real-world data and visualizations. In: *Proceedings of the 47th ACM Technical Symposium on Computing Science Education* (Vol. 1, pp. 18–23).
8. Charles, P., Grothoff, C., Saraswat, V., Donawa, C., Kielstra, A., Ebcioglu, K., & Sarkar, V., (2005). X10: An object-oriented approach to non-uniform cluster computing.

ACM Sigplan Notices, 40(10), 519–538.

9. Cormode, G., & Muthukrishnan, S., (2005). An improved data stream summary: The count-min sketch and its applications. *Journal of Algorithms, 55*(1), 58–75.
10. Driscoll, J. R., Sarnak, N., Sleator, D. D., & Tarjan, R. E., (1986). Making data structures persistent. In: *Proceedings of the Eighteenth Annual ACM Symposium on Theory of Computing* (Vol. 1, pp. 109–121).
11. Edwards, H. C., Trott, C. R., & Sunderland, D., (2014). Kokkos: Enabling manycore performance portability through polymorphic memory access patterns. *Journal of Parallel and Distributed Computing, 74*(12), 3202–3216.
12. ElGamal, A. F., (2013). An educational data mining model for predicting student performance in programming course. *International Journal of Computer Applications, 70*(17), 22–28.
13. Fujimoto, A., Tanaka, T., & Iwata, K., (1986). Arts: Accelerated ray-tracing system. *IEEE Computer Graphics and Applications, 6*(4), 16–26.
14. Goodrich, M. T., Tamassia, R., & Goldwasser, M. H., (2013). *Data Structures and Algorithms in Python* (Vol. 1, pp. 978–1011). Hoboken: Wiley.
15. Goodrich, M. T., Tamassia, R., & Goldwasser, M. H., (2014). *Data Structures and Algorithms in Java* (Vol. 1, pp. 3–7). John Wiley & sons.
16. Goodrich, M. T., Tamassia, R., & Mount, D. M., (2011). *Data Structures and Algorithms in C++* (Vol. 1, pp. 2–6). John Wiley & Sons.
17. Gu, J., Li, Z., & Lee, G., (1997). Experience with efficient array data flow analysis for array privatization. In: *Proceedings of the Sixth ACM SIGPLAN Symposium on Principles and Practice of Parallel Programming* (Vol., 1, pp. 157–167).
18. Harris, C. R., Millman, K. J., Van, D. W. S. J., Gommers, R., Virtanen, P., Cournapeau, D., & Oliphant, T. E., (2020). Array programming with NumPy. *Nature, 585*(7825), 357–362.
19. Heintze, N., (1994). Set-based analysis of ML programs. *ACM SIGPLAN Lisp Pointers, 7*(3), 306–317.
20. Kim, D. K., Kim, M., & Park, H., (2008). Linearized suffix tree: An efficient index data structure with the capabilities of suffix trees and suffix arrays. *Algorithmica, 52*, 350–377.
21. Kulik, J. A., Kulik, C. L. C., & Bangert-Drowns, R. L., (1985). Effectiveness of computer-based education in elementary schools. *Computers in Human Behavior, 1*(1), 59–74.
22. Lao, B., Wu, Y., Nong, G., & Chan, W. H., (2021). Building and checking suffix array simultaneously by induced sorting method. *IEEE Transactions on Computers, 71*(4), 756–765.
23. Lin, D. K., Simpson, T. W., & Chen, W., (2001). Sampling strategies for computer experiments: Design and analysis. *International Journal of Reliability and Applications, 2*(3), 209–240.

24. Manber, U., & Myers, G., (1993). Suffix arrays: A new method for on-line string searches. *SIAM Journal on Computing, 22*(5), 935–948.
25. McKinney, W., (2010). Data structures for statistical computing in python. In: *Proceedings of the 9th Python in Science Conference* (Vol. 445, No. 1, pp. 51–56).
26. McKinney, W., (2011). Pandas: A foundational python library for data analysis and statistics. *Python for High Performance and Scientific Computing, 14*(9), 1–9.
27. Mehlhorn, K., (2013). *Data Structures and Algorithms 1: Sorting and Searching* (Vol. 1, pp. 4–8). Springer Science & Business Media.
28. Millman, K. J., & Aivazis, M., (2011). Python for scientists and engineers. *Computing in Science & Engineering, 13*(2), 9–12.
29. Mitzenmacher, M., (2001). Compressed bloom filters. In: *Proceedings of the Twentieth Annual ACM Symposium on Principles of Distributed Computing* (Vol. 1, pp. 144–150).
30. Morris, M. D., Moore, L. M., & McKay, M. D., (2008). Using orthogonal arrays in the sensitivity analysis of computer models. *Technometrics, 50*(2), 205–215.
31. Papazafiropulos, N., Fanucci, L., Leporini, B., Pelagatti, S., & Roncella, R., (2016). Haptic models of arrays through 3D printing for computer science education. In: *Computers Helping People with Special Needs: 15th International Conference, ICCHP 2016, Linz, Austria, July 13–15, 2016, Proceedings, Part I 15* (Vol. 1, pp. 491–498). Springer International Publishing.
32. Reynolds, J. C., (2002). Separation logic: A logic for shared mutable data structures. In: *Proceedings 17th Annual IEEE Symposium on Logic in Computer Science* (Vol. 1, pp. 55–74). IEEE.
33. Rosenschein, J. S., & Zlotkin, G., (1994). *Rules of Encounter: Designing Conventions for Automated Negotiation Among Computers* (Vol. 1, pp. 3–6). MIT press.
34. Samet, H., (1984). The quadtree and related hierarchical data structures. *ACM Computing Surveys (CSUR), 16*(2), 187–260.
35. Urban, J. M., & Quilter, L., (2005). Efficient process or chilling effects-takedown notices under section 512 of the digital millennium copyright act. *Santa Clara Computer & High Tech. LJ, 22*(1), 621.
36. Vaidya, J., & Clifton, C., (2005). Secure set intersection cardinality with application to association rule mining. *Journal of Computer Security, 13*(4), 593–622.
37. Van, D. W. S., Colbert, S. C., & Varoquaux, G., (2011). The NumPy array: A structure for efficient numerical computation. *Computing in Science & Engineering, 13*(2), 22–30.
38. Verma, N., Jia, H., Valavi, H., Tang, Y., Ozatay, M., Chen, L. Y., & Deaville, P., (2019). In-memory computing: Advances and prospects. *IEEE Solid-State Circuits Magazine, 11*(3), 43–55.
39. Vigna, S., (2008). Broadword implementation of rank/select queries. In: *Experimental Algorithms: 7th International Workshop, WEA 2008 Provincetown, MA, USA, May 30-June 1, 2008 Proceedings 7* (Vol. 1, pp. 154–168). Springer Berlin Heidelberg.

40. Virtanen, P., Gommers, R., Oliphant, T. E., Haberland, M., Reddy, T., Cournapeau, D., & Van, M. P., (2020). SciPy 1.0: Fundamental algorithms for scientific computing in python. *Nature Methods, 17*(3), 261–272.
41. Wang, Y., Huang, J., & Lei, J., (2011). The formal design models of a universal array (UA) and its implementation. *International Journal of Software Science and Computational Intelligence (IJSSCI), 3*(3), 69–89.
42. Wiebe, M., Rocklin, M., Alumbaugh, T. J., & Terrel, A., (2014). Blaze: Building a foundation for array-oriented computing in python. In: *Proceedings of the 13th Python in Science Conference* (Vol. 1, pp. 99–102).

CHAPTER 4

ALGORITHM SELECTION

UNIT INTRODUCTION

The effectiveness of code can be considerably impacted by the data structure. Even seemingly unrelated data structures, like the set and array, may harm or make a program under excessive stress (Raschka, 2018).

After choosing a specific data structure, there is still another crucial variable that can have a significant impact on the effectiveness of code: selecting the right algorithm to employ.

Although the term algorithm implies complexity, the process is quite simple. An algorithm is a specific method for addressing a problem (Kerschke et al., 2019). For instance, an algorithm might be used to prepare a cereal bowl. The algorithm for making cereal follows these four steps:

i. Take a bowl.
ii. Fill the bowl with cereal.
iii. Fill the bowl with milk.
iv. Place a spoon inside the bowl (Rice, 1976).

An algorithm is a procedure for carrying out a specific operation in computing terms. Deletion, searching, insertion, and reading are the four main processes examined previously. This chapter explains multiple ways to approach a task. In other words, various algorithms can carry out a specific operation.

To learn how to make the code writing fast or slow—even to the point at which it breaks down under extreme stress. A brand-new data structure is examined for this purpose, called an ordered array (Leyton-Brown et al., 2003). Many available algorithms are searched for various orders and learn how to pick the best one.

Learning Objectives

After the chapter, readers will be able to comprehend the following:

- Recognize the significance of algorithms for data structures.
- A conceptual basis for ordered arrays.
- Method for looking for a value in ordered arrays.
- The fundamental concept of binary search or comparison to linear search.

Key Terms

1. Algorithms
2. Binary Search
3. Data Structures
4. Linear Search
5. Ordered arrays
6. Sorting
7. Searching

4.1. ORDERED ARRAYS

The ordered array and the array are nearly similar. The only distinction is that ordered arrays demand the values be consistently maintained in – you guessed it – order (Swarztrauber, 1984). In other words, whenever a value gets added, it is added to the appropriate cell, maintaining the array's sort order. In contrast, values can be inserted at the end of a regular array without considering the sequence of items.

As an illustration, consider the array [3, 17, 80, and 202]:

3	17	80	202

To add the number 75 in a conventional array, the number 75 can be added at the last position, as seen below (Chen, 2001):

3	17	80	202	75
				↑

As mentioned in the previous chapter, the computer can complete this in a single step.

To insert the value 75 in an ordered array, it is placed in the appropriate location to maintain the items' ascending order (Mohammed et al., 2021):

3	17	75	80	202
		↑		

This is more easily said than done, though. The 75 cannot be dropped into the appropriate slot by the computer in a single motion. It must first identify the proper location for the 75 to be inserted before shifting other values to create room for it. Let's dissect this procedure in detail.

Restarting from the initially ordered array (Puglisi et al., 2007):

3	17	80	202

Step #1: Examine the number located at index 0 to find out whether the 75 should be inserted to the left or the right of it:

KEYWORD

Ordered array is an array in which elements are arranged in a sorted order either in ascending or descending order.

3	17	80	202

75 has to be added someplace to its right because 75 is bigger than 3, which is known. The following cell must be inspected because it is unknown which cell needs to be placed.

Step #2: The value in the following cell is examined (Baase, 2009):

3	17	80	202

Continue since 75 is higher than 17

Step #3: Look at the value in the subsequent cell:

3	17	80	202

Number 80, bigger than the 75 and desired to insert, has been found. This 75 must be positioned directly to the left of 80 to keep the sequence of this ordered array since it reached the first value bigger than 75. To do so, move some data around to accommodate the 75.

Step #4: The last value is moved to the right (Manber & Myers, 1993).

3	17	80		202

Step #5: Place the previous-to-last value to the right (Amestoy et al., 2004):

3	17		80	202

Step #6: Finally, place the number 75 in its proper location:

3	17	75	80	202

It becomes apparent that while adding to an organized array, A search must be performed to determine the exact location for the insertion. This is a significant efficiency distinction between standard and ordered arrays (Christou et al., 2012).

While an ordered array is less efficient for insertion than a regular array, it has a concealed superpower when it occurs during the search operation.

KEYWORD

Linear search is the simplest approach employed to search for an element in a data set.

4.2. SEARCHING AN ORDERED ARRAY

The procedure for locating a specific value within a regular array: examine each cell individually, from left to right, until the desired value is found. This procedure is known as linear search (Kumar, 2013). Let's compare linear search with a conventional array and an ordered array.

Consider the case having the standard array [17, 3, 75, 202, and 80]. The value 22 can theoretically be found everywhere in the array; to search for it—which is not the case in this example, every element must be searched. To locate the value before approaching the array's end that's the sole situation that can halt our search before it ends (Bentley & Sedgewick, 1997).

But even if the value isn't in the array, a search may stop early with an ordered array while trying to find a 22 in the sorted array [3, 17, 75, 80, 202]. The 22 can't possibly be anywhere to the right of the 75, so stop looking as soon as you reach there.

Here is an example of a linear search using an ordered array in Ruby.

```
def linear_search(array, value)
array each do |element|
if element == value
return value
elsif element > value
break
end
end
return nil
end
```

In light of this, linear search typically needs fewer steps in an array with order than in a regular array. Despite this, a scan is required in every cell if the value looking for is equal to or higher than the final number (Parmar & Kumbharana, 2015).

The efficiency of ordered and regular arrays doesn't seem to differ significantly at first glance.

But that's because the potential of algorithms has not yet been fully realized. And soon, that will alter.

Up until this point, assuming that linear search is the only method for finding a value inside an ordered array. However, linear search is merely one feasible algorithm, i.e., one specific value search method. It involves searching every single cell until the desired value is found. However, it isn't the only approach available for finding values.

An ordered array benefits over a standard array because it supports a different searching algorithm. This method is called binary search, as it is significantly faster than linear search (Mehlhorn, 2013).

4.3. BINARY SEARCH

Did you Know?

Aristotle, an ancient Greek thinker, first described the divide-and-conquer strategy, upon which binary search is founded.

Maybe someone has played this game as a child or may play it with their children now: Think of a number between one and 100. Continue guessing the number one considering, and one will indicate if you need to estimate higher or lower (Nowak, 2009).

Once already knew the way to play the game. No one would begin the game by selecting the number 1. but would start with 50, which is exactly in the middle (Bentley, 1975).

Why? Because by choosing 50, regardless of whether advised to estimate higher or lower, half of the possible numbers get eliminated!

If one guessed 50 and were told to predict higher, one would choose 75 to eliminate fifty percent of the leftover numbers. If advised to predict lower after one guessed 75, one would choose 62 or 63. Thus, select the halfway point to eliminate half of the leftover numerals.

Visualize this procedure with a game in which one must predict a number between 1 and 10 instead (Lieberman & Allebach, 1997):

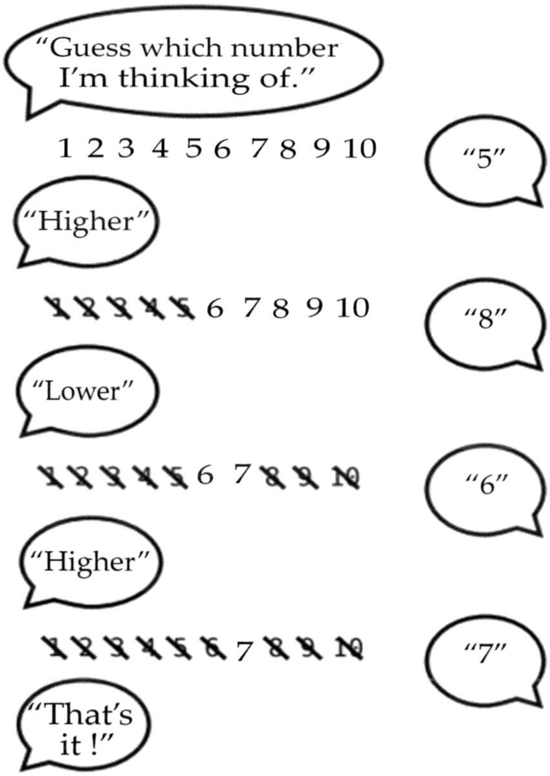

Figure 4.1. Illustration of game for binary search (Source: Jay Wengrow, Creative Commons License).

Binary search can be described as follows, in a nutshell.

The main benefit of an array that is ordered to a regular array is the availability of a binary search instead of a linear search (Alhroob et al., 2020). With a typical array, binary search is impossible because the values may be in any sequence.

Suppose having a 9-element ordered array to observe this in action. Since the computer cannot tell the value that each cell holds, arrays shall represent as follows (Zhang et al., 2013):

?	?	?	?	?	?	?	?	?

Let's assume that one wants to look inside this ordered array for the value 7. A binary search will help do this:

Step #1: Start looking in the center cell. Since the array's length is known, one can divide it by two to get the correct memory address and jump to this cell. Look at that cell's value:

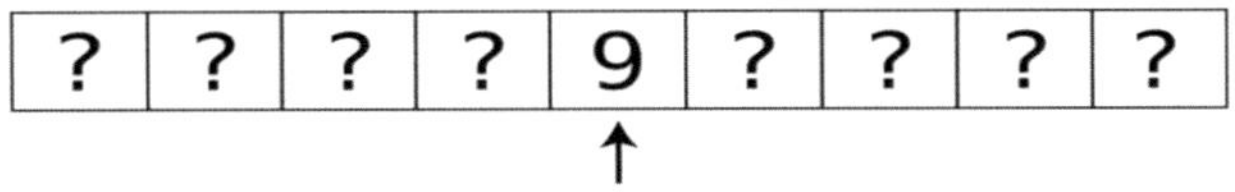

One can infer the position of the seven is to its left because the revealed value is a 9. Effectively deleted all cells to the proper (right) side of the nine from the array, which is half of the array. (and the 9 itself) (Liu et al., 2022):

Step #2: Look at the cells' middle value to the left of number 9. Given that there are two center values, we arbitrarily select the left one (Crawford et al., 2017):

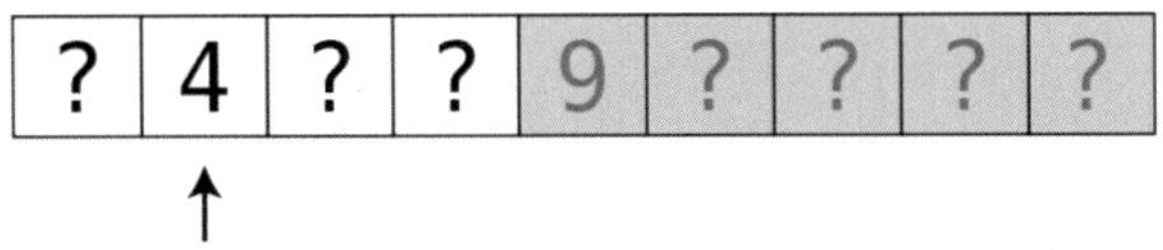

The 4 indicates that the 7 has to lie to its right. Remove 4 as well as adjacent cell:

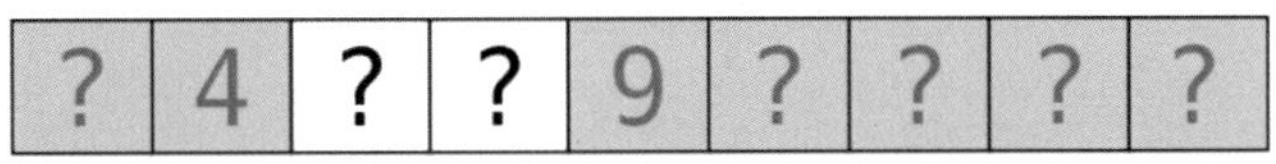

Step #3: There are two additional compartments where the seven can fit. Arbitrarily select the one on the left (Liu et al., 2019):

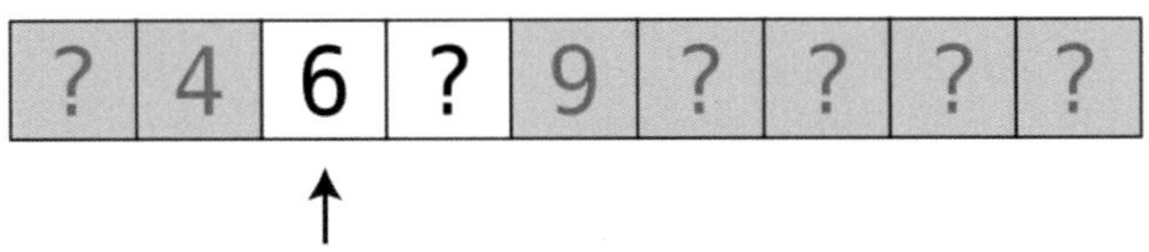

Step #4: We examine the last remaining cell. (If it is absent, there is no 7 in this ordered array.)

In four stages, seven are located successfully. Even though this is the identical number of steps in a linear search needed in this example, the strength of binary search is shortly demonstrated (Jennison et al., 1991).

Here is a Ruby implementation of binary search:

```
def binary_search(array, value)
lower_bound = 0
array _bound = upper.length – 1
while lower_bound <= upper_bound do
midpoint = (upper_bound + lower_bound) / 2
value_at_midpoint = array[midpoint]
if value < value_at_midpoint
upper_bound = midpoint – 1
elsif value > value_at_midpoint
lower_bound = midpoint + 1
elsif value == value_at_midpoint
return midpoint
end
end
return nil
end
```

4.4. BINARY SEARCH VS. LINEAR SEARCH

The binary search technique does not significantly outperform the linear search algorithm for ordered arrays of small size (Berman & Collin, 1974). Now examine what transpires with larger arrays, though.

The maximum amount of steps required for search with an array of 100 values:

Search linearly: 100 steps. Seven steps for binary search.

Using a linear search, one must look at every element to see if the value looking for is in the last cell or is higher compared to the value in the last cell. This would require 100 steps for an array of size 100.

But when utilizing binary search, every guess cuts down the number of cells that potentially scan by half. To eliminate a startling fifty cells in the first guess

Take a second look and will notice a pattern:

The binary search method requires two steps to find anything in a list of size 3, which is the maximum number of steps possible (Bentley, 1979).

KEYWORD

Binary search is an efficient algorithm for finding an item from a sorted list of items.

There are seven cells in total to twice the present amount of cells on an array of cells, and then add one more cell so that the total number remains odd to keep things simple. Using binary search, the number of steps that may be taken to find something in such an array is three.

If double it once more (and add one), then the greatest number of steps required to locate something utilizing binary search is four. This is the case even if the sorted array has 15 members.

The pattern appears that the number of steps required for binary search will rise by just one each time the number of objects in the arranged array is doubled. This pattern develops when double the number of items in the array.

This pattern is exceptionally useful: The binary search technique will add an excess of a single additional step for each time that doubles the amount of data (Das & Khilar, 2013).

Compare this to the method of linear search. Having three items, the process could take up to three steps. No one can have more than seven stages for any element. Up to 100 steps are required to reach the number 100. A linear search will have the same stages as an item within the database. When using a linear search, the number of necessary steps will increase by a factor of two if the same factor increases the number of elements in an array (Balogun, 2020). In binary search, increase the number of steps by one if the number of elements in the array increases is increased by a factor of two.

This graph enables everyone to see how the performance of binary search compares to that of linear search (Kumari et al., 2012):

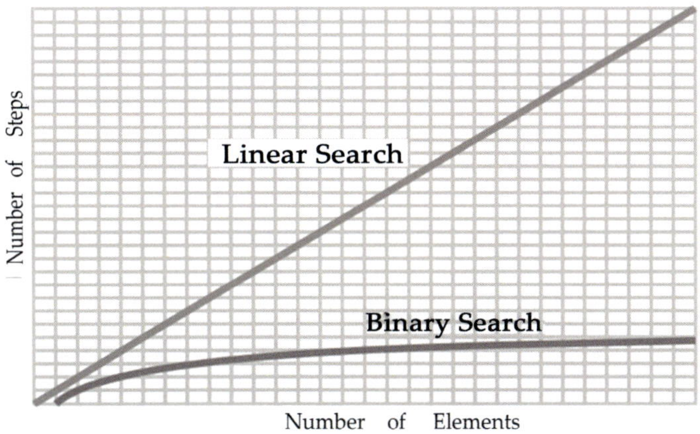

Figure 4.2. Graph of performance comparison between linear and binary search (Source: Brain Macdonald, Creative Commons License).

Now see how this works out for arrays that are even more massive. When searching through an array with 10,000 elements, a linear approach could take as many as 10,000 steps, while a binary search could take as few as 13 steps. A linear search may take as many as one million steps for an array with a size of 1 million, whereas a binary search could take as few as twenty steps for the same size array (Sreelaja, 2021).

Once more, it is important to consider that structured arrays are not always faster in all circumstances. Inserting data into ordered arrays takes significantly longer than into regular arrays. The trade-off, however, is as follows: While utilizing an ordered array, the insertion process is slightly slower, but the search process is a lot quicker. Always evaluating applications is required to determine what would be a better fit (Bajwa et al., 2015).

And this is the point where talking about algorithms. There are frequently several ways to accomplish a specific computing task and the algorithm that might significantly impact how quickly the code runs.

It's also critical to understand that, in most cases, there isn't a single data structure or method that is ideal in every circumstance (Gambhir et al., 2016). Always utilize sorted arrays just because they provide binary search. Standard arrays might be preferable when expecting to explore the data frequently but merely add data, as their insertion is quicker. Counting each competing algorithm's steps that each competing algorithm takes is the best way to compare them.

Did you Know?

Ada Lovelace, a British mathematician, and author who lived in the nineteenth century created one of the first computer programs.

ACTIVITY 4.1

Use a binary search technique to look up a certain element within an ordered array.

Plot the runtimes of the linear search and binary search methods for big arrays to compare how well they work.

SUMMARY

Because they govern how data may be handled, modified, and searched, algorithms are important in data structures. Binary search is one typical algorithm that is used to order arrays. A data structure known as an ordered collection comprises a group of components sorted in either a descending or ascending order. An ordered array can be effectively searched for a particular element using the binary search technique. With ordered arrays, binary search dramatically lowers the number of comparisons required for locating an element. Overall, algorithms like binary search are critical for data structures like ordered arrays. They can greatly increase the effectiveness of activities like searching, resulting in speedier and more productive systems.

REVIEW QUESTIONS

1. Why algorithms are important in data structures.
2. What effect do algorithms have on how well data structures perform?
3. Describe an ordered array & how data structures use it.
4. How binary search boosts the effectiveness of looking through ordered arrays.
5. How may algorithm selection impact the effectiveness of data structures?

MULTIPLE CHOICE QUESTIONS

1. What is the primary function of algorithms in data structures?

a. To store data efficiently
b. To retrieve data quickly
c. To manipulate and process data
d. To secure data storage

2. What is binary search?

a. An algorithm for sorting elements in an array
b. An algorithm for searching for a component in an unordered list
c. An algorithm for searching for an element in an ordered list
d. None of the above

3. What is the advantage of using binary search with ordered arrays?

a. It can reduce the number of comparisons needed to find an element
b. It can increase the number of comparisons required to find an element
c. It can only be used with small arrays
d. None of the above

4. **What is an ordered array?**
   a. A data structure that stores elements in random order
   b. A data structure that stores elements in ascending or descending order
   c. A data structure that stores elements in a hash table
   d. None of the above
5. **Select the best description to explain what a binary search algorithm is.**
   a. Put the elements in order, check each item in turn.
   b. Elements do not need to be in order, compare to the middle value, split the list in order and repeat
   c. Elements do not need to be in order, check each item in turn.
   d. Put the elements in order, compare with the middle value, split the list in order and repeat.

Answers to Multiple Choice Questions

1. (c) 2. (c) 3. (a) 4. (b) 5. (d)

REFERENCES

1. Alhroob, A., Alzyadat, W., Imam, A. T., & Jaradat, G. M., (2020). The genetic algorithm and binary search technique in the program path coverage for improving software testing using big data. *Intelligent Automation & Soft Computing, 26*(4), 3–9.
2. Amestoy, P. R., Davis, T. A., & Duff, I. S., (2004). Algorithm 837: AMD, an approximate minimum degree ordering algorithm. *ACM Transactions on Mathematical Software (TOMS), 30*(3), 381–388.
3. Baase, S., (2009). *Computer Algorithms: Introduction to Design and Analysis* (Vol. 1, pp. 2–5). Pearson Education India.
4. Bajwa, M. S., Agarwal, A. P., & Manchanda, S., (2015). Ternary search algorithm: Improvement of binary search. In: *2015 2nd International Conference on Computing for Sustainable Global Development (INDIACom)* (Vol. 1, pp. 1723–1725). IEEE.
5. Balogun, G. B., (2020). *A Comparative Analysis of the Efficiencies of Binary and Linear Search Algorithms* (Vol. 1, pp. 5–8).
6. Bentley, J. L., & Sedgewick, R., (1997). Fast algorithms for sorting and searching strings. In: *Proceedings of the Eighth Annual ACM-SIAM Symposium on Discrete Algorithms* (Vol. 1, pp. 360–369).
7. Bentley, J. L., (1975). Multidimensional binary search trees used for associative searching. *Communications of the ACM, 18*(9), 509–517.
8. Bentley, J. L., (1979). Multidimensional binary search trees in database applications. *IEEE Transactions on Software Engineering, 3*(4), 333–340.

9. Berman, G., & Collin, A. W., (1974). A modified list technique allowing binary search. *Journal of the ACM (JACM), 21*(2), 227–232.
10. Chen, W., (2001). New algorithm for ordered tree-to-tree correction problem. *Journal of Algorithms, 40*(2), 135–158.
11. Christou, M., Crochemore, M., Flouri, T., Iliopoulos, C. S., Janoušek, J., Melichar, B., & Pissis, S. P., (2012). Computing all subtree repeats in ordered trees. *Information Processing Letters, 112*(24), 958–962.
12. Crawford, B., Soto, R., Astorga, G., García, J., Castro, C., & Paredes, F., (2017). Putting continuous metaheuristics to work in binary search spaces. *Complexity, 1*, 3–7.
13. Das, P., & Khilar, P. M., (2013). A randomized searching algorithm and its performance analysis with binary search and linear search algorithms. *International Journal of Computer Science & Applications (TIJCSA), 1*(11), 2–7.
14. Gambhir, A., Vijarania, M., & Gupta, S., (2016). Implementation and application of binary search in 2-D array. *Int. J. Inst. Ind. Res., 2*(1), 30, 31.
15. Jennison, B. K., Allebach, J. P., & Sweeney, D. W., (1991). Efficient design of direct-binary-search computer-generated holograms. *JOSA A, 8*(4), 652–660.
16. Kerschke, P., Hoos, H. H., Neumann, F., & Trautmann, H., (2019). Automated algorithm selection: Survey and perspectives. *Evolutionary Computation, 27*(1), 3–45.
17. Kumar, P., (2013). Quadratic search: A new and fast searching algorithm (an extension of classical binary search strategy). *International Journal of Computer Applications, 65*(14), 1–10.
18. Kumari, A., Tripathi, R., Pal, M., & Chakraborty, S., (2012). Linear search versus binary search: A statistical comparison for binomial inputs. *International Journal of Computer Science, Engineering and Applications, 2*(2), 29–30.
19. Leyton-Brown, K., Nudelman, E., Andrew, G., McFadden, J., & Shoham, Y., (2003). A portfolio approach to algorithm selection. In: *IJCAI* (Vol. 3, pp. 1542–1543).
20. Lieberman, D. J., & Allebach, J. P., (1997). Efficient model based halftoning using direct binary search. In: *Proceedings of International Conference on Image Processing* (Vol. 1, pp. 775–778). IEEE.
21. Liu, J. P., & Tsai, C. M., (2022). Binary computer-generated holograms by simulated-annealing binary search. In: *Photonics* (Vol. 9, No. 8, p. 581). MDPI.
22. Liu, J. P., Yu, C. Q., & Tsang, P. W., (2019). Enhanced direct binary search algorithm for binary computer-generated Fresnel holograms. *Applied Optics, 58*(14), 3735–3741.
23. Manber, U., & Myers, G., (1993). Suffix arrays: A new method for on-line string searches. *SIAM Journal on Computing, 22*(5), 935–948.
24. Mehlhorn, K., (2013). *Data Structures and Algorithms 1: Sorting and Searching* (Vol. 1, pp. 4–8). Springer Science & Business Media.
25. Mohammed, A. S., Amrahov, Ş. E., & Çelebi, F. V., (2021). Interpolated binary search: An efficient hybrid search algorithm on ordered datasets. *Engineering Science and Technology, an International Journal, 24*(5), 1072–1079.

26. Mozes, S., Onak, K., & Weimann, O., (2008). Finding an optimal tree searching strategy in linear time. In: *SODA* (Vol. 8, pp. 1096–1105).
27. Nowak, R., (2009). Noisy generalized binary search. *Advances in Neural Information Processing Systems, 22*(1), 3–6.
28. Parmar, V. P., & Kumbharana, C. K., (2015). Comparing linear search and binary search algorithms to search an element from a linear list implemented through static array, dynamic array and linked list. *International Journal of Computer Applications, 121*(3), 1–6.
29. Puglisi, S. J., Smyth, W. F., & Turpin, A. H., (2007). A taxonomy of suffix array construction algorithms. *ACM Computing Surveys (CSUR), 39*(2), 4–9.
30. Raschka, S., (2018). *Model Evaluation, Model Selection, and Algorithm Selection in Machine Learning, 1,* 4–10.
31. Rice, J. R., (1976). The algorithm selection problem. In: *Advances in Computers* (Vol. 15, pp. 65–118). Elsevier.
32. Sreelaja, N. K., (2021). Ant colony optimization based light weight binary search for efficient signature matching to filter ransomware. *Applied Soft Computing, 111*(1), 107–635.
33. Swarztrauber, P. N., (1984). FFT algorithms for vector computers. *Parallel Computing, 1*(1), 45–63.
34. Zhang, D., Wei, L., Leung, S. C., & Chen, Q., (2013). A binary search heuristic algorithm based on randomized local search for the rectangular strip-packing problem. *INFORMS Journal on Computing, 25*(2), 332–345.

CHAPTER 5

STACKS AND QUEUES

UNIT INTRODUCTION

A stack only provides access to the most recently inserted data item. One can see the next-to-last item introduced, if the item is removed etc. This ability is beneficial in numerous programming scenarios (Brandenburg, 1988). This section investigates the use of stacking to determine whether the parentheses and commas in the source file of a computer program are uniformly distributed. Stacking is also indispensable for decoding the weakest (analyzing) equations like 3*(4+5).

Stacking is helpful when programmers use complex data structure algorithms. Most microprocessors, including those found in computers, utilize a stack-based architecture. The returned address and arguments are placed on a stack before the stack is cleared when an associated function is called. Stacking operations are incorporated within the microprocessor (Shavit & Taubenfeld, 2016).

Earlier portable calculators utilized a stack-based architecture. Instead of using parentheses to input arithmetic expressions it pushed the intermediate outcomes onto a stack.

A line is a British term for the procession (the type in which individuals wait). To queue up in UK means creating a line. In computing, a queue has evolved into an identical data structure to a stack, except that the first item added to a backlog is eliminated first. (FIFO). The last item added to a pile is the first to be eliminated. (LIFO) (Pierson & Rodger, 1998).

A queue works identically to the ticketing line: the first person who arrives at the queue's rear is the first to reach the front to purchase a ticket. Final in line appears to be the only one who purchased a ticket (or, if the event is sold out, the final individual who did not purchase a ticket). Figure 5.1 depicts how this appears (Park & Ahmed, 2017).

Figure 5.1. Image of how a queue works (Source: Jeff Durham, Creative Commons License).

Learning Objectives

At the chapter's end, students will get the ability to comprehend the following:

- Understand the concepts of stacks and queues and their applications in computer science
- Difference between LIFO (last in, first out) and FIFO (first in, first out) data structures
- Basic operations of stacks and queues, including push, pop, enqueue and dequeue
- Understand how to implement stacks and queues using arrays and linked list
- Fundamental concept of priority queues and their implementation

Key Terms

1. Array Implementation
2. Dequeue
3. Enqueue

4. Function Calls
5. FIFO
6. LIFO
7. Linked List
8. Overflow
9. Push
10. Pop
11. Task Scheduling
12. Underflow

5.1. UNDERSTANDING STACKS

To better comprehend the concept of a tower, examine some analogies. The United States Postal Service supplies the first. Upon receiving the mail, many people arrange it on the foyer table or place it in an "in" basket at work (Hanciles et al., 1997). Then, in the spare time, they organize the accumulated correspondence in reverse order. Accept the letter at the stack's highest point first, then respond appropriately by paying the bill, tossing it, etc.

The initial letter has been discarded, and the next letter, now at the top of the heap, is examined and dealt with. Get the letters at the bottom of any stack eventually. (it is currently on top). Figure 5.2 shows a stack of letters (Kanetkar, 2019).

The "do what's essential first" approach is suitable so that every communication can be processed appropriately. There is an opportunity that the invoices being held will not be paid on time or that the letters at the lowest point of the stack will not be read for days.

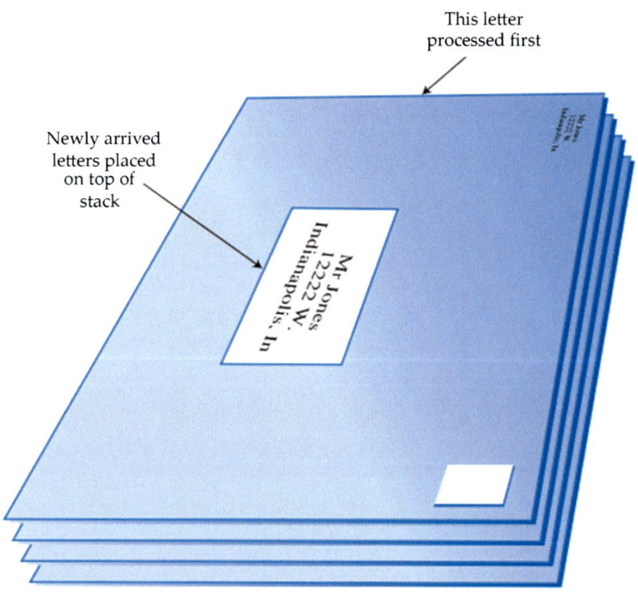

Figure 5.2. Image of a stack of letters (Source: Robert Lafore, Creative Commons License).

Many individuals do not strictly adhere to this approach. Take mail from the stack's lowest part as an example, and start with the earliest letter. Or, before processing the mail, they may search through it and position the letters in the highest priority on top. In such cases, the email system is replaced by a computing science stack. A queue is created when letters are eliminated from the bottom; a priority queue is created when letters are prioritized. In the next hour, these options will be discussed.

A second analogy for a stack is the duties completed on a typical workday. Working on a time-consuming project

(A) when a coworker requests some help with another one

(B) (Tan & Seng, 2010). Any member of Accounting stops by to talk about travel costs

(C) while working on B. During this meeting, one might answer an urgent call from Sales or briefly troubleshoot a large product. (

D). Restart Project B after call D is over, project B after meeting C is over, and Project A after Project B is finished (at last!). Tasks with a lower priority be "stacked up" and waiting for completion.

Pushing is placing a data point at the summit of the hierarchy. Removing an object from the summit of a tall structure is called "popping" it (Stigall & Sharma, 2018). These include the most basic tasks on a stack.

Last-In-First-Out (LIFO) refers to a storage mechanism where the last item added is the first to be removed.

Remember

Stacks are used in many programming languages to keep track of function calls. When a function is called, its parameters and local variables are added to the stack. When the function returns, they are removed from the stack.

5.1.1. The Stack Workshop Applet

Utilize a Workshops applet of Stack to understand how stacks function. Figure 5.3 depicts the four icons appearing when this applet is launched: New, Push, Pop, or Peek (Stojanova et al., 2017). Will discuss these next.

This Stack Workshops applet seems array-based. An array containing information items is observed. A stack limits access despite relying on an array of values, so no one can access every data entry as with an array.

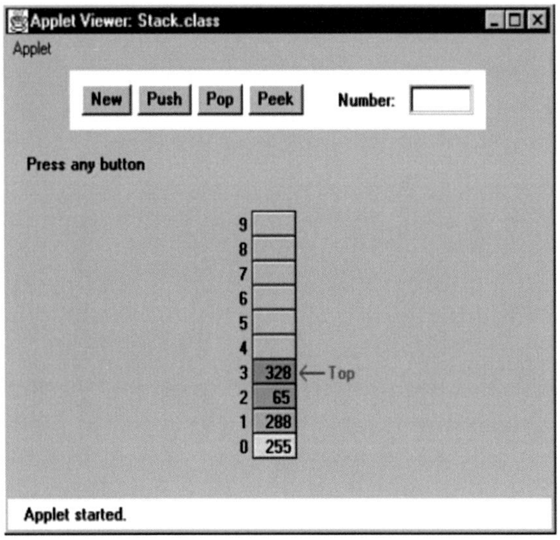

Figure 5.3. Illustration of the stack workshop applet (Source: Tonya Simpson, Creative Commons License).

5.1.1.1. New

Four data items are already entered into the stack at the beginning of the Workshop applet. The New button will start a brand-new stack off empty if that's what is required (Case et al., 2010). The three buttons after that perform the key stack operations.

5.1.1.2. Push

To add an object to the stack, click the Push icon. After once tapping this button, enter the key's contents to push the object. A few more keystrokes will move the entered item to the peak of the stack after it has been entered into the text field.

The topmost part of the stack, or the most recent item inserted, is always shown by a red arrow (Celinski et al., 2017). The Top arrow is incremented (moved up) throughout the insertion procedure in one step (button click), and the data item is inserted into the cell in the following phase. Reversing the order would replace the current item at the top. Maintaining these two phases correctly while writing the code for implementing a stack is crucial.

Pushing a new item when the stack of items is full results in a message that says, "Can't insert: stacking is full." (The array that implements an ADT stack fills up even though an ADT stack shouldn't logically do so.)

5.1.1.3. Pop

Use the Pop icon to eliminate data from the highest part of the stack. When a pop() routine returns a result, the popped value displays in the Numbers text field (Boyapati & Darga, 2007).

Again, note the two necessary steps: The item is first taken out of the cell that Top points to, after which Top decreases to indicate the greatest occupied cell. The order utilized in the initial push operation is reversed in this.

When an item is eliminated from the array using the pop operation, the cell color turns gray to indicate it has done so. This slightly misrepresents how computer memory works because deleted objects stay in an array until new data is written over them (Nikander & Virrantaus, 2007). However, they are theoretically gone, the applet illustrates, because they can't be accessible once the Top marker goes below their position.

The top arrows indicate –1, below the lowest cell, when the last Item on the stack has been removed. This shows that there is nothing on the stack. When the stack is empty, the message "Can't pop: Stacking is blank" tries to pop an item.

5.1.1.4. Peek

The two most important stack operations are push and pop (Rodger, 2002). However, reading values at the highest point of the stacks with no deleting can sometimes be helpful. This is done using the peek operation. Press a Peek button several times to copy the category value of the items at the peak of the stack into the Numeric text box. Nonetheless, the object doesn't disappear from the stack; it stays there.

Look at the top item briefly. The stacked user cannot see any additional parts by design.

5.1.1.5. Stack Size

Because stacks are frequently brief, transitory data structures, a stack is demonstrated with ten cells (Di Benedetto et al., 2011). Stacks in actual applications could require a little bit more space, but still astonishing how little space a stack uses. For instance, a stack of merely a few dozen cells can parse a very long mathematical expression.

KEYWORD

Stack is an abstract data type (ADT), that is popularly used in most programming languages. It is named stack because it has the similar operations as the real-world stacks, for example – a pack of cards or a pile of plates, etc.

After reviewing what stacks are used for, examine how they are implemented in C++ (Wiener & Pinson, 2000).

5.1.2 Stack Implementation in C++

Let's have to take a look at Stack. cpp, an application that implements a stack using the StackX class. The code below implements this class and includes a short main() function (Keith & Martin, 1994).

```
THE Stack.cpp PROGRAM
#include <iostream>
#include <vector>
using namespace std;
class StackX
{
private:
int maxSize;
<double> stackVect;
int top;
public:
StackX(int s) : maxSize(s), top(-1)
{
stackVect.reserve(maxSize);
}
void push(double j)
{
stackVect[++top] = j;
}
double pop()
{
return stackVect[top--];
```

```
}
double peek()
{
return stackVect[top];
}
bool isEmpty()
{
return (top == -1);
}
bool isFull()
{
return (top == maxSize-1);
}
};
int main()
{
StackX theStack(10);
theStack.push(20);
theStack.push(40);
theStack.push(60);
theStack.push(80);
while( !theStack.isEmpty() )
{
double value = theStack.pop();
cout << value << " ";
}
cout << endl;
```

```
return 0;

} //end main()
```

The main() function builds a stack with a capacity of 10, adds four items to this stack, and then pops each item off the stack one at a time until the stack is empty (Baumgartner & Russo, 1995). Here is the result:

```
80 60 40 20
```

Observe how the data are presented in reverse order. The 80 shows up first in the output since the final item was pushed & was the first one popped.

KEYWORD

Data item is a container of data that is registered with the server. The set of data items registered with the server comprises the server's data store.

The data members in this iteration within StackX class are of type double. This can be altered to anything else, such as object types.

5.1.3. StackX Class Member Functions

Like in earlier applications, a vector is the class's data storage method. It is known as stackVect here.

The function Object() [native code] creates a brand-new stack of whatever size is specified in its argument. The variables hold the stack's maximum size (the vectors). The data members of the vector are the vector itself, with the variable at the top, which stores an index of the item at the top of the stack (Drocco et al., 2020).

To store a data item, the push() function within the member moves top-up so that the points area is immediately above the previous top. Keeping in mind that before inserting the object, the top is increased (Hogan, 2014).

The member function pop() returns the top-most value and then decreases the top (Dubois-Pelerin & Zimmermann, 1993). However, the value is still available in the vector even though the item is effectively rendered unreachable and removed from the stack.

A member's peek() method returns the value at the peak of the stacks without changing it. Stack being blank or full, the member method isEmpty(), and full () returns true correspondingly. If a stack is empty, the peak variable is at -1; if the stacking is full, it is at maxSize-1. Push() and pop() are seen in Figure 5.4 (Blunk & Fischer, 2014).

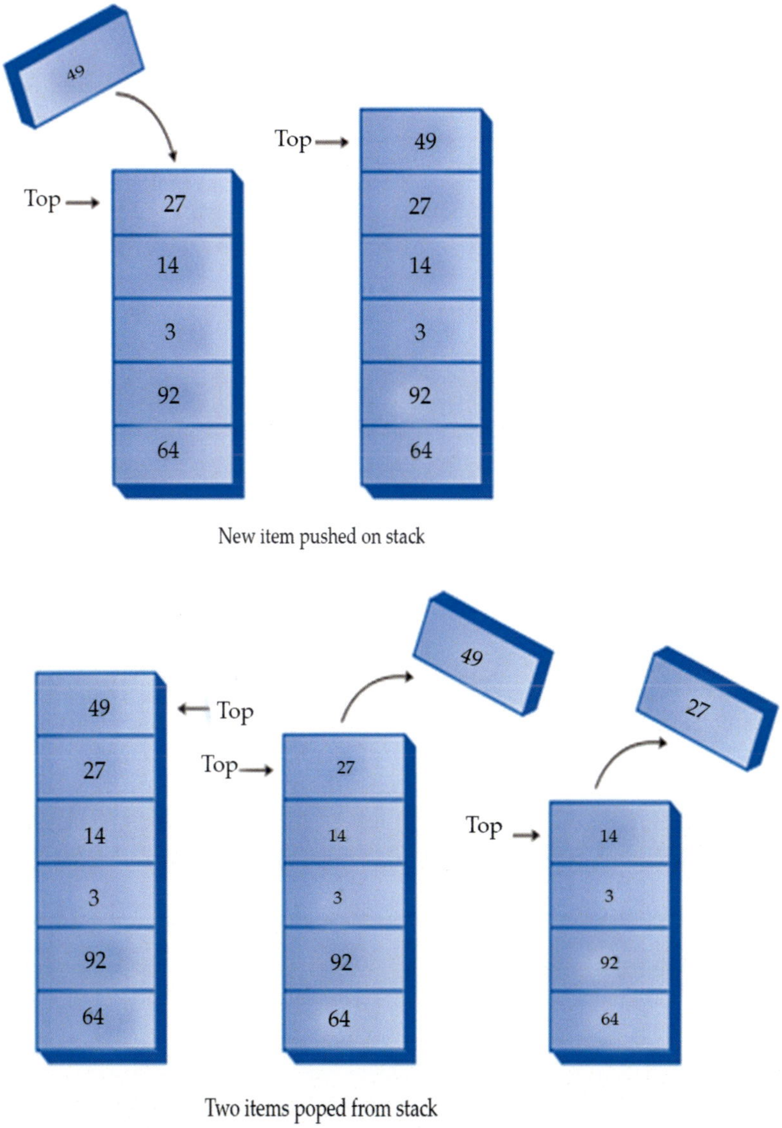

Figure 5.4. Operation of the StackX class member functions (Source: Robert Lafore, Creative Commons License).

5.1.4. Error Handling

There are various approaches to handling stack faults. To push something onto a full stack? Or remove something from an empty stack?

In Stack. Cpp, the class user control over how to handle these failures. While pushing a new item, one makes sure the stack isn't already full (Thomas, 2016):

```
if( !theStack.isFull() )

theStack.push(item);
```

```
else

cout << "Can't insert, stack is full";
```

This code portion is left aside from the main() procedure in the interests of simplicity (and, in any case, in this small application, recognizing the condition of the stack is not complete due to its recent initialization). Test the empty stack when pop() is used in main().

KEYWORD

Stack class represents a last-in-first-out (LIFO) stack of objects.

Internal tests for these issues are provided by several stack classes in the member functions push() and pop() (Serebryany et al., 2018). Throwing an exception that can be collected and handled by the class user is a good approach for a stack class in C++ when such issues are found.

After learning the basics of programming a stack, let's examine several applications that use stacks to address issues.

5.1.5. Delimiter Matching

Parsing specific types of text strings is one frequent application for stacks. The programs processing the strings are often compilers, and the strings are typically coded in a machine's language (Vandevoorde & Josuttis, 2002).

A program that determines what is involved by looking at the text limitations in a user-typed piece of text. Even while it fails to be just one line of real C++ code (although it might be), this text should use delimiters similarly to how C++ does. The delimiters are the brackets [and], parentheses [and], and braces. The rule states that the same closure separator must come after every initial delimiter (on the left), and so on. In a string, delimiters that open later must be sealed over delimiters that open earlier. Here are a few instances:

c[d]

a{b[c]d}e

a{b(c]d}e

a[b{c}d]e}

a{b(c)

5.1.5.1. Opening Delimiters on the Stack

The program reads each character from the string individually and adds opening delimiters to a stack while locating them. The software attempts to match the final delimiter read to the input by bursting the gaping delimiter at the leading edge of the stack while the closed delimiter reads the input (Sibertin-Blanc et al., 1995). An error has occurred if the delimiters are of different types (for instance, there is an initial brace yet a closing parenthesis). Additionally, Suppose a delimiter remains on the stack. In that case, an error has occurred after the parse has finished or if there isn't an opening delimited on the stacks to match the concluding one.

KEYWORD

String is generally considered as a data type and is often implemented as an array data structure of bytes (or words) that stores a sequence of elements, typically characters, using some character encoding.

Let's examine the behavior of a typical valid string on the stack:

a{b(c[d]e)f}

The stack is depicted in Table 5.1 as every character in the string is read (Martin, 1990). The entries in the following column list the stack's contents from left to right.

After reading the first instance of each original delimiter, add to the stack in order. The first delimiter from the input was retrieved and matched with each terminating delimiter from the stack. Starting delimiter was removed at the top of each stack. It's fine if paired off. Non-delimiter characters are ignored and are not added to the stack (Langsam et al., 1996).

Table 5.1. Stack contents matching delimiter (Source: Robert Lafore, Creative Commons License)

Character Examine	Include Contents
a	
{	{
b	{
(	{(
c	{(
[	{([
d	{([
]	{(
e	{(
)	{
f	{
}	

This technique is effective because created-finally delimiter pairs should be terminated first (Batty et al., 2013). This reflects the last-in-first-out property of the array.

KEYWORD

Parsing is the process of analyzing a string of symbols, either in natural language, computer languages or data structures, conforming to the rules of a formal grammar.

5.1.5.2. Code for brackets. cpp in C++

Below is a display of the brackets.cpp processing program's source code. The parsing member method, check(), has been added to Bracket Checker (Vandevoorde & Josuttis, 2002).

```
THE brackets.cpp PROGRAM
#include <iostream>
#include <string>
#include <vector>
using namespace std;
class StackX
{
private:
int maxSize;
vector<char> stackVect;
int top;
public:
StackX(int s) : maxSize(s), top(-1)
{ stackVect.resize(maxSize); }
void push(char j)       //put item on top of stack
{ stackVect[++top] = j; }
char pop()       //take item from top of stack
{ return stackVect[top--]; }
char peek()      //peek at top of stack
{ return stackVect[top]; }
```

```
bool isEmpty()
{ return (top == -1); }
};
class BracketChecker
{
private:
string input;
public:
BracketChecker(string in) : input(in)
{ }
void check()
{
int stackSize = input.length();
StackX theStack(stackSize);
bool isError = false;
for(int j=0; j<input.length(); j++)
{
char ch = input[j];
switch(ch)
{
case '{':
case '[':
case '(':
theStack.push(ch);
break;
case '}':
case ']':
```

```
case ')':
if( !theStack.isEmpty() )
{
char chx = theStack.pop();
if( (ch=='}' && chx!='{') ||
(ch==']' && chx!='[') ||
(ch==')' && chx!='(') )
{
isError = true;
cout << "Mismatched delimeter:. "
<< ch << " at " << j << endl;
}
}
else
{
isError = true;
cout << "Misplaced delimiter: "
<< ch << " at " << j << endl;
}
break;
default:
}
}
if( !theStack.isEmpty() )
cout << "Missing right delimiter" << endl;
else if( !isError )
cout << "OK" << endl;
```

```
}
};
int main()
{
string input;
while(true)
{
cout << "Enter string containing delimiters "
<< "(no whitespace): ";
cin >> input;
if( input.length() == 1 )
break;
BracketChecker theChecker(input);
theChecker.check();
}
return 0;
}
```

KEYWORD

Object-oriented programming is a computer programming model that organizes software design around data, or objects, rather than functions and logic

StackX class in previous program is used by the check() procedure. Be mindful of how simple it is to use this class. The code required is all in one location. One benefit of object-oriented programming is this (Bonfanti et al., 2020).

The check() procedure on this BracketChecker structure is invoked when This text string is used as input to generate a BracketChecker object created by the main() function after it has repeatedly received a line of data from the user. The checker() member function shows any problems it discovers; otherwise, it determines that the delimiters' syntax is correct (Fülöp et al., 2022).

The check() method returns the wrong character detected there and the character number (beginning at 0 on the left) where it identified the issue.

a{b(c]d}e

the results of check() are

Mismatched delimiter:] at 5

5.1.6 Utilizing the Stack as an Analytical Tool

Noting the usefulness of the brackets.cpp initiative's stack. An array is created to do the same function as the stack. Still, it might have also needed to worry about maintaining an index for the most recent character that was added in addition to other bookkeeping duties. The stack is simpler to utilize conceptually (Hock et al., 2019). The program is simpler to understand and less prone to errors since the stack restricts accessibility to its contents via the push() & pop() member methods.)

5.1.7. Efficiency of Stacks

A stack can add items and remove them in continuous O(1) time. The duration is very short and independent of the number of items in the stack (Campoli et al., 2019). There is no need for contrasts or maneuvers. Of course, there is only one item to which access is limited by design.

Did you Know?

The "hot potato" is an example of a queue. Players stand in circle and pass a ball around while music plays. When the music stops, the player holding the ball is out.

5.2. QUEUES

Like stacks, queues are a programming tool. And can also simulate events like people standing in line in a bank, waiting for a flight to take off, or messages that need to be sent over the Internet.

The computer's operating system (or the network) has several queues that quietly perform their duties. Print jobs are held in a printer queue until a printer becomes available (Carriero et al., 1986). While typing on the keyboard, a queue also saves keystroke information. Because the keystroke sits in the queue till a word processor can read it and won't be lost while utilizing a program for writing, the machine is short-engaged in another process when a key is pressed. Using a queue ensures that the keystrokes remain sequential until they are processed.

5.2.1. The Applet Queue Workshop

Launch the applet associated with the Queue Workshop. As shown in Figure 5.5, there will be four items in the backlog (Mendelson et al., 2006). The applet illustrates an array-based queue. While connected lists are also frequently used to create queues, this is a prevalent strategy.

Two fundamental queue procedures are inserting an item at the end of the queue and removing an item from the front. This is comparable to someone standing in the back of the queue of moviegoers and then, after paying for a ticket and moving to the head of the line, leaving (Paznikov & Anenkov, 2019).

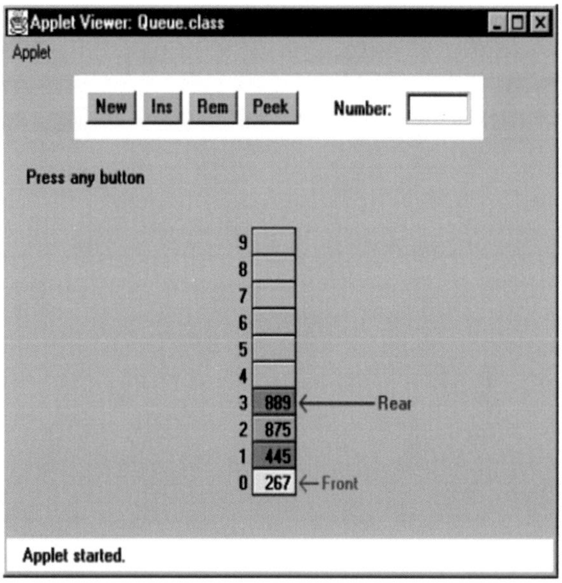

Figure 5.5. Image of the queue workshop applet (Source: Mike Henry, Creative Commons License).

Everyone uses the terms "push" and "pop" to describe the insertion and removal of items from a stack. With queues, standardization hasn't advanced as far (Prakash et al., 1994). In contrast to removal, which may be referred to as delete, get, or deque, insert is sometimes known as put, add, or enqueue. The back, tail, or end of the queue are further names for the back, where items are inserted. The front, where objects are removed, is sometimes referred to as the head. The terms insertion, and the front, will be used.

5.2.1.1. Inserting a New Item

A new item can be inserted by clicking the Ins key in The queue Workshops applet. An invitation to input the key value for another item in the Figure text field is present after the first hit; this must be a number between 0 and 999 (Moir et al., 2005). Repeatedly pressing this key will add items to the back of the line and move the Reverse arrow.

5.2.1.2. Removing an Item

The Rem button can also be used to remove the item currently in front of the line (Payer et al., 2011). The item is deleted, its value has been saved in the Number form (corresponding to the delete), and the Front indicator is raised. The cell of the applet containing the removed item is shaded gray to signify removal. This will continue in memory in a typical implementation, but Front would have moved on. In Figure 5.6, insertion and deletion operations are shown.

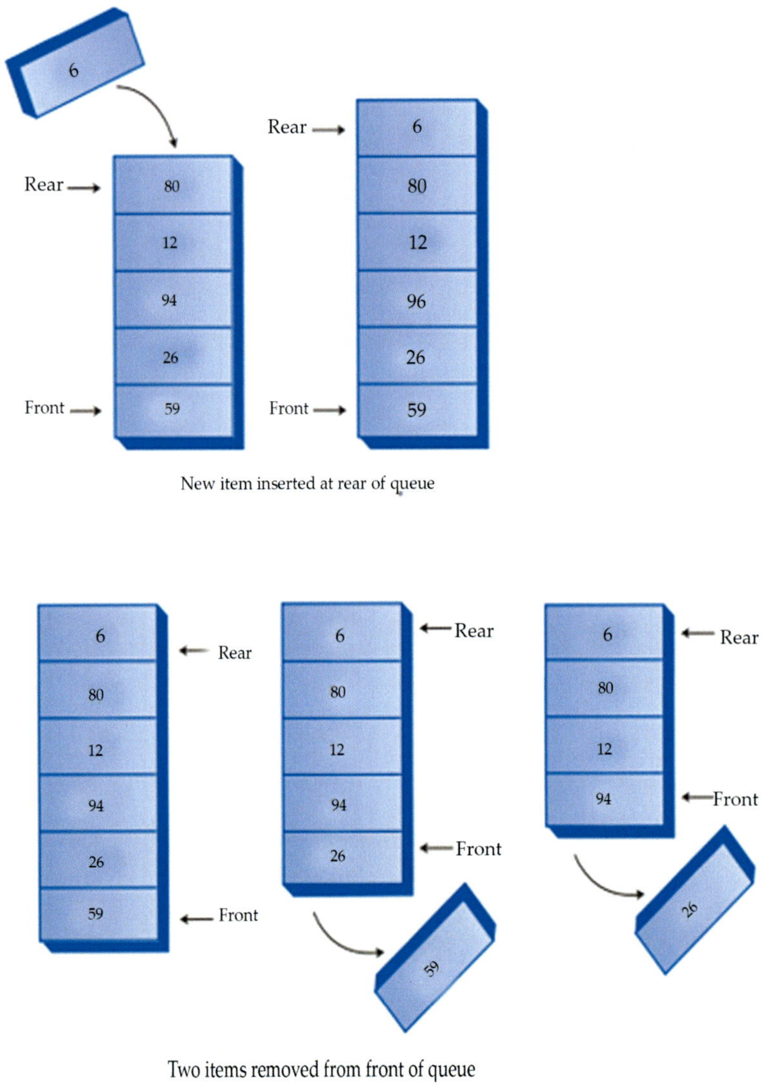

Figure 5.6. Operation of the queue class member functions (Source: Dan Schref, Creative Commons License).

The components in a queue do not always extend to array index 0, unlike in a stack. As seen in Figure 5.7, the Front will point to a higher index cell once some items have been deleted (Flajolet et al., 1980).

As seen in figure, the front gets a lower value and is positioned beneath the Rear in the list in this illustration. This isn't always the case, further discovered in a second.

5.2.1.3. Peeking at an Item

The peek queue operation is also demonstrated. Without taking the item out of the queue, this determines the worth of the things at the front. (Peek is sometimes referred to by many other names when used with a queue, just as insert and remove) (Langdon, 1998). The value from the Front is sent to the Numbers box when clicking the Peek button. The line has not changed. The value at the head of the queue is returned by the peek() member function. Although some queue implementations provide member functions called rearPeek() and frontPeek(), users normally want to know what is about to be removed rather than what was recently inserted (Kogan & Petrank, 2012).

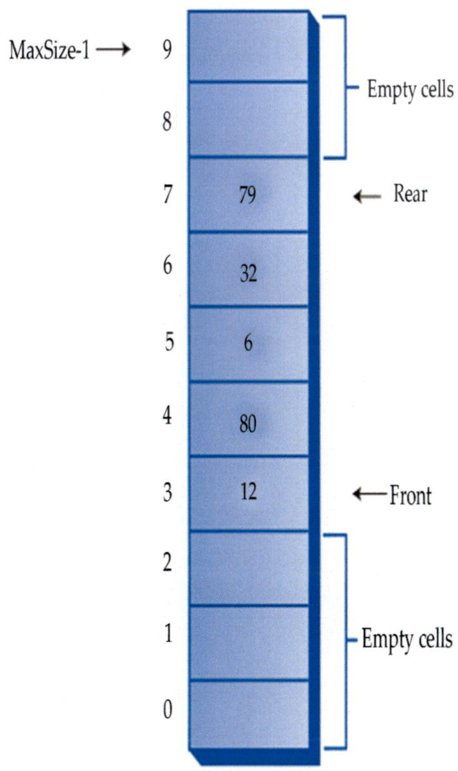

Figure 5.7. Representing a queue with some items removed (Source: Tonya Simpson, Creative Commons License).

5.2.1.4. Creating a New Queue with a New

Utilize the button labeled New to begin with a blank queue if that is what is desired (Pierson & Rodger, 1998).

5.2.1.5. The Empty and Full Errors

The error message received can't be removed, and the list is empty if the user tries to eliminate a product when no further items are in the queue. Warning "Can't insert, the queue is full" is seen if attempting to insert something when all the cells have become filled (Breen & Monro, 1994).

5.2.2. A Circular Queue

The front arrow in the Workshops applet goes upward toward The greater number is included in the array when a new item is added to the queue (Nageshwara & Kumar, 1988). The Rear also rises when an item is removed. To verify it, perform the following procedures on the Workshop applet.

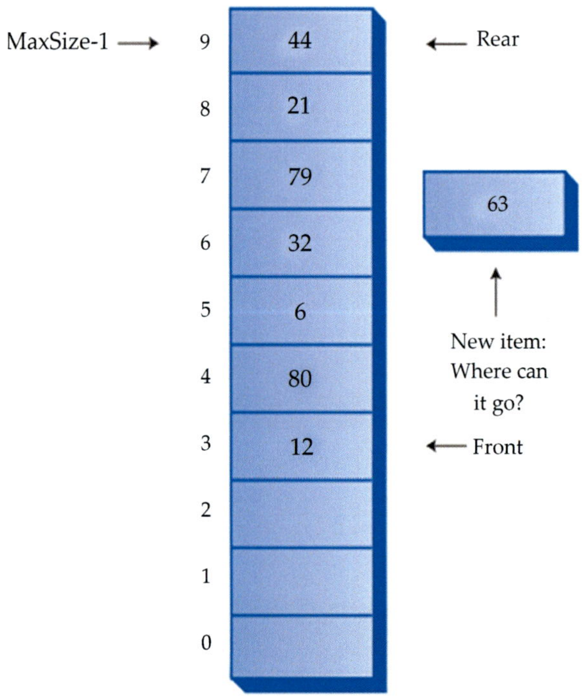

Figure 5.8. Representation of rear arrow at the end of array (Source: Brian Gill, Creative Commons License).

Moving the front and the back of the queue forward presents a problem since. Eventually, the back of the queue will be after the conclusion of the list (the highest index). Even though Rem deleted the vacant cells at the start of the array, it is unable to add an item because Rear is at its limit. But can it? Figure 5.8 depicts this circumstance.

Remember

Queues are used in operating systems to manage tasks that need to be executed in a specific order.

5.2.3. C++ Code for a Queue

The Queue class in the queue.cpp program has member procedures insert(), delete(), size(), peak(), isFull(), and isEmpty() (Demaine et al., 2007).

The main() method creates the five-cell queue, which then adds four things, takes away three, and finally adds four more. The wraparound feature is activated after the sixth insertion. Then, everything is taken out and put on the show. The result appears as follows:

40 50 60 70 80

The program Queue.cpp is shown in the code below (Herlihy et al., 2003).

THE Queue.cpp PROGRAM

```
#include <iostream>

#include <vector>

using namespace std;

class Queue

{

private:

int maxSize;

vector<int> queVect;

int front;

int rear;

int nItems;

public:

Queue(int s) : maxSize(s), front(0), rear(-1), nItems(0)

{ queVect.resize(maxSize); }

void insert(int j) //put item at rear of queue
```

```
{
if(rear == maxSize-1)
rear = -1;
queVect[++rear] = j;
nItems++;
}
int remove()
{
int temp = queVect[front++];
if(front == maxSize)
front = 0;
nItems--;
return temp;
}
int peekFront()
{ return queVect[front]; }
bool isEmpty()
{ return (nItems==0); }
bool isFull()
{ return (nItems==maxSize); }
int size()
{ return nItems; }
};
int main()
{
Queue theQueue(5);
theQueue.insert(10);
```

```
theQueue.insert(20);
theQueue.insert(30);
theQueue.insert(40);
theQueue.remove();
theQueue.remove();
theQueue.remove();
theQueue.insert(50);
theQueue.insert(60);
theQueue.insert(70);
theQueue.insert(80);
while( !theQueue.isEmpty() )
{
int n = theQueue.remove();
cout << n << " ";
}
cout << endl;
return 0;
}
```

A method in which the nItems data member of the Queue class includes both front and back and the present total number of items in the queue. All queue versions lack this data component (Brodal & Okasaki, 1996).

KEYWORD

Queue is defined as a linear data structure that is open at both ends and the operations are performed in First In First Out (FIFO) order.

5.2.4. Insert() Constituent Function

The queue is not regarded as complete by the insert() method. Despite not being illustrated by main() is frequently used only once, invoking isFull() to get a false return value (Rihani et al., 2015). (Including the fullness check within the insert() method and raising an exception if a try is made to insert information onto a full line is preferable.) Typically, insertion includes incrementing the rear while inserting at the present location of the rear. During maxSize-1, the back is seen at the highest point of the array (vector), but it has to shift to the lowest point before the increment. Rear is set to -1 for the rear to become 0, the bottom of the array. Then nItems is increased.

5.2.5. The Remove() Class Method

The delete() function does not consider the queue to be empty. Before executing remove(), it should be validated that it is true by calling isEmpty(), or remove() can incorporate this error-checking (Shavit & Lotan, 2000).

KEYWORD

Error checking is a test that evaluates ability to spot errors in sets of data or text.

Always begin removal by getting the value at the front, then increase the front. The front must then be looped around to 0, albeit if doing so extends it past the final portion of the array. While the possibility is investigated, the return on value is momentarily held. Then nItems is decreased.

5.2.6. The Peek() Member Function

The peek() member function is straightforward: it returns the value at front. (Shavit & Taubenfeld, 2016). Some implementations permit peeking into the array's back row as well; these functions go by the names peekFront() and peekRear(), respectively, or simply front() and back().

5.2.7. Empty(), is Full(), and size() Member Functions

The information inferred by the member functions size(), isFull(), and isEmpty() is provided. Each depends upon the nItems information members, which both check to see if it is 0, return maxSize or its value.

5.2.8. Constructing Queue Class without an Item Count

Fact that the Queue class includes the information within its member nItems means that the member procedures insert() and delete() must increment and decrease this value (Brodal, 2013). This may not seem like a significant penalty; however, it could affect performance with many deletions and insertions.

As a result, some queue implementations do not provide an item count and instead compute the queue's capacity and state using both the front and the back data members. Empty(), was full (), and size() algorithms are somewhat difficult because the series of objects may be fractured or contiguous following this operation.

A peculiar issue also develops. When a line is full, the front & rear pointers adopt particular places but can also assume identical positions while the line is null. The row could then seem both full & empty at once (Goodrich et al., 2013). Creating an array (vector) of a single cell bigger than the number of items allowed can solve this problem. The following code demonstrates a Queue class that utilizes this no-count strategy. Using the no-count implementation in this class (Zhan, 1997).

KEYWORD

Data members include members that are declared with any of the fundamental types, as well as other types, including pointer, reference, array types, bit fields, and user-defined types.

THE Queue CLASS WITHOUT nItems

```
class Queue
{
private:
int maxSize;
vector<int>(queVect);
int front;
int rear;
public:
{
queVect.resize(maxSize);
}
void insert(int j)
{
if(rear == maxSize-1) rear = -1;
queVect[++rear] = j;
}
int remove()
{
```

```
int temp = queVect[front++];
if(front == maxSize)
front = 0;
return temp;
}
int peek()
{
return queVect[front];
}
bool isEmpty()
{
return ( rear+1==front || (front+maxSize-1==rear) );
}
bool isFull()
{
return ( rear+2==front || (front+maxSize-2==rear) );
}
int size()
{
if(rear >= front)
return rear-front+1;
else
return (maxSize-front) + (rear+1);
}
};
```

Observe how complicated member functions size(), isEmpty(), & isFull() are. Since it is rarely necessary for practice, going into great depth about this no-count strategy.

5.2.9. Efficiency of Queues

Items can be added to and withdrawn in a list in O(1) time, just like with a stack. The wraparound function may cause some deletions and insertions to take noticeably longer than others, but the Big O time is unaffected (Vuillemin, 1978).

Moving on from queues, discuss the second important topic of this hour, an associated data structure known as a priority sequence.

5.3. PRIORITY QUEUES

Compared to the stacks or the queue, the queue of priorities is a more complex data structure. However, it comes in handy in an unforeseen broad range of circumstances. A priority queue has a front & back, similar to a conventional line, with objects put in the back and taken out of the front of the line (Hassin & Haviv, 1997). In contrast, in a queue with priority, the product with the lowest key (or, in some executions, the item in the largest key) stays at the front, as the items are organized by key value. When introduced, items are positioned properly to maintain order.

Here's how the priority queue's similarity to mail sorting works. Place each letter the mailman brings into the queue of unread letters based on its importance. The highest position on the list is for urgent calls (such as a phone company regarding disconnecting your modem line) (Choi & Chang, 1999). In contrast, the bottom is for messages that may wait for an additional leisurely response. (such as a letter from Aunt Mabel).

KEYWORD

Priority queue is an abstract data-type similar to a regular queue or stack data structure.

When responding to mail, select the letter from the summit of the list to ensure that the most urgent correspondence is addressed first. Figure 5.9 depicts this (Maertens et al., 2006).

Programmers frequently employ priority queues as tools, just like stacks and queues having a variety of uses in some computer systems. Programs may be put in a priority queue in a preempt multitasking OS (Laevens & Bruneel, 1998). For example, the application in the highest priority gets a time slice to do next. People frequently seek out the cheapest option because they believe it to be the most practical or quick solution.). As a result, the product with the lowest key is given top priority. In this discussion, even if there are other circumstances when the top key has the most importance.

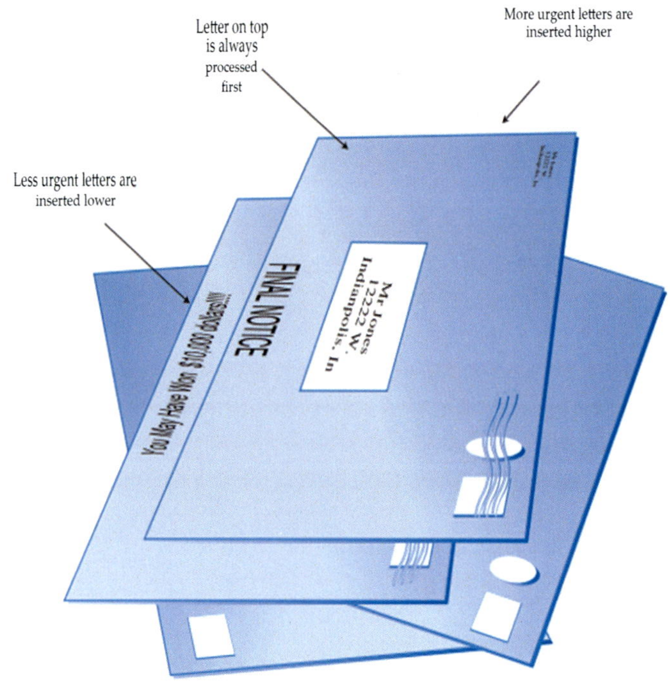

Figure 5.9. Illustration of letters in a priority queue (Source: Mike Henry, Creative Commons License).

The product with the lowest key should be accessible quickly and have a priority queue for speedy insertion (Ritha & Robert, 2010). Due to this, priority queues are frequently constructed using the heap data structure, as just mentioned. Instead, use a simple array to illustrate a priority queue. Although this method has a slow insertion speed, it is easier to use and more appropriate when there aren't many things, while insertion speed isn't important.

5.3.1. Applet for the PriorityQ Workshop

The workshop applet handles the item's order in a priority queue with an array. In an ascending-priority queue, the item with the lowest key is the one that is accessed with remove and has the highest priority (A weakest-priority queue would be utilized if the highest-key item needed to be retrieved) (Vuillemin, 1978).

The smallest item has the smallest key and is located on the array's highest percentage index, while the largest item is still at index 0. The configuration when an applet is launched is shown in Figure 5.10. There are initially five things in the queue (Adiri & Yechiali, 1974).

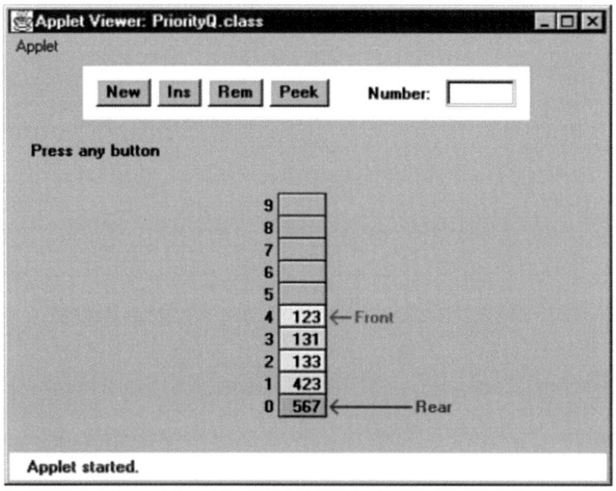

Figure 5.10. Illustration of the priority queue workshop applet (Source: Richard Wright, Creative Commons License).

5.3.1.1. Inserting a New Item

Try adding something. The Number data element must have the key value of the new item entered. Choose a number to be placed in the middle of the queue's values. Consider choosing 300, as shown in Figure 5.10 (Kleinrock & Finkelstein, 1967). And note how objects with smaller keys migrate up to create a room when a person strikes them repeatedly. Ins. A black arrow indicates the object that is shifting. The new object is fitted into the freshly generated space once the ideal placement has been determined.

Keep in mind that this priority queue implementation does not use a wraparound. Due to the necessity of locating the correct in-order position, insertion is slow, whereas deletion is quick. Implementing a wraparound wouldn't make things better. The bottom part of the array contains the Reverse arrow, which stays stationary and continually points to index 0 (Nageshwara & Kumar, 1988).

5.3.1.2. Delete an Item

Elimination is quick and easy because the front arrow leads to the top of the updated list (Kaufman, 1984). After all, the item to be erased always appears at the beginning of the list. There is no need for comparisons or shifting.

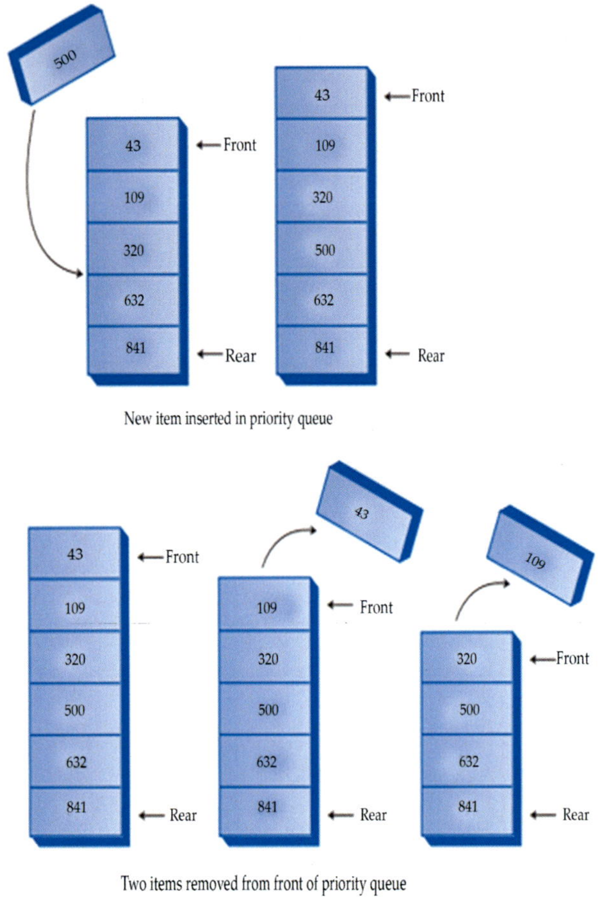

Figure 5.11. Operation of the priority queue class member functions (Source: Mike Henry, Creative Commons License).

Although are not strictly necessary, provided Front and Rear arrows within the PriorityQ Workshops applet to enable a comparison with a typical queue. The algorithms add items in order rather than at the back since are aware that the initial item of the line always appears at the apex of the list at nItems-1. Figure 5.11 demonstrates how the PriorityQ classes' member functions operate (Muzakkari et al., 2020).

5.3.1.3. Peek and New

A minimum item's value can be viewed without eliminating it through the Peek button. Additionally, an unfilled priority queue may be created with the New button.

5.3.2. The Priority Queue in C++

Here is a basic array-based prioritized queue's C++ source code (Alexander et al., 2012).

THE priorityQ.cpp PROGRAM

```
#include <iostream>

#include <vector>

using namespace std;

class PriorityQ

{

int maxSize;

vector<double> queVect;

int nItems;

public:

PriorityQ(int s) : maxSize(s), nItems(0)

{ queVect.resize(maxSize); }

void insert(double item)

{

int j;

if(nItems==0)

queVect[nItems++] = item;

else

{

for(j=nItems-1; j>=0; j--)

{

if( item > queVect[j] )

queVect[j+1] = queVect[j];

else
```

```
break;
}
queVect[j+1] = item;
nItems++;
}
}
double remove()
{ return queVect[--nItems]; }
double peekMin()
{ return queVect[nItems-1]; }
bool isEmpty()
{ return (nItems==0); }
bool isFull()
{ return (nItems == maxSize); }
};
int main()
{
PriorityQ thePQ(5);
thePQ.insert(30);
thePQ.insert(50);
thePQ.insert(10);
thePQ.insert(40);
thePQ.insert(20);
while( !thePQ.isEmpty() )
{
double item = thePQ.remove();
cout << item << " ";
```

```
}
cout << endl;
return 0;
}
```

Five objects are randomly placed into the main() function, removed, and then shown. Always start by deleting the smallest component to determine the outcome (Jain et al., 2015).

10, 20, 30, 40, 50

A member's insert() function verifies whether any items exist; if none exist, add them at position 0. If not, the function begins at the head of the enumeration & moves current items up until it finds the right spot for the new product. The items are then incremented when a new item has been added (Rönngren & Ayani, 1997). Note that before executing insert, utilize isFull() if there's a risk if the priority list has become full. ().

Since the front remains nItems-1 and the rear is usually 0, rear and front data components are no longer necessary in the Queue class.

The remove() method, which lowers nItems or removes the first item in the list, is the definition of simplicity. The peekMin() member method is comparable, except that nItems is not decremented. isEmpty() and isFull() verify whether nItems is equal to 0 or maxSize, respectively.

5.3.3. Effectiveness of Priority Queues

Due to the necessity of transferring items to replace the void left through a removed item, a transfer is required. Employing a priority queue in this situation requires O(N) time for entry but only O(1) time for deletion (Sanders, 2000).

ACTIVITY 5.1

Write a code to implement a stack using an array data structure. Then tests its implementation with different inputs to see if it behaves as expected.

Write a code to implement a queue using a linked list data structure. Then tests its implementation with different inputs to see if it behaves as expected.

SUMMARY

Stacks and queues are two important data structures in computer science and programming. They are both abstract data types that allow elements to be added and removed in a specific order. A stack is a Last In, First Out (LIFO) data structure and it operates like a stack of plates, where the most recent item added to the stack is the first one to be removed. Elements can only be added or removed from the top of the stack. Common operations on a stack include push and pop. A queue is a First In, First Out (FIFO) data structure and it operates like a line of people waiting for a ticket, where the first person in line is the first to be served. Elements can only be added to the back of the queue and removed from the front. Common operations on a queue include enqueue and dequeue. Both stacks and queues have many practical applications in computer science and programming, such as in algorithms for parsing expressions, searching and sorting data, and processing jobs in parallel.

REVIEW QUESTIONS

1. What is a stack and what is Last In, First Out (LIFO) property?
2. What are the common operations performed on a stack?
3. What is a queue and what are the common operations performed on a queue?
4. What are the practical applications of stacks and queues in computer science and programming?
5. What is a priority queue and how is it different from a regular queue?

MULTIPLE CHOICE QUESTIONS

1. What is the Last In, First Out property?

a. The first element added is the first element to be removed
b. The last element added is the first element to be removed
c. Elements can be added and removed in any order
d. Elements can only be added to the back and removed from the front

2. **Which data structure has a LIFO property?**
   a. Stack
   b. Queue
   c. Priority queue
   d. Binary search tree
3. **Which data structure has a FIFO property?**
   a. Stack
   b. Queue
   c. Priority queue
   d. Binary search tree
4. **In what situation would you use a stack instead of a queue?**
   a. When you need to process elements in the order they were added
   b. When you need to process elements in reverse order of insertion
   c. When you need to remove elements in order of priority
   d. None of the above
5. **The process of inserting an element in the stack is called?**
   a. Enqueue
   b. Insert
   c. Push
   d. Pop

Answers to Multiple Choice Questions

1. (b) 2. (a) 3. (b) 4. (b) 5. (c)

REFERENCES

1. Adiri, I., & Yechiali, U., (1974). Optimal priority-purchasing and pricing decisions in nonmonopoly and monopoly queues. *Operations Research, 22*(5), 1051–1066.
2. Alexander, M., MacLaren, A., O'Gorman, K., & White, C., (2012). Priority queues: Where social justice and equity collide. *Tourism Management, 33*(4), 875–884.
3. Batty, M., Dodds, M., & Gotsman, A., (2013). Library abstraction for C/C++ concurrency. *ACM SIGPLAN Notices, 48*(1), 235–248.
4. Baumgartner, G., & Russo, V. F., (1995). Signatures: A language extension for improving type abstraction and subtype polymorphism in C++. *Software: Practice and Experience, 25*(8), 863–889.

5. Blunk, A., & Fischer, J., (2014). A highly efficient simulation core in C++. In: *Proceedings of the Symposium on Theory of Modeling & Simulation-DEVS Integrative* (Vol. 1, pp. 1–8).
6. Bonfanti, S., Gargantini, A., & Mashkoor, A., (2020). Design and validation of a C++ code generator from abstract state machines specifications. *Journal of Software: Evolution and Process, 32*(2), e2205.
7. Boyapati, C., & Darga, P., (2007). Efficient software model checking of data structure properties. In: *Dagstuhl Seminar Proceedings; Schloss Dagstuhl-Leibniz-Zentrum für Informatik,* (Vol. 1, pp. 2–9).
8. Brandenburg, F. J., (1988). On the intersection of stacks and queues. *Theoretical Computer Science, 58*(1–3), 69–80.
9. Breen, E. J., & Monro, D. H., (1994). An evaluation of priority queues for mathematical morphology. *Mathematical Morphology and its Applications to Image Processing, 1*, 249–256.
10. Brodal, G. S., & Okasaki, C., (1996). Optimal purely functional priority queues. *Journal of Functional Programming,* 6(6), 839–857.
11. Brodal, G. S., (2013). *A Survey on Priority Queues* (Vol. 1, pp. 150–163). Space-Efficient Data Structures, Streams, and Algorithms: Papers in Honor of J. Ian Munro on the Occasion of His 66th Birthday.
12. Campoli, L., Oblapenko, G. P., & Kustova, E. V., (2019). KAPPA: Kinetic approach to physical processes in atmospheres library in C++. *Computer Physics Communications, 236*, 244–267.
13. Carriero, N., Gelernter, D., & Leichter, J., (1986). Distributed data structures in Linda. In: *Proceedings of the 13th ACM SIGACT-SIGPLAN Symposium on Principles of Programming Languages* (Vol. 1, pp. 236–242).
14. Case, A., Marziale, L., & Richard, III. G. G., (2010). Dynamic recreation of kernel data structures for live forensics. *Digital Investigation, 7*(1), S32–S40.
15. Celinski, T. M., Dijkstra, B. A., Ribeiro, L. G., Souza, M. A., & Celinski, V. G., (2017). Development of learning objects and their application in teaching and learning data structures and their algorithms. *Iberoamerican Journal of Applied Computing, 7*(2), 6–8.
16. Choi, B. D., & Chang, Y., (1999). Single server retrial queues with priority calls. *Mathematical and Computer Modeling, 30*(3, 4), 7–32.
17. Demaine, E. D., Iacono, J., & Langerman, S., (2007). Retroactive data structures. *ACM Transactions on Algorithms (TALG), 3*(2), 13–15.
18. Di Benedetto, M., Corsini, M., & Scopigno, R., (2011). SpiderGL: A graphics library for 3D web applications. *International Archives of the Photogrammetry, Remote Sensing and Spatial Information Sciences, 38(5W16)* (Vol. 1, 467–474).
19. Drocco, M., Castellana, V. G., & Minutoli, M., (2020). Practical distributed programming in C++. In: *Proceedings of the 29th International Symposium on High-Performance*

Parallel and Distributed Computing (Vol. 1, pp. 35–39).

20. Dubois-Pelerin, Y., & Zimmermann, T., (1993). Object-oriented finite element programming: III. An efficient implementation in C++. *Computer Methods in Applied Mechanics and Engineering, 108*(1, 2), 165–183.
21. Flajolet, P., Françon, J., & Vuillemin, J., (1980). Sequence of operations analysis for dynamic data structures. *Journal of Algorithms, 1*(2), 111–141.
22. Fülöp, E., Gyén, A., & Pataki, N., (2022). C++ source code rejuvenation for an improved exception specification. In: *2022 IEEE 16th International Scientific Conference on Informatics (Informatics)* (Vol. 1, pp. 94–99). IEEE.
23. Goodrich, M. T., Tamassia, R., & Goldwasser, M. H., (2013). *Data Structures and Algorithms in Python* (Vol. 1, pp. 978–1011). Hoboken: Wiley.
24. Hanciles, B., Shankararaman, V., & Munoz, J., (1997). Multiple representation for understanding data structures. *Computers & Education, 29*(1), 1–11.
25. Hassin, R., & Haviv, M., (1997). Equilibrium threshold strategies: The case of queues with priorities. *Operations Research, 45*(6), 966–973.
26. Herlihy, M., Luchangco, V., & Moir, M., (2003). Obstruction-free synchronization: Double-ended queues as an example. In: *23rd International Conference on Distributed Computing Systems, 2003; Proceedings.* (Vol. 1, pp. 522–529). IEEE.
27. Hock, P., Nakayama, K., & Arai, K., (2019). A tool for C++ header generation. *International Journal of Advanced Computer Science and Applications, 10*(7), 3–8.
28. Hogan, R. J., (2014). Fast reverse-mode automatic differentiation using expression templates in C++. *ACM Transactions on Mathematical Software (TOMS), 40*(4), 1–16.
29. Jain, M., Bhagat, A., & Shekhar, C., (2015). Double orbit finite retrial queues with priority customers and service interruptions. *Applied Mathematics and Computation, 253*, 324–344.
30. Kanetkar, Y., (2019). *Data Structures Through C: Learn the Fundamentals of Data Structures Through C* (Vol. 1, pp. 2–5). BPB publications.
31. Kaufman, J. S., (1984). Approximation methods for networks of queues with priorities. *Performance Evaluation, 4*(3), 183–198.
32. Keith, M. J., & Martin, M. C., (1994). Genetic programming in C++: Implementation issues. *Advances in Genetic Programming, 2*(1), 285–310.
33. Kleinrock, L., & Finkelstein, R. P., (1967). Time dependent priority queues. *Operations Research, 15*(1), 104–116.
34. Kogan, A., & Petrank, E., (2012). A methodology for creating fast wait-free data structures. *ACM SIGPLAN Notices, 47*(8), 141–150.
35. Laevens, K., & Bruneel, H., (1998). Discrete-time multiserver queues with priorities. *Performance Evaluation, 33*(4), 249–275.
36. Langdon, W. B., (1998). *Genetic Programming and Data Structures: Genetic Programming+ Data Structures= Automatic Programming* (Vol. 1, pp. 5–10).

37. Langsam, Y., Augenstein, M. J., & Tenenbaum, A. M., (1996). *Data Structures Using C and C++* (Vol. 2, No. 1, pp. 2–6). Prentice Hall Press.
38. Maertens, T., Walraevens, J., & Bruneel, H., (2006). On priority queues with priority jumps. *Performance Evaluation, 63*(12), 1235–1252.
39. Martin, B., (1990). The separation of interface and implementation in C++. *Hewlett-Packard Laboratories, 3*(1), 8–10.
40. Mendelson, R., Tarjan, R. E., Thorup, M., & Zwick, U., (2006). Melding priority queues. *ACM Transactions on Algorithms (TALG), 2*(4), 535–556.
41. Moir, M., Nussbaum, D., Shalev, O., & Shavit, N., (2005). Using elimination to implement scalable and lock-free FIFO queues. In: *Proceedings of the Seventeenth Annual ACM Symposium on Parallelism in Algorithms and Architectures* (Vol. 1, pp. 253–262).
42. Muzakkari, B. A., Mohamed, M. A., Kadir, M. F., & Mamat, M., (2020). Queue and priority-aware adaptive duty cycle scheme for energy efficient wireless sensor networks. *IEEE Access, 8*(1), 17231–17242.
43. Nageshwara, R. V., & Kumar, V., (1988). Concurrent access of priority queues. *IEEE Transactions on Computers, 37*(12), 1657–1665.
44. Nikander, J., & Virrantaus, K., (2007). Learning environment of spatial data algorithms. In: *International Cartographic Conference ICC, Moscow, ICC* (Vol. 1, pp. 1–5).
45. Park, B., & Ahmed, D. T., (2017). Abstracting learning methods for stack and queue data structures in video games. In: *2017 International Conference on Computational Science and Computational Intelligence (CSCI)* (Vol. 1, pp. 1051–1054). IEEE.
46. Payer, H., Roeck, H., Kirsch, C. M., & Sokolova, A., (2011). Scalability versus semantics of concurrent FIFO queues. In: *Proceedings of the 30th Annual ACM SIGACT-SIGOPS Symposium on Principles of Distributed Computing* (Vol. 1, pp. 331, 332).
47. Paznikov, A. A., & Anenkov, A. D., (2019). Implementation and analysis of distributed relaxed concurrent queues in remote memory access model. *Procedia Computer Science, 150*(1), 654–662.
48. Pierson, W. C., & Rodger, S. H., (1998). Web-based animation of data structures using JAWAA. *ACM SIGCSE Bulletin, 30*(1), 267–271.
49. Prakash, S., Lee, Y. H., & Johnson, T., (1994). A nonblocking algorithm for shared queues using compare-and-swap. *IEEE Transactions on Computers, 43*(5), 548–559.
50. Rihani, H., Sanders, P., & Dementiev, R., (2015). Multiqueues: Simple relaxed concurrent priority queues. In: *Proceedings of the 27th ACM Symposium on Parallelism in Algorithms and Architectures* (Vol. 1, pp. 80–82).
51. Ritha, W., & Robert, L., (2010). Fuzzy queues with priority discipline. *Applied Mathematical Sciences, 4*(12), 575–582.
52. Rodger, S. H., (2002). Using hands-on visualizations to teach computer science from beginning courses to advanced courses. In: *Second Program Visualization*

Workshop (Vol. 1, pp. 103–112).

53. Rönngren, R., & Ayani, R., (1997). A comparative study of parallel and sequential priority queue algorithms. *ACM Transactions on Modeling and Computer Simulation (TOMACS), 7*(2), 157–209.
54. Sanders, P., (2000). Fast priority queues for cached memory. *Journal of Experimental Algorithmics (JEA), 5*(1), 7–10.
55. Serebryany, K., Stepanov, E., Shlyapnikov, A., Tsyrklevich, V., & Vyukov, D., (2018). *Memory Tagging and How it Improves C/C++ Memory Safety* (Vol. 1, pp. 3–7).
56. Shavit, N., & Lotan, I., (2000). Skiplist-based concurrent priority queues. In: *Proceedings 14th International Parallel and Distributed Processing Symposium: IPDPS 2000* (Vol. 1, pp. 263–268). IEEE.
57. Shavit, N., & Taubenfeld, G., (2016). The computability of relaxed data structures: Queues and stacks as examples. *Distributed Computing, 29*(1), 395–407.
58. Sibertin-Blanc, C., Hameurlain, N., Touzeau, P., & France, P. A., (1995). Syroco: A C++ implementation of cooperative objects. In: *Workshop on Petri Nets and Object-Oriented Models of Concurrency* (Vol. 1, pp. 4–8).
59. Stigall, J., & Sharma, S., (2018). Usability and learning effectiveness of game-themed instructional (GTI) module for teaching stacks and queues. In: *SoutheastCon 2018* (Vol. 1, pp. 1–6). IEEE.
60. Stojanova, A., Stojkovikj, N., Kocaleva, M., Zlatanovska, B., & Martinovska-Bande, C., (2017). Application of VARK learning model on "data structures and algorithms" course. In: *2017 IEEE Global Engineering Education Conference (EDUCON)* (Vol. 1, pp. 613–620). IEEE.
61. Tan, B., & Seng, J. L. K., (2010). Notice of retraction: Game-based learning for data structures: A case study. In: *2010 2nd International Conference on Computer Engineering and Technology* (Vol. 6, pp. V6–718). IEEE.
62. Thomas, D. B., (2016). Synthesisable recursion for C++ HLS tools. In: *2016 IEEE 27th International Conference on Application-Specific Systems, Architectures and Processors (ASAP)* (Vol. 1, pp. 91–98). IEEE.
63. Vandevoorde, D., & Josuttis, N. M., (2002). *C++ Templates: The Complete Guide, Portable Documents* (Vol. 1, pp. 3–9). Addison-Wesley Professional.
64. Vuillemin, J., (1978). A data structure for manipulating priority queues. *Communications of the ACM, 21*(4), 309–315.
65. Wiener, R., & Pinson, L. J., (2000). *Fundamentals of OOP and Data Structures in Java* (Vol. 1, pp. 2–8). Cambridge University Press.
66. Zhan, F. B., (1997). Three fastest shortest path algorithms on real road networks: Data structures and procedures. *Journal of Geographic Information and Decision Analysis, 1*(1), 69–82.

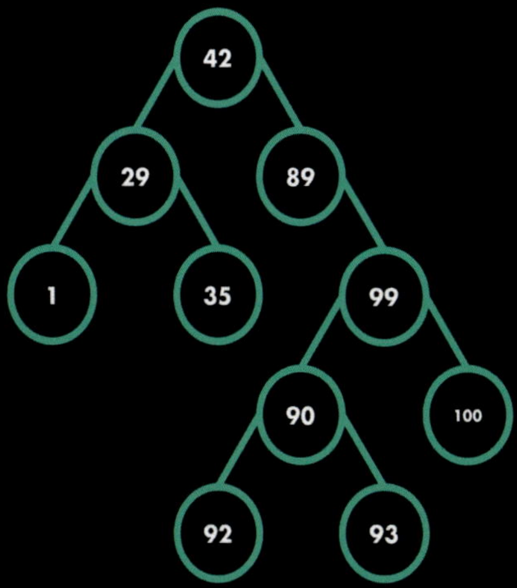

CHAPTER 6

TREES

UNIT INTRODUCTION

A tree is made up of nodes and edges. Figure 6.1 depicts a tree (Snyder, 1982). The nodes and edges of a tree are shown in this illustration as circles and lines, respectively. A great deal of theoretical knowledge about trees has been examined in great detail as abstract mathematical entities (Culler et al., 2004).

Nodes are the standard items in any type of data structure, including persons, cars, airplane bookings, etc. Nodes are frequently used to represent data items in computer applications. Objects express entities from the real world in object-oriented programming (OOP) languages like C++ (Raymond, 1989). Such data elements had previously been kept in lists and arrays.

The lines (edges) linking the nodes display the connections between them. Generally speaking, the lines represent comfort: A line connecting two nodes enables the software to traverse the nodes quickly and easily (Plaisant et al., 2002). Only a path that crosses through the lines allows one to move from node to node. Typically, movement occurs from the bottom downward along the margins. When a program is written in C++, pointers express edges.

A tree typically begins with a single node at the very top, with lines joining to additional nodes on another row, and so on (Dung et al., 2007). As a result, trees have tiny crowns and massive bases. Programs usually start operations from the little end of a tree, even though this could seem backward compared to physical trees. Moving the tree upward, like reading literature, may be easier to think about.

There are numerous tree varieties. Figure 6.1 depicts a tree in which every node has a maximum of two offspring (Friedman & Supowit, 1987). Students will become clear in a moment. But in this hour, talk about a particular kind of tree known as the binary tree. A binary tree can only have two children per node. Multi-way trees are more general trees where nodes may possess more than two children.

Did you Know?

A tree is actually an instance of a more general category called a graph.

After discussing some broad elements of trees, some terminology for different tree sections is examined.

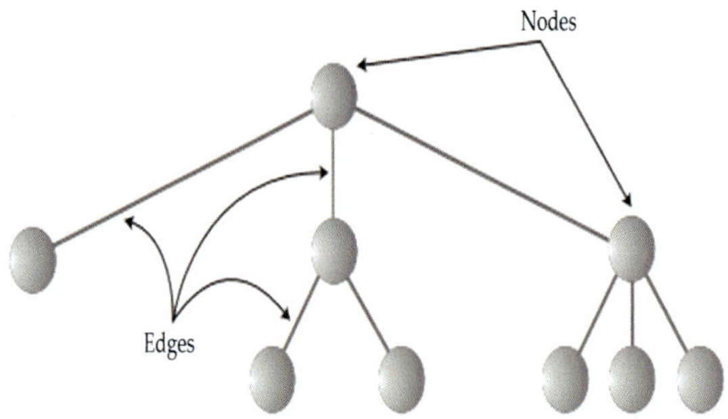

Figure 6.1. Illustration of tree with more than two children (Source: Narasimha Karumanchi, Creative Commons License).

Learning Objectives

At the chapter's end, students will get the ability to comprehend the following:

- The basic concept of trees and important tree terminologies
- Understanding basic binary tree operations
- The process of finding, inserting and deleting a node in the tree
- The concept of traversing the tree
- The efficiency of binary trees

Key Terms

1. Binary Search Trees
2. Deleting
3. Decision Trees
4. Edges
5. Graph Algorithms

6. Insertion
7. In-order Traversal
8. Leaves
9. Nodes
10. Pre-order Traversal
11. Searching
12. Trees

6.1. TREE TERMINOLOGY

Specific characteristics of trees are described using a variety of terminology. Fortunately, most of these phrases connect to actual trees or familial relationships (such as parents and children), making them easy to recall. Many of these words describe a binary tree in Figure 6.2 (Klein & Ravi, 1995).

6.1.1. Path

Think about moving between nodes by using the edges that link them. A path is a name given to the generated collection of parts (Hayes, 1976).

6.1.2. Root

Root of a tree is the highest node. In a tree, there's only one root. Only if one path connects each node to the root across the edges and nodes is it considered a tree. A non-tree is depicted in Figure 6.3 (Bolognesi & Brinksma, 1987). It breaks this rule.

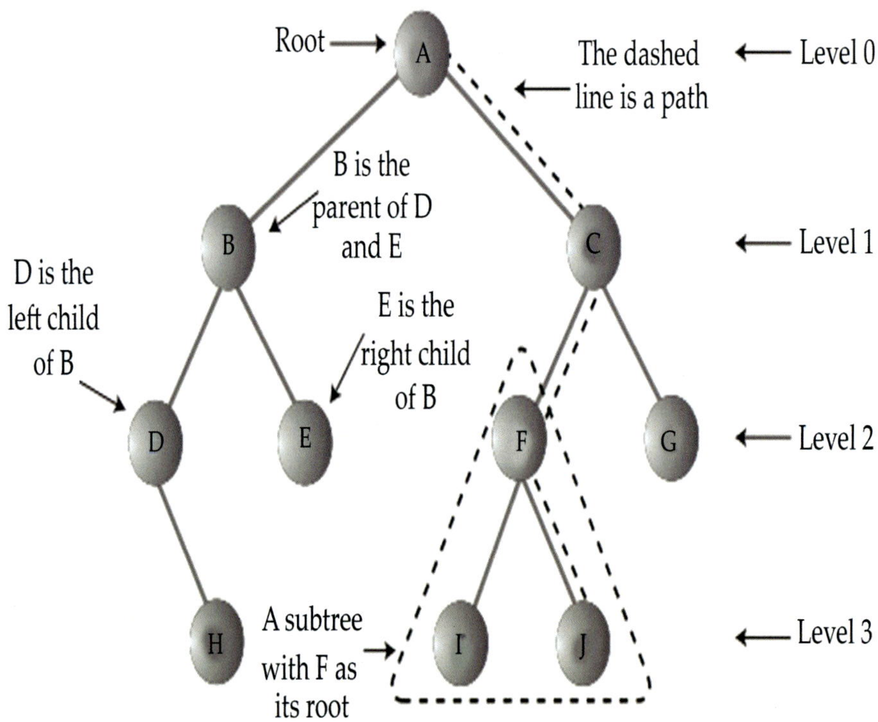

Figure 6.2. Image of tree terms (Source: Sobhan, Creative Commons License).

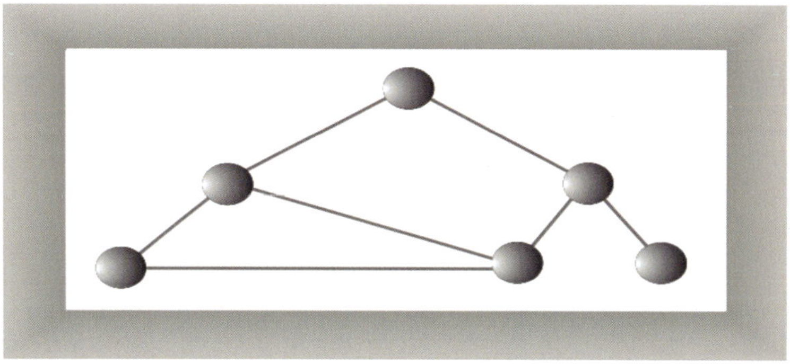

Figure 6.3. Representation of a non-tree (Source: Vamshi Krishna, Creative Commons License).

6.1.3. Parent

Every node (apart from the root) has one edge going up to another node (Joshi, 1987). The parent node is the node that is located above it.

6.1.4. Child

A line or multiple lines connecting a node to another node can run downward. Children nodes are directly beneath a specific node (Parhami, 2006).

6.1.5. Leaf

Leaf nodes, or just leaves, are nodes with no children. A tree can only have one root, although it can have many leaves.

6.1.6. Sub-tree

The root of a subtree can be any node that has children, children of children, and so forth (Singh, 2009). Thinking of a node as a family, its sub-tree will contain all its offspring.

6.1.7. Visiting

The program's control reaches a node as visited to perform some operation on it, such as displaying it or evaluating the value of a single data member (Grama et al., 2003). A node doesn't seem to have been visited if a user passes over it while traveling between nodes.

6.1.8. Traversing

To move through a tree is to go through each node in a particular order (Schuld et al., 2015). For instance, going over each node in the order of increasing key value. In the following hour, it is observed that there are additional ways to climb a tree.

6.1.9. Levels

A node's level describes how many generations away it is from the root. Assuming the root has level zero, its offspring will be level one, their grandchildren level 2, and so on.

6.1.10. Keys

A key value often refers to one data item within an object (Shneiderman, 1992). This value is utilized while looking for the object or working with it in various ways. Typically, the most significant value of an item of information is depicted in the circle symbolizing the node (this will be depicted in numerous figures below).

KEYWORD

Binary tree is a rooted tree that is also an ordered tree in which every node has at most two children.

6.1.11. Binary Trees

A binary tree is one in which each node can have a maximum of two offspring (Luellen et al., 2005). Due to their simplicity, popularity, and widespread application, binary trees are the main topic of this hour's discussion.

Figure 6.2 shows how each node's left and right children in a binary structure correlate to their locations when a picture of the tree is displayed. In a binary tree, a node doesn't have a maximum number of children; it could have just one left child, one right child, or none (making it a leaf) (Sudkamp, 2007).

The formal name for this particular binary tree is the binary search tree. The left child of this tree needs to possess a key smaller than its parent, and the right child must have a key equal to or larger than its parent. The binary search tree can be seen in Figure 6.4.

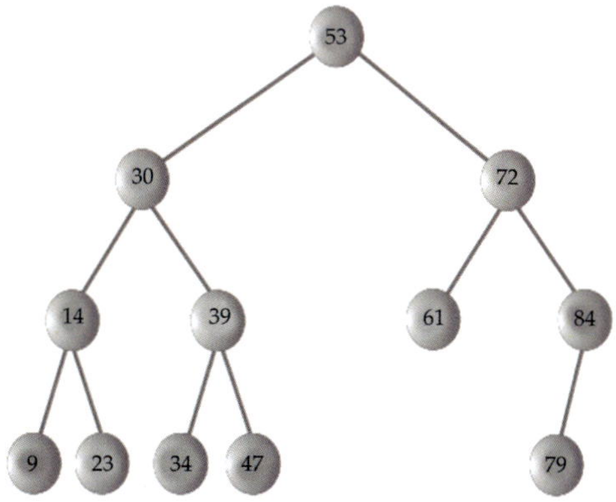

Figure 6.4. Image of a binary search tree (Source: Kalyani Tummala, Creative Commons License).

After learning the description of the components of a tree, the structure of a tree that most people are already familiar with is examined.

6.2. TREE ANALOGY IN COMPUTER

The hierarchical structure of files in a system of computers is an example of a frequently encountered tree. The main directory of a particular device is the tree's root, and its children comprise the one-level directories that go down from the root directory, having several subdirectories (Halasz & Moran, 1982). Files constitute leaves in this tree because they do not have any children.

A hierarchy file structure isn't a binary tree because a directory may have many children. A comprehensive pathname, such as C:SALESEASTNOVEMBERSMITH.DAT, represents the path from the root node toward the SMITH.DAT leaf's node. Root and path, used to describe file structures, are taken from tree theory (Perlin & Fox, 1993). The trees discussed here differ significantly from a hierarchical file structure. Subdirectories in a file hierarchy carry pointers to different subdirectories or files and don't store any data themselves. Data is only found in files. Every node in a tree has information in it. (a personnel record, car part specifications, or whatever). All nodes (excluding leaves) carry other nodes' pointers (Weiser, 1999).

Did you Know?

Trees can be used to implement efficient sorting algorithms such as heapsort and binary search tree sort.

6.3. BASIC BINARY TREE OPERATIONS

Identifying the node with a specific key and adding a new node are basic binary-tree procedures. These actions are demonstrated using a Tree Workshop applet and examining the accompanying C++ code (Hamouda et al., 2020).

6.3.1. The Tree Workshop Applet

Launching the applet for the Binary Tree Workshop. A screen similar to that in Figure 6.5 appears (Li et al., 2010). The tree displayed in the Workshops applet will also not match the tree because it is generated randomly.

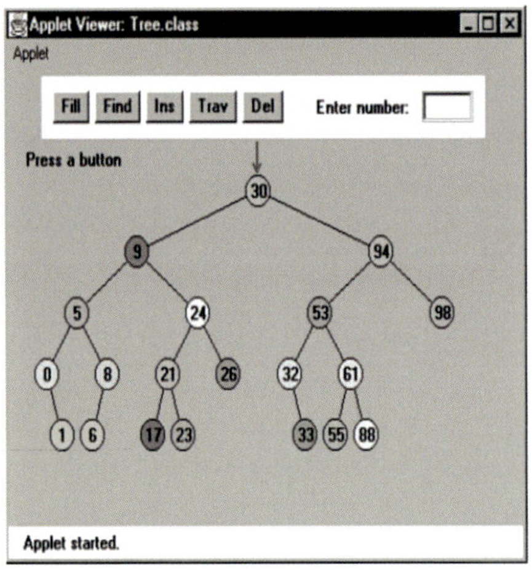

Figure 6.5. Illustration of applet from binary tree workshop (Source: Narasimha Karumanchi, Creative Commons License).

6.3.1.1. Binary Tree Workshop Applet Uses

The nodes exhibit variable values for key (0–99). A real tree will have a greater variety of essential values (Gurwitz, 1995). For example, If the number of people who work for Social Security is utilized as the key value, then the range of potential values is from 0 to 999,999,999.

A Workshop applet's maximum depth is 5, meaning there can only be a maximum of 5 layers between the root & bottom of the row, another distinction between it and a real tree (Siltaneva & Mäkinen, 2002). This limitation ensures that every node in the tree is visible on the monitor. There are, theoretically, an infinite number of levels in a real tree.

Always create a new tree using the Workshop applet.

6.3.1.2. Constructing Tree using Workshop Applet

i. "Fill" is selected from the menu.

ii. The total nodes of the tree will need to be entered in response to a prompt. This ranges from one to 31 (Yi & Tan, 2016). However, 15 will provide a typical tree.

iii. To create a new tree, enter the number and click Fill twice. Theories can be tested by making trees with various amounts of nodes.

6.3.1.3. Unbalanced Trees

As shown in the following figure, the resulting trees are unbalanced, with most nodes on both sides of the root. Certain sub-trees may be out of balance (Benoit et al., 2005).

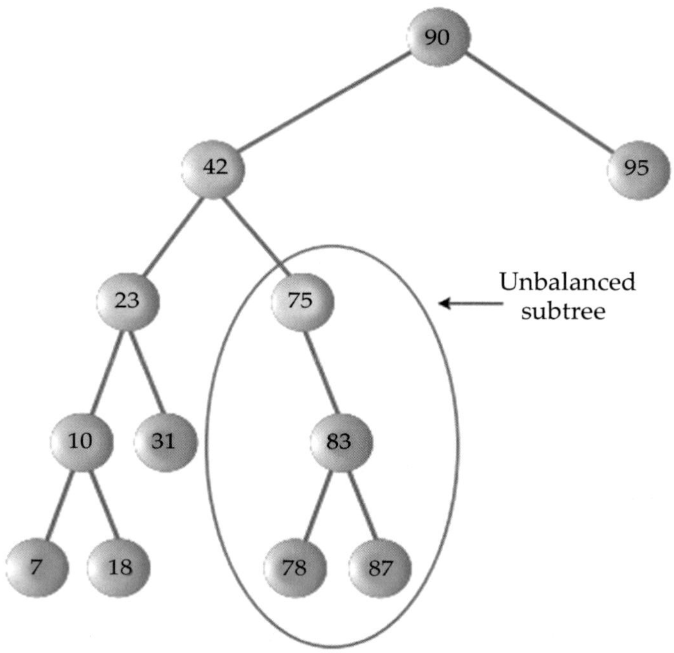

Figure 6.6. Representation of an out balanced tree without balanced sub tree (Source: Sobhan, Creative Commons License).

The order in which the data pieces are introduced causes trees to go out of balance (Cano et al., 2011). The tree will appear roughly balanced if these essential values are put at random. Nevertheless, a series of ascensions (11, 18, 33, 42, 65, etc.) or a descending sequence is produced. Each value becomes a right child if it is increasing and a left offspring if it is decreasing; as a result, the tree may not be in a state of equilibrium. Although the Workshop applet's key values are produced randomly, some brief descending or ascending sequences will inevitably be formed, resulting in local imbalances. Try building up trees by entering an ordered series of objects to observe what happens once discovered and how the items are added to the tree's structure using the Workshops applet.

When using Fill to build the tree, obtain all the nodes asked for many of them. The number of nodes a branch can support will depend on how unbalanced the tree's structure gets. That's because the applet's tree can only grow up to five levels deep; a real tree wouldn't be a problem.

Unbalanced trees may not be a major issue for larger trees if a tree is constructed from information elements whose key values appear in random order because it is unlikely that a long run of consecutive numbers will occur. However, significant values may be presented in a certain sequence, such as when a data entry worker stacks the personnel files in ascending order of employee numbers prior to entering the data. This is an example of how important values may be presented. When this occurs, trees' productive capacity place, the productive capacity of trees may be considerably reduced.

6.3.2. Illustrating the Tree in C++ Code

KEYWORD

Node class is simply a class representing a node in a data structure. Data structures like lists, trees, maps, etc. consist of so-called nodes

Examine the C++ implementation of the binary tree. There are various techniques for expressing a tree in computer memory, just as for other data structures. The most prevalent method places nodes in random memory locations and connects them with pointers pointing to their descendants (Johnsson, 1987). (A tree can also be represented in memory as an array, but disregard it for now.).

6.3.2.1. The Node Class

To construct an object of the nodes class. These objects contain information about the preserved objects or pointers for the node's two offspring (Tueno & Janneck, 2021). This is how it seems.

```
class Node
{
public:
int iData; //data item (key)
double dData;  //data item
Node* pLeftChild;       //left child node
Node* pRightChild;      //right child node
//
//constructor
Node() : iData(0), dData(0.0), pLeftChild(NULL),
```

```
        pRightChild(NULL)
    { }
    //
    void displayNode()      //display ourself: {75, 7.5}
    {cout << '{' << iData << ," " << dData << "} ";
    }}; //class Node ends
```

Some programmers may include a pointer to the parent of a node. It complicates some processes while simplifying others, so it is not included. The code of this object's member function displayNode(), which shows the node's data, is irrelevant to this topic even though it exists (Sleator & Tarjan, 1983).

The class Node can be created using additional methods. Instead of just including the information items in the node, one could also provide a pointer to an object that uniquely identifies the data item (Davoodi et al., 2017):

```
    class Node
    {Person* p1;            //pointer for Person object
    Node* pLeftChild;       //pointer for left child
    Node* pRightChild;      //pointer for right child};
```

This makes it more conceptually clear the node & data items it carries are not the same, but it leads to slightly more sophisticated code, so stick with the first way.

6.3.2.2. The Tree Class

In addition, a class may be used to generate the tree, which is the object that comprises all the nodes. Its class name is Tree. Its sole data member is a Node* variable associated with the root. All of the other nodes are reachable from the root (Lucas, 1987). Consequently, they don't need data members.

Tree class includes many member functions, including those for inserting and searching, traversing the tree in various ways, and displaying it (Pănoiu et al., 2005). Here is a simplified version:

```
    class Tree
    {
```

KEYWORD

Member functions are operators and functions that are declared as members of a class.

```
private:
Node* pRoot;    //first node of tree
public:
//-------------------------------------------------------------
Tree() : pRoot(NULL) //constructor
{ }
//-------------------------------------------------------------
Node* find(int key)     //find node with given key
{ /*body not shown*/ }
//-------------------------------------------------------------
void insert(int id, double dd) //insert new node
{ /*body not shown*/ }
//-------------------------------------------------------------
void traverse(int traverseType)
{ /*body not shown*/ }
//-------------------------------------------------------------
void displayTree()
{ /*body not shown*/ }
//-------------------------------------------------------------
}; //end class Tree
```

6.3.2.3. The main() Function

A means of manipulating the tree is required. Here is an example of how to build a tree, add three nodes to it, and finally search for a single one of them using a main() method (Hassan, 1986):

```
int main()
{
Tree theTree;    //make a tree
theTree.insert(50, 1.5);//insert 3 nodes
```

```
theTree.insert(25, 1.7);
theTree.insert(75, 1.9);
Node* found = theTree.find(25); //find node with key 25
if(found != NULL)
cout << "Found the node with key 25" << endl;
else
cout << "Could not find node with key 25" << endl;
return 0;
} // end main()
```

The main() procedure in Listing 6.1 offers a basic interface to insert data, search for items, and carry out other tasks using the keyboard (Miao et al., 2006).

Specific tree operations are examined, such as identifying and adding a node. The issue of removing a node is also discussed.

6.4. FINDING A NODE

The most basic of the main tree operations is to locate a node that matches a particular key. Remember that each node in a tree of binary searches represents information-containing objects, which could be objected to as representing people. A key is an employee number and names, addresses, phone numbers, salaries, and other data members (Gupta et al., 2016). Alternately, they might stand in for auto parts, having a part number as the fundamental value and information for stock level, cost, etc. The Workshop applet denotes the qualities of each node with a number and corresponding color. These two traits are present when a node is created and continue to exist throughout the node's lifetime.

KEYWORD

Workshop applets are graphics-based demonstration programs that show what trees and other data structures look like.

6.4.1. Locating a Node with the Workshop Applet

Given a key value, select a node to display in the Workshop applet by looking at it and choosing one preferably close to a tree's base.

For explanation, assume to choose to locate the node in Figure 6.7 representing the object with key value 57 (Chawra & Gupta,

2020). Of course, a distinct tree is obtained, and an alternate key value is chosen once the Workspace applet is run.

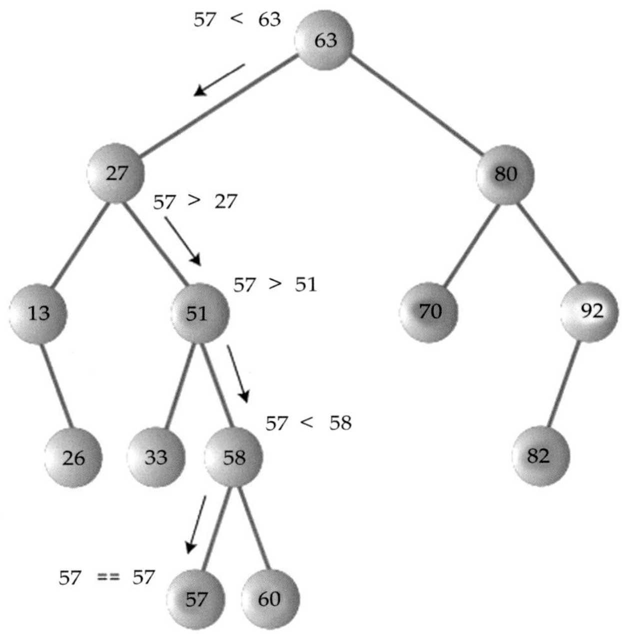

Figure 6.7. Illustration of finding the node number 57 (Source: Ram Mohan, Creative Commons License).

6.4.1.1. To Do: Search for a Node

i. Select the Find option. The popup will ask how much the node is worth (Zhou et al., 2014).
ii. Type 57. Press Find twice more.
iii. Keep pressing the Find button. The prompt will say Coming to a left child or Coming to a right child when the Workshop applet searches for the chosen node, & A single level will be descended by the red arrow in either a right or left direction (Fortune et al., 1980).

The arrow in Figure 6.7 begins with the root. Software contrasts root value, 63, with the key value, 57. The software understands the requested node lies on the tree's left side because the key is smaller, either the root's left child or a descendant of this child. Comparing 57 and 27 will reveal that the requested node is on the correct sub-tree of 27, as the root's left child has the value of 27. The direction of the arrow is in the direction of node 51, the subtree's base. Once more, node 51 is greater than 57 (Guha & Khuller, 1998). As a result, 57 is shifted to the left after 58 has been moved to the right. Again, the contrast reveals that 57 matches the node's key value. The workshop application displays a message indicating that the node has been located. On the discovered node, a serious program would run, showing its information or changing one of its information.

6.4.2. C++ Code for Finding a Node

Here is the code the locate() method uses, which is a Tree class member function.

```
Node* find(int key)      //find node with given key
{  //(assumes non-empty tree)
Node* current = pRoot;                //start at root
while(current->iData != key)  //while no match,
{
if(key < pCurrent->iData)      //go left?
pCurrent = pCurrent->pLeftChild;
else       //or go right?
pCurrent = pCurrent->pRightChild;
if(pCurrent == NULL)  //if no child,
return NULL;     //didn't find it
}
return pCurrent; //found it
} //end find()
```

This procedure stores the pointer from the node examined in the variable current. The argument keyword represents the value to be found. The routine begins at the beginning (Wilkov, 1972). (It has to; this is the only node it can access directly.) Pcurrent has also been set to its base.

The value to get the key is then compared with the key values in the current node's iData member within the while loop. PCurrent represents the left child of the node if a key has a lower value than this data member. If the key is larger than 0, current has been configured as the right child within the node, also known as the node's iData data member.

6.4.3. Unable to Locate the Node

When pCurrent becomes undefined, it is impossible to locate the following child nodes in the sequence; at the end of the line of code, before discovering the node looked for, it is impossible to exist. We return NULL to make this clear (Smalheiser et al., 2009).

6.4.4. Found the Node

Suppose the while loop's condition is not met. In such a case, allowing escape from the lowest level of that loop, indicating that the iData data associated with pCurrent match key, signifying that the node wanted has been located to ensure the program that performed find() may utilize any of the node's information to return to the node (Bholowalia & Kumar, 2014).

KEYWORD

Node is a data structure that stores a value that can be of any data type and has a pointer to another node

6.4.5. Efficiency of the Find Operation

The number of layers below a node is located and the time it takes to locate it. There can only be five tiers and a maximum of 31 nodes in the Workshop applet (Tang et al., 2006). As a result, any node with as few as 5 comparisons can be located. The base two logarithms are O(log2 N) or O(log N) time.

6.5. INSERTING A NODE

To locate the appropriate location before inserting a node. Similar to the method explained in the chapter on the discovery, finding a node that no more exists is analogous to doing this. A path from the root leads to the appropriate node, which serves as the starting point for the most recent node (George & Liu, 1979). Depending on whether or not the new node's key is less than or higher than the parent's, the newly created node is connected to this parent either left child after being located.

6.5.1. Using the Workshop Applet to Add a Node

With the Workshop applet, adding a node is similar to finding an existing node.

Include a Node

i. Select "Ins" from the menu (McLennan et al., 2007).

ii. Write the name corresponding to the node's value for the key for a node that needs to be placed. A brand-new node having a value of 45 might be added. Put this in the text box.

iii. Continue to press the Ins button. The newly created node will be attached when the red arrow drops to the insertion site (Shivaratri et al., 1992).

The program searches for the appropriate location to insert a node as its initial phase. Figure 6.8a depicts how it appears.

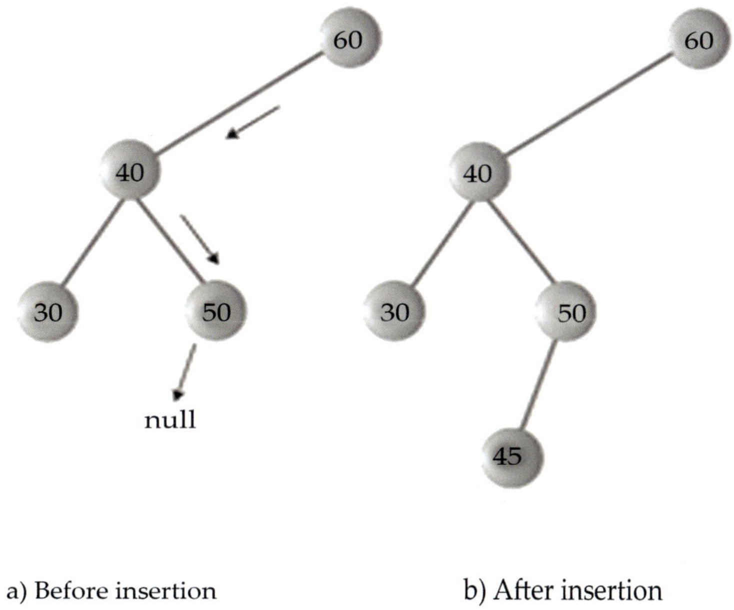

Figure 6.8. Representation of adding a node (Source: Vamshi Krishna, Creative Commons License).

Since 45 is greater than 40, but below 60, one can reach node 50. The pLeftChild data component is Empty since 45 is now smaller than 50, heading left, but 50 lacks a child to its left. The insertion function of the node understands where to attach the new node when it comes across this NULL (Dakin, 1965). As seen in Figure 6.8b, the Workshop applet accomplishes this by constructing an additional node containing the value 45 and linking it to the child node to the left of 50.

6.5.2. Inserting a Node in C++

The insert() function creates the new node, which then utilizes its arguments to fill it with data (Alakeel, 2010).

The other step is to insert() to choose where to put the new node. The method for doing this is much the same as locating a node, which is covered in the chapter on find(). The main distinction is that it runs into a NULL node when looking for a node, and the node seeking doesn't exist (Yen, 1972). If necessary, create a node while attempting to insert one before returning.

The data item supplied as an input id is the value that needs to be looked for. The while loop treats a node with an identical key value with the assumption that it is simply over the key value and uses true of the state because Locating a node whose id value matches another one. Discuss duplicate nodes once more.

KEYWORD

Return statement ends the execution of a function, and returns control to the calling function.

In genuine trees, a site to add a node is continually found unless memory is exhausted; Using a return statement, the while loop is completed after adding the new node.

Code insert() function's is shown below (Nardelli et al., 2003):

```
void insert(int id, double dd) //insert new node
{
Node* pNewNode = new Node;      //make new node
pNewNode->iData = id;       //insert data
pNewNode->dData = dd;
if(pRoot==NULL)       //no node in root
pRoot = pNewNode;
else      //root occupied
{
Node* pCurrent = pRoot;      //start at root
Node* pParent;
while(true)       //(exits internally)
{
pParent = pCurrent;
if(id < pCurrent->iData)       //go left?
{
pCurrent = pCurrent->pLeftChild;
if(pCurrent == NULL)  //if end of the line,
{  //insert on left
```

```
pParent->pLeftChild = pNewNode;
return;
}
} //end if go left
else     //or go right?
{
pCurrent = pCurrent->pRightChild;
if(pCurrent == NULL)  //if end of the line
{          //insert on right
pParent->pRightChild = pNewNode;
return;
}
} //end else go right
} //end while
} //end else not root
} //end insert()
```

To keep track of the most recent non-NULL node across, create a new variable called pParent . (50 in the figure). This is required because upon learning that the previous value of pCurrent lacked an appropriate child and was set to NULL (Ishida et al., 1995). Without saving pParent, the Current location track would be lost.

The previous non-NULL node determined, pParent, should have the proper child pointer changed to the new node to insert the new node. If the left grandchild of pParent cannot be found, attach the newly generated nodes towards the left child; if the right child is not found, join the new node child. The left offspring of 50 and 45 are shown attached in Figure 6.8.

6.6. DELETING A NODE

How is the node taken away? Unfortunately, the deleting process requires a lot of work and effort. Thus, it is outside the purview of this book. The applet for the Tree Workshop has a Del button. To observe how certain nodes are removed in various ways. Any node with no offspring can be deleted quickly and simply by removing it. A node is eliminated by linking its child with its parent if it has just one child (Lewis & Yannakakis, 1980). However, deleting a node with two children is challenging.

Some programs label a node as "deleted" to avoid the complicated process. Despite not being erased, algorithms may choose to leave it.

KEYWORD

Traversing is a process in which each element of a data structure is accessed. Accessing an element of data structure means visiting every element at least once

6.7. TRAVERSING TREE

A tree can be traversed by going through every node in a specific order (Soule, 1977). Finding, adding, and removing nodes are more frequent operations than this one. The fact that traversing is not extremely quick is one explanation for this. Theoretically, however, exploring a tree may have unexpected practical implications.

A tree can be crossed in three easy ways. , postorder, inorder and Preorder are their names. Let's first look at the order in which binary search trees use most frequently.

6.7.1. Inorder Traversal

A tree of binary searches will be explored in ascending order depending on their key values during an in-order traversal (Chen & Das, 1992). This is one method of making a list with the order of the information in a binary tree.

Recursion is the easiest approach for carrying out a traverse. This is how it goes. A node is sent as the input when using a recursive algorithm to iterate across the tree. This node serves as the root at first. Only three tasks must be completed by the function.

- Explore the left subtree of the node using itself.
- Stop the node.
- Invoke the node's right subtree by calling it (Frisken & Perry, 2002).

Remember that visiting a node means doing something to it: displaying it, writing it to a file, or whatever.

Traversals work with any binary tree, not just with binary search trees. The traversal mechanism doesn't pay any attention to the key values of the nodes; it only concerns itself with whether a node has children.

6.7.2. C++ Code for Traversing

Before examining how traversal appears in the Workshop applet, display the real code for in order traverse because it is so straightforward. The three processes already mentioned are carried out by the method inOrder(). The node visit consists of presenting the node's contents (Brinck, 1985). As with every recursive function, the procedure must have a base case—the circumstance under which it returns immediately without invoking itself. This occurs when the node supplied as an input to inOrder() is NULL. Here is the inOrder() member function's code:

```
void inOrder(Node* pLocalRoot)
{
if(pLocalRoot != NULL)
{
inOrder(pLocalRoot->pLeftChild);    //left child
cout << pLocalRoot->iData << " ";   //display node
inOrder(pLocalRoot->pRightChild);   //right child
}
}
```

Initial calls to this member function include the root as a parameter (Baeza-Yates et al., 1994):

```
inOrder(root);
```

After that, the function operates independently and keeps calling itself until no more nodes are visited.

6.7.3. Moving Through a 3-Node Tree

Look at a simple example to understand how this recursive traversal method functions. Figure 6.9 displays a tree with just the root (A), a left-handed kid (B), and a right-handed child (C) as the nodes (C).

KEYWORD

Recursive function is a function that repeats or uses its own previous term to calculate subsequent terms and thus forms a sequence of terms.

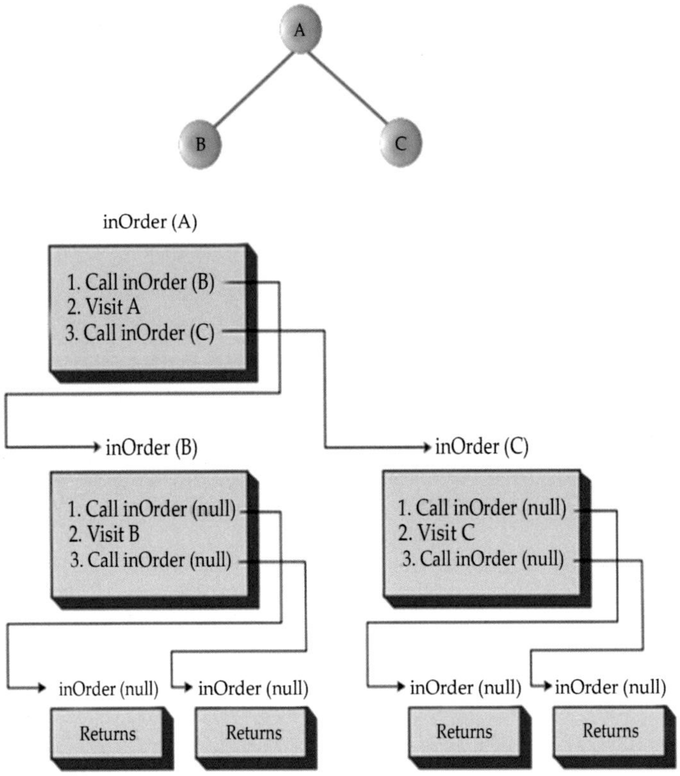

Figure 6.9. Flowchart of applying a 3-node tree's inorder () member method (Source: Kalyani Tummala, Creative Commons License).

Following are the Traversal Steps to complete this task (InOrder).

i. Call inOrder() first, passing root A as an input parameter. Refer to this version of inOrder() as inOrder.(A)

ii. Using B as a parameter, inOrder(A) first uses inOrder() with the left-hand child, A. Called this the second iteration of inOrder() inOrder.(B).

iii. inOrder(B) is now invoked with its left offspring as an argument. The argument is NULL since it has no remaining children. This generates a call to inorder(), referred to as inOrder.(NULL) (Wald et al., 2006).

iv. At this point, three calls to InOrder() have been made: inOrder(A), inOrder(B), & inOrder.(NULL). On the other hand, inOrder(NULL) returns immediately if the argument is NULL (Chen et al., 1996).

iv. At this point, inOrder(B) continues by visiting B, which we'll presume means displaying it.

v. The right child is passed as an input to inOrder (B), which then executes inOrder()again. Once more, this parameter is NULL. Therefore the second in order (NULL) function returns right away (Wilson et al., 2021).

vi. inOrder (B) returns after doing tasks 1 through 3. (and thereby ceases to exist).

vii. Just returned to inOrder (A) after traversing A's left child.

viii. After visiting A, we call inOrder () once more, passing C as an input to create inOrder.(C). Since inOrder(C) has no offspring, like inOrder(B), task 1 returns without taking any further action, task 2 travels to C, and task 3 does nothing.

ix. The command now goes to inOrder (B). (A).

x. But now that inOrder(A) is finished, it returns, and the traverse is completed (Ong, 2006).

The nodes were visited sequentially and investigated in the order of A, B, and C. This would be the binary search tree's ascending key order.

Similar techniques are used to handle more complex trees. The inOrder() method constantly runs for each node until the whole tree has been traversed.

6.7.4. Using the Workshop Applet to Traverse

Press Trav repeatedly to observe a traverse in the Workshop applet. (Input of numbers is not necessary)

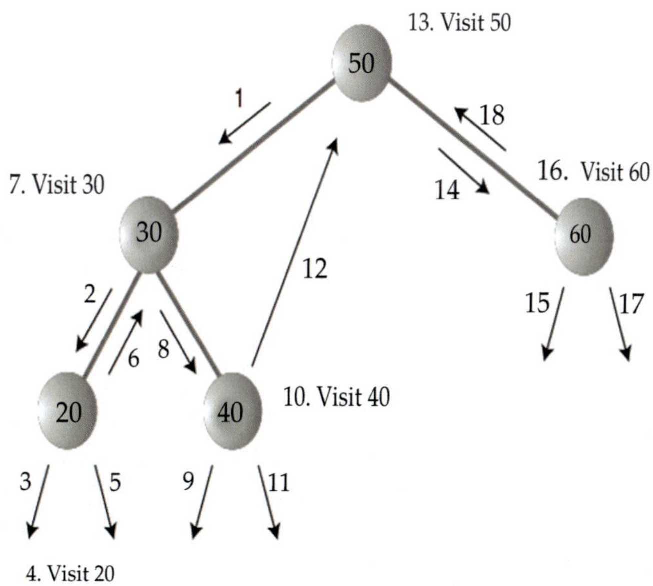

Figure 6.10. Image of traversing a tree in order (Source: Kiran, Creative Commons License).

When the tree in Figure 6.10 is traversed in order using the Tree Workshop applet, the results are displayed in Table 6.1

(Revelles et al., 2000). This one is a little more advanced than the 3-node tree that was previously displayed. The root is where the red arrow begins. The order of node keys & the accompanying messages is shown in Table 6.2. On the Workshop applet screen's bottom, the key sequence is visible.

Table 6.1. Tabular data of workshop applet traversal (Source: Laxmi, Creative Commons License)

Step Number	The Red Arrow on Node	Message	List of Nodes visited
1	50	Check the left, kid.	
2	30	Check the left, kid.	
3	20	Check the left, kid.	
4	20	Travel to this node.	
5	20	Verify a correct child	20
6	20	Proceed to the prior subtree's root.	20
7	30	Travel to this node.	20
8	30	Verify the correct offspring	20 30
9	40	Examine a left child	20 30
10	40	Travel to this node.	20 30
11	40	Verify the correct offspring	20 30 40
12	40	Proceed to the prior subtree's root.	20 30 40
13	50	Travel to this node.	20 30 40
14	50	Verify the correct offspring	20 30 40 50
15	60	Examine a left child	20 30 40 50
16	60	Travel to this node.	20 30 40 50
17	60	Verify the correct offspring	20 30 40 50 60
18	60	Proceed to the prior subtree's root.	20 30 40 50 60
19	50	Done traversal	20 30 40 50 60

The routine visits each node travels its left subtree, and then visits its right subtree for each node. This may not be immediately apparent. For example, this occurs in phases 2, 7, and 8 for node 30 (Karapinar et al., 2012).

It's not as difficult as it first appears. Utilizing the Tree Workspace applet, explore different trees to comprehend better what's going on.

6.7.5. Postorder and Preorder Traversals

In addition to in order, the tree can also be traversed in preorder and postorder. It is reasonably obvious to navigate a tree in order. Postorder and pre-traversal are less obvious. Nevertheless, these traversals are beneficial when analyzing algebraic expressions or creating programs that explore. Let's examine why that must be the case.

An algebraic expression involving the binary operators for arithmetic +, -, /, and * can be represented by a tree of binary values (Jakobsson et al., 2003). The other nodes have names for variables (A, B, and C), whereas the root node has an operator. Each subtree is expressed as an algebraic expression.

Figure 6.11 depicts a binary tree that represents an algebraic expression (Berman et al., 2007)

A*(B+C)

This is called infix notation, the standard notation used in algebra. The right inorder sequence A*B+C will be generated by traversing the tree in order but must be manually introduced by parentheses.

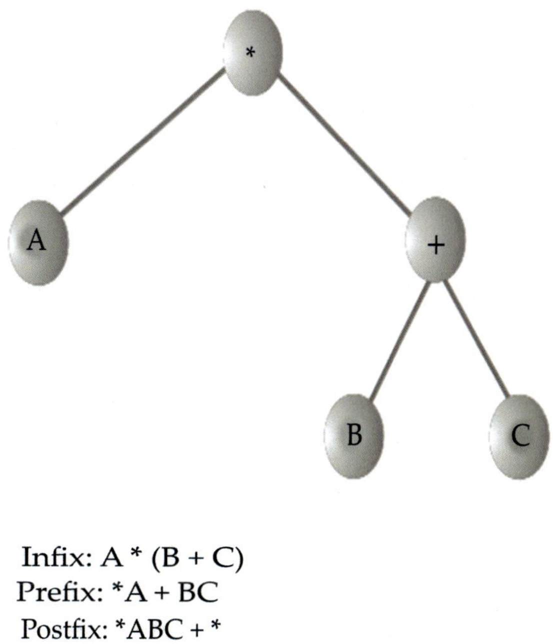

Figure 6.11. Image of an algebraic expression represented by a tree (Source: Laxmi, Creative Commons License).

What relevance does this have to preorder as well as postorder traversals? Think about what's involved. The same three procedures used in order are carried out for these additional traversals but in an alternate sequence. The preorder() member function's sequence is as follows:

i. Check out the node.
ii. Invoke it to investigate the node's left subtree.
iii. To navigate the correct subtree of a node, summon itself.

The expression would be produced by traversing the tree in Figure 6.11 using preorder (Popov et al., 2007).

*A+BC

This refers to Prefix notation. Yet another acceptable approach to depicting an algebraic expression. One wonderful feature is that there is no need for parenthesis; the expression makes sense without them. Every of the operators is applied to the expression's next two elements, starting on the left. These two items are A and +BC in the case of the first operator, *. In order notation, the final phrase is B+C because +BC means to "apply + to the following two elements within the expression," namely B and C (Hapala & Havran, 2011). We get A*(B+C) in order by adding that to the original phrase *A+BC (preorder).

KEYWORD

Algebraic expressions are the idea of expressing numbers using letters or alphabets without specifying their actual values.

Change one type of algebraic notation to another by utilizing various traversals.

The three activities are arranged once more in the post-order traversal member function:

i. Utilize itself to traverse the node's left subtree.
ii. Utilize itself to find the node's correct subtree.
iii. Go to the node (Barringer & Akenine-Möller, 2013).

The expression for the tree depicted in Figure 6.11 would be produced through a postorder traverse of the nodes.

ABC+*

Postfix notation describes this concept. Every operator applies to the two items on its left, beginning with the rightmost operator. A & BC+ are the first to receive the *. Add the + to both B and C by repeating the method for BC+. As an infix, this gives us (B+C). It provides an A*(B+C) infix when added to the original ABC+* (postfix) equation.

With additional ingenious ways to employ the various traversals than constructing different sorts of algebraic expressions. Utilize postorder traversal to eliminate all the nodes once the tree is destroyed.

6.8. THE EFFICIENCY OF BINARY TREES

Most tree operations entail descending a tree level by level to locate a specific node. How lengthy is this procedure? About fifty percent of a tree's terminals are on its lowest level. (In actuality, the bottom row has one extra node than the remainder of the tree.) Most queries, insertions, & deletion require identifying a node at the lowest level, which accounts for about 50% of all operations. (The final quarter of these processes requires locating a node at the next-lowest level, etc.)

During a search, one node on every level must be visited. By knowing the number of levels, we can estimate how long it will take to perform these operations.

Table 6.2 illustrates the levels required to house a specific number of nodes, assuming a full tree (Fei & Liu, 2006).

Did you Know?

The Fibonacci sequence, a mathematical sequence that appears frequently in nature can be represented as a binary tree.

Table 6.2. Levels for a Described Number of Nodes (Source: Narasmiha, Creative Commons License)

Quantity of Nodes	Count of Levels
1	1
3	2
7	3
15	4
31	5
….	….
1023	10
….	….
32,767	15
….	….
1,048,575	20
….	….
33,554,432	25
…..	….
1,073,741,824	30

This problem is comparable to the ordered array problem that was dealt with in "Ordered Arrays" Hour 3. In that situation, the number of binary comparisons was equivalent to the base-2 logarithmic for the array's number of cells. Here, refer to the first column's number of nodes as N and the second column's number of levels as L, N is one fewer than two increased to the value of L, or N = 2L – 1.

When multiplying both ends of the formula by one, we get

N+1 = 2L

This is comparable to (Wu et al., 2012)

L = log2(N+1)

Thus, a base-2 log of N determines the time required to perform typical tree operations. Such operations need O(log N) time in the Big O notation.

If the tree is incomplete, an analysis is difficult. For any amount of tree levels, the average search times for the non-complete tree will be shorter than those for the whole tree since lower levels will see fewer searches.

The tree is superior to the several data-storage structures discussed thus far (Ruskey & Hu, 1977). Typically takes 500,000 comparisons to locate the desired item in a 1,000,000-item unordered array or linked list. However, a network of 1,000,000 objects only requires 20 comparisons.

Finding an item in an ordered array is just as easy, but inserting a new item typically involves shifting 500,000 objects. A tree with 1,000,000 elements can be added with 20 or fewer comparisons and a quick connection process. Similar to relocating 500,000 items on average to remove one item out of a 1,000,000-item array. Even without considering deletion, removing time is also inversely associated with the logarithmic of the overall number without considering deletion, removing time is also inversely associated with the logarithmic of the overall amount of nodes (Qu et al., 2020). Because of this, a tree offers the highest efficiency level of efficiency for all common data-storage operations.

More quickly, while any of the operations traverses, the traversals usually aren't done frequently in a normal huge database. When a tree is used to process, algebraic or analogous phrases get more suitable, generally not too long (Qing-Yun & Fu, 1983).

ACTIVITY 6.1

Write down code to implement a binary search tree and then use it to perform operations such as inserting, deleting, and searching for nodes.

SUMMARY

In computer science and programming, a tree is a widely used data structure that is used to represent hierarchical relationships between elements. Trees consist of nodes, which are connected by edges, and have a root node that serves as the starting point for the tree. Each node in a tree can have one or more child nodes, which are connected to it by edges. A node that has no children is called a leaf node, while a node with one or more children is called an internal node. Trees are used in a variety of applications such as file systems, compiler construction and graph algorithms. Some common types of trees used in programming include binary trees, binary search trees, balanced trees, heap and trie.

REVIEW QUESTIONS

1. What is a tree and how is it different from a linear data structure?
2. What is the root node of a tree and what is its significance?
3. What is a binary tree and what are its properties?
4. What is a leaf node in a tree and how is it different from an internal node?
5. How are trees used in real-world applications, such as file systems and databases?

MULTIPLE CHOICE QUESTIONS

1. What is a tree in computer science?

a. A linear data structure
b. A non-linear data structure
c. A data structure for storing key-value pairs
d. None of the above

2. What is a binary search tree?

a. A tree with at most two children per node
b. A tree with at most three children per node
c. A tree where each node has exactly two children
d. None of the above

3. What is the height of a tree?

a. The number of nodes in the tree
b. The number of edges in the tree
c. The distance between the root node and the deepest leaf node
d. None of the above

4. **What is the purpose of self-balancing trees like AVL trees?**
   a. To store data more efficiently than traditional binary trees
   b. To ensure that the tree remains balanced and efficient for searching and sorting
   c. To allow for multiple parents for each node in the tree.
   d. None of the above
5. **What is a full binary tree?**
   a. Each node has exactly zero or two children
   b. Each node has exactly two children
   c. All the leaves are at the same level
   d. Each node has exactly one or two children

Answers to Multiple Choice Questions

1. (d) 2. (a) 3. (c) 4. (b) 5. (a)

REFERENCES

1. Alakeel, A. M., (2010). A guide to dynamic load balancing in distributed computer systems. *International Journal of Computer Science and Information Security, 10*(6), 153–160.
2. Baeza-Yates, R., Cunto, W., Manber, U., & Wu, S., (1994). Proximity matching using fixed-queries trees. In: *CPM* (Vol. 94, pp. 198–212).
3. Barringer, R., & Akenine-Möller, T., (2013). Dynamic stackless binary tree traversal. *Journal of Computer Graphics Techniques, 2*(1), 38–49.
4. Benoit, D., Demaine, E. D., Munro, J. I., Raman, R., Raman, V., & Rao, S. S., (2005). Representing trees of higher degree. *Algorithmica, 43*(1), 275–292.
5. Berman, P., Karpinski, M., & Nekrich, Y., (2007). Optimal trade-off for Merkle tree traversal. *Theoretical Computer Science, 372*(1), 26–36.
6. Bholowalia, P., & Kumar, A., (2014). EBK-means: A clustering technique based on elbow method and k-means in WSN. *International Journal of Computer Applications, 105*(9), 2–6.
7. Bolognesi, T., & Brinksma, E., (1987). Introduction to the ISO specification language LOTOS. *Computer Networks and ISDN Systems, 14*(1), 25–59.
8. Brinck, K., (1985). The expected performance of traversal algorithms in binary trees. *The Computer Journal, 28*(4), 426–432.
9. Cano, A., Gémez-Olmedo, M., & Moral, S., (2011). Approximate inference in Bayesian networks using binary probability trees. *International Journal of Approximate Reasoning, 52*(1), 49–62.

10. Chawra, V. K., & Gupta, G. P., (2020). Load balanced node clustering scheme using improved memetic algorithm based meta-heuristic technique for wireless sensor network. *Procedia Computer Science, 167,* 468–476.
11. Chen, C. C. Y., & Das, S. K., (1992). Breadth-first traversal of trees and integer sorting in parallel. *Information Processing Letters, 41*(1), 39–49.
12. Chen, M. S., Park, J. S., & Yu, P. S., (1996). Data mining for path traversal patterns in a web environment. In: *Proceedings of 16th International Conference on Distributed Computing Systems* (Vol. 1, pp. 385–392). IEEE.
13. Culler, D., Estrin, D., & Srivastava, M., (2004). Guest editors' introduction: Overview of sensor networks. *Computer, 37*(08), 41–49.
14. Dakin, R. J., (1965). A tree-search algorithm for mixed integer programming problems. *The Computer Journal, 8*(3), 250–255.
15. Davoodi, P., Raman, R., & Satti, S. R., (2017). On succinct representations of binary trees. *Mathematics in Computer Science, 11*(1), 177–189.
16. Dung, P. M., Mancarella, P., & Toni, F., (2007). Computing ideal sceptical argumentation. *Artificial Intelligence, 171*(10–15), 642–674.
17. Fei, B., & Liu, J., (2006). Binary tree of SVM: A new fast multiclass training and classification algorithm. *IEEE Transactions on Neural Networks, 17*(3), 696–704.
18. Fortune, S., Hopcroft, J., & Wyllie, J., (1980). The directed subgraph homeomorphism problem. *Theoretical Computer Science, 10*(2), 111–121.
19. Friedman, S. J., & Supowit, K. J., (1987). Finding the optimal variable ordering for binary decision diagrams. In: *Proceedings of the 24th ACM/IEEE Design Automation Conference* (Vol. 1, pp. 348–356).
20. Frisken, S. F., & Perry, R. N., (2002). Simple and efficient traversal methods for quadtrees and octrees. *Journal of Graphics Tools, 7*(3), 1–11.
21. George, A., & Liu, J. W., (1979). An implementation of a pseudoperipheral node finder. *ACM Transactions on Mathematical Software (TOMS), 5*(3), 284–295.
22. Grama, A., Kumar, V., Gupta, A., & Karypis, G., (2003). *Introduction to Parallel Computing* (Vol. 1, pp. 2–7). Pearson Education.
23. Guha, S., & Khuller, S., (1998). Approximation algorithms for connected dominating sets. *Algorithmica, 20*(1), 374–387.
24. Gupta, S. K., Kuila, P., & Jana, P. K., (2016). Genetic algorithm approach for k-coverage and m-connected node placement in target based wireless sensor networks. *Computers & Electrical Engineering, 56*(1), 544–556.
25. Gurwitz, C., (1995). Achieving a uniform interface for binary tree implementations. In: *Proceedings of the Twenty-Sixth SIGCSE Technical Symposium on Computer Science Education* (Vol. 1, pp. 66–70).
26. Halasz, F., & Moran, T. P., (1982). Analogy considered harmful. In: *Proceedings of the 1982 Conference on Human Factors in Computing Systems* (Vol. 1, pp. 383–386).

27. Hamouda, S., Edwards, S. H., Elmongui, H. G., Ernst, J. V., & Shaffer, C. A., (2020). BTRecurTutor: A tutorial for practicing recursion in binary trees. *Computer Science Education, 30*(2), 216–248.

28. Hapala, M., & Havran, V., (2011). Kd□tree traversal algorithms for ray tracing. In: *Computer Graphics Forum* (Vol. 30, No. 1, pp. 199–213). Oxford, UK: Blackwell Publishing Ltd.

29. Hassan, M., (1986). A fault-tolerant modular architecture for binary trees. *IEEE Transactions on Computers, 100*(4), 356–361.

30. Hayes, J. P., (1976). A graph model for fault-tolerant computing systems. *IEEE Transactions on Computers, 25*(09), 875–884.

31. Ishida, K., Kakuda, Y., & Kikuno, T., (1995). A routing protocol for finding two node-disjoint paths in computer networks. In: *Proceedings of International Conference on Network Protocols* (Vol. 1, pp. 340–347). IEEE.

32. Jakobsson, M., Leighton, T., Micali, S., & Szydlo, M., (2003). Fractal Merkle tree representation and traversal. In: *CT-RSA* (Vol. 2612, pp. 314–326).

33. Johnsson, S. L., (1987). Communication efficient basic linear algebra computations on hypercube architectures. *Journal of Parallel and Distributed Computing, 4*(2), 133–172.

34. Joshi, A. K., (1987). An introduction to tree adjoining grammars. *Mathematics of Language, 1,* 87–115.

35. Karapinar, Z., Senturk, A., Zavrak, S., Kara, R., & Erdogmus, P., (2012). Binary apple tree: A game approach to tree traversal algorithms. In: *2012 International Conference on Information Technology Based Higher Education and Training (ITHET)* (Vol. 1, pp. 1–3). IEEE.

36. Klein, P., & Ravi, R. J. J. A., (1995). A nearly best-possible approximation algorithm for node-weighted Steiner trees. *Journal of Algorithms, 19*(1), 104–115.

37. Lewis, J. M., & Yannakakis, M., (1980). The node-deletion problem for hereditary properties is NP-complete. *Journal of Computer and System Sciences, 20*(2), 219–230.

38. Li, T., Wang, G., & Chen, J., (2010). A modified binary tree codification of drainage networks to support complex hydrological models. *Computers & Geosciences, 36*(11), 1427–1435.

39. Lucas, J. M., (1987). The rotation graph of binary trees is Hamiltonian. *Journal of Algorithms, 8*(4), 503–535.

40. Luellen, J. K., Shadish, W. R., & Clark, M. H., (2005). Propensity scores: An introduction and experimental test. *Evaluation Review, 29*(6), 530–558.

41. McLennan, G., Ferguson, J. S., Thomas, K., Delsing, A. S., Cook-Granroth, J., & Hoffman, E. A., (2007). The use of MDCT-based computer-aided pathway finding for mediastinal and perihilar lymph node biopsy: A randomized controlled prospective trial. *Respiration, 74*(4), 423–431.

42. Miao, L., Qi, H., Ramanath, R., & Snyder, W. E., (2006). Binary tree-based generic

demosaicking algorithm for multispectral filter arrays. *IEEE Transactions on Image Processing, 15*(11), 3550–3558.

43. Nardelli, E., Proietti, G., & Widmayer, P., (2003). Finding the most vital node of a shortest path. *Theoretical Computer Science, 296*(1), 167–177.
44. Ong, C. H., (2006). On model-checking trees generated by higher-order recursion schemes. In: *21st Annual IEEE Symposium on Logic in Computer Science (LICS'06)* (Vol. 1, pp. 81–90). IEEE.
45. Pănoiu, M., Muscalagiu, I., Osaci, M., & Iordan, A., (2005). Multimedia educational software for binary tree and their application present. *Annals of the Faculty of Engineering Hunedoara, 3*(3), 4–8.
46. Parhami, B., (2006). *Introduction to Parallel Processing: Algorithms and Architectures* (Vol. 1, pp. 4–8). Springer Science & Business Media.
47. Perlin, K., & Fox, D., (1993). Pad: An alternative approach to the computer interface. In: *Proceedings of the 20th Annual Conference on Computer Graphics and Interactive Techniques* (Vol. 1, pp. 57–64).
48. Plaisant, C., Grosjean, J., & Bederson, B. B., (2002). Spacetree: Supporting exploration in large node link tree, design evolution and empirical evaluation. In: *IEEE Symposium on Information Visualization, 2002: INFOVIS 2002* (Vol. 1, pp. 57–64). IEEE.
49. Popov, S., Günther, J., Seidel, H. P., & Slusallek, P., (2007). Stackless KD□tree traversal for high performance GPU ray tracing. In: *Computer Graphics Forum* (Vol. 26, No. 3, pp. 415–424). Oxford, UK: Blackwell Publishing Ltd.
50. Qing-Yun, S., & Fu, K. S., (1983). A method for the design of binary tree classifiers. *Pattern Recognition, 16*(6), 593–603.
51. Qu, Z., Li, J., Bao, K. H., & Si, Z. C., (2020). An unordered image stitching method based on binary tree and estimated overlapping area. *IEEE Transactions on Image Processing, 29*(1), 6734–6744.
52. Raymond, K., (1989). A tree-based algorithm for distributed mutual exclusion. *ACM Transactions on Computer Systems (TOCS), 7*(1), 61–77.
53. Revelles, J., Urena, C., & Lastra, M., (2000). *An Efficient Parametric Algorithm for Octree Traversal, 1,* 6–10.
54. Ruskey, F., & Hu, T. C., (1977). Generating binary trees lexicographically. *SIAM Journal on Computing, 6*(4), 745–758.
55. Schuld, M., Sinayskiy, I., & Petruccione, F., (2015). An introduction to quantum machine learning. *Contemporary Physics, 56*(2), 172–185.
56. Shivaratri, N. G., Krueger, P., & Singhal, M., (1992). Load distributing for locally distributed systems. *Computer, 25*(12), 33–44.
57. Shneiderman, B., (1992). Tree visualization with tree-maps: 2-D space-filling approach. *ACM Transactions on Graphics (TOG), 11*(1), 92–99.
58. Siltaneva, J., & Mäkinen, E., (2002). A comparison of random binary tree generators. *The Computer Journal, 45*(6), 653–660.

59. Singh, A., (2009). An artificial bee colony algorithm for the leaf-constrained minimum spanning tree problem. *Applied Soft Computing, 9*(2), 625–631.
60. Sleator, D. D., & Tarjan, R. E., (1983). Self-adjusting binary trees. In: *Proceedings of the Fifteenth Annual ACM Symposium on Theory of Computing* (Vol. 1, pp. 235–245).
61. Smalheiser, N. R., Torvik, V. I., & Zhou, W., (2009). Arrowsmith two-node search interface: A tutorial on finding meaningful links between two disparate sets of articles in MEDLINE. *Computer Methods and Programs in Biomedicine, 94*(2), 190–197.
62. Snyder, L., (1982). Introduction to the configurable, highly parallel computer. *Computer, 15*(01), 47–56.
63. Soule, S., (1977). A note on the nonrecursive traversal of binary trees. *The Computer Journal, 20*(4), 350–352.
64. Sudkamp, T. A., (2007). *Languages and Machines: An Introduction to the Theory of Computer Science, 3/E* (Vol. 1, pp. 3–7). Pearson Education India.
65. Tang, J., Hao, B., & Sen, A., (2006). Relay node placement in large scale wireless sensor networks. *Computer Communications, 29*(4), 490–501.
66. Tueno, A., & Janneck, J., (2021). A method for securely comparing integers using binary trees. *Cryptology ePrint Archive, 2*(1), 3–9.
67. Wald, I., Ize, T., Kensler, A., Knoll, A., & Parker, S. G., (2006). Ray tracing animated scenes using coherent grid traversal. In: *ACM SIGGRAPH 2006 Papers* (Vol. 1, pp. 485–493).
68. Weiser, M., (1999). The computer for the 21st century. *ACM SIGMOBILE Mobile Computing and Communications Review, 3*(3), 3–11.
69. Wilkov, R., (1972). Analysis and design of reliable computer networks. *IEEE Transactions on Communications, 20*(3), 660–678.
70. Wilson, L., Vaughn, N., & Krasny, R., (2021). A GPU-accelerated fast multipole method based on barycentric Lagrange interpolation and dual tree traversal. *Computer Physics Communications, 265*(1), 108017.
71. Wu, H., Zeng, Y., Feng, J., & Gu, Y., (2012). Binary tree slotted ALOHA for passive RFID tag anticollision. *IEEE Transactions on Parallel and Distributed Systems, 24*(1), 19–31.
72. Yen, J. Y., (1972). Finding the lengths of all shortest paths in n-node nonnegative-distance complete networks using ½ N3 additions and N3 comparisons. *Journal of the ACM (JACM), 19*(3), 423, 424.
73. Yi, J., & Tan, G., (2016). Binary-tree encryption strategy for optical multiple-image encryption. *Applied Optics, 55*(20), 5280–5291.
74. Zhou, J., Zhang, Y., & Cheng, J., (2014). Preference-based mining of top-K influential nodes in social networks. *Future Generation Computer Systems, 31*(1), 40–47.

CHAPTER 7

SEARCH ALGORITHMS IN DATA STRUCTURES

UNIT INTRODUCTION

Relational databases have evolved as a powerful technical tool for data transfer and manipulation over the last few years. Rapid improvements in data technology and science have had a substantial influence on how data is represented in current years (Abiteboul et al., 1995; 1997; 1999). In database technology, a new issue has emerged that restricts the effective representations of the data using classical tables. Data are shown as graphs and trees in several database systems. Certain applications, on either side, need a specific database system to manage time and uncertainty. To overcome the issues faced in database systems, significant research is being done (Adalı & Pigaty, 2003; Shaw et al., 2016).

At the moment, the researchers are looking at the possibility of developing models for "next-generation database systems," or databases that may reflect new data kinds and provide unique manipulation capabilities while still enabling regular search operations. Next-generation databases effectively handle structured documents, Web, network directories, and XML by modeling data in the format of trees and graphs (Altınel & Franklin, 2000; Almohamad & Duffuaa, 1993) (Figure 7.1).

In addition, modern database system utilizes tree or graph models for the representation of data in a variety of applications, including picture databases, molecular databases, and commercial databases. Due to the enormous importance of tree and graph database systems, several methods for tree and graph querying are now being developed (Altman, 1968; Amer-Yahia et al., 2001, 2002). Certain applications, including databases for commercial package delivery, meteorological databases, and financial databases, require temporal uncertainty coupled with database items in addition to querying and analyzing trees and graphs (Atkinson et al., 1990; Andries & Engels, 1994).

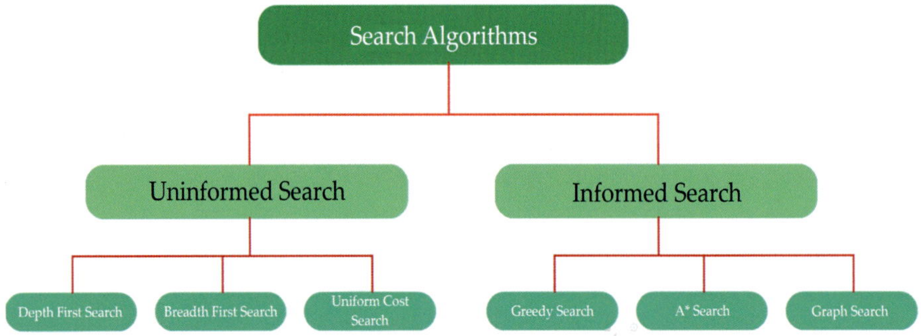

Figure 7.1. Categorization of search algorithms (Source: geeksforgeeks, Creative Commons License).

In the discipline of computer science, effective searching and sorting are considered essential and widely encountered difficulties. For example, the goal of a search algorithm for the gathering of things is to discover and differentiate a specific object from the rest. The search algorithm, on either side, may do a recognition analysis of a certain object that does not exist in the system (Baeza-Yates, 1989; Baeza-Yates et al., 1994). Database objects frequently contain key values that serve as the foundation for a search. Furthermore, certain data values contain information that will be obtained when an item is discovered (Baeza-Yates & Gonnet, 1996; Baeza-Yates & Ribeiro-Neto, 1999). A telephonic book, for example, provides a list of contacts with various contact information. Following the inclusion of some search inputs, the search algorithm is utilized to find specific contact details. It is common knowledge that certain data, such as a name or a number, is connected with such key values. Consider a search scenario in which you're looking for a single key-value pair (such as name). A list or an array is frequently used to hold the collection of things. The ith element (i.e., A[i]) normally correlates to the key value for the ith item present in a collection of n (number of) objects in a specific array A (i.e., A [1, …, n]) (Barrow & Burstall, 1976; Barbosa et al., 2001; Boag et al., 2002).

Did you Know?

Google's search algorithm known as PageRank was named after Google cofounder Larry Page and is based on the idea of analyzing links between web pages to determine their relevance.

The objects are frequently sorted utilizing key values (e.g., in a phone book), but this does not always necessary. Based upon the data's sorting condition, several search methods can be necessary to find the information (such as either sorted or not sorted). For a specific search algorithm, the inputs are the number of objects (i.e., n), an array of items (i.e., A), and the key-value pairs to be used in locating the objects (i.e., x). This explains the many kinds of search algorithms that are available (Boncz et al., 1998, 1999).

LEARNING OBJECTIVES

At the chapter's end, students will get the ability to comprehend the following:

- The basic concept of search algorithms in data structures
- Understanding the concept of ordered and unordered linear search
- Learn about binary search in data structures
- The process of searching in trees and graphs

KEY TERMS

1. Artificial Intelligence
2. Binary Search
3. Linear Search
4. Graph Search
5. Machine Learning
6. Search Algorithms
7. Tree Search

7.1. UNORDERED LINEAR SEARCH

Consider the assumption that every given array is not fundamentally ordered. This could correlate to unsorted collection evaluations that do not have alphabetical sorting in the first place. As an example, what would be the best way for a student to acquire her or his exam results? To find his or her exam, she or he would look through the entire collection of examinations in a chronological manner (Boole, 1916; Bowersox et al., 2002). This search is related to algorithms that use unordered linear search results (Figure 7.2).

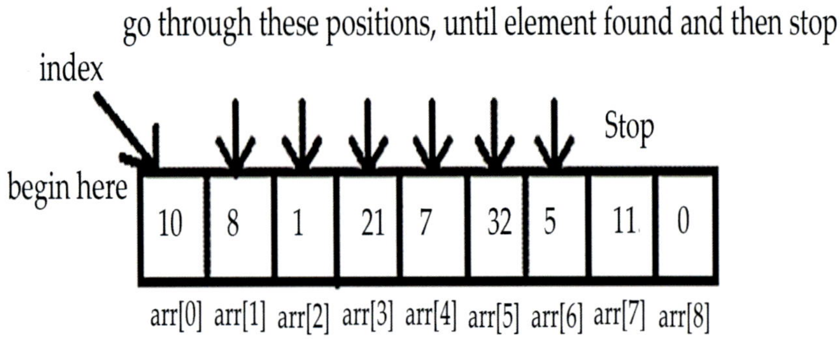

Figure 7.2. Explanation of linear search (Source: Karuna Sehgal, Creative Commons License).

The following is a typical case of an Unordered Linear Search:

Input: An objects array; n shows the number of objects; the x-key value is being determined.

Output: return point "*i*," if not, return note "x not found."

i. Perform the x comparison with every array (A) element A from the beginning.
ii. If x is the ith element in array A, returns point "i" once the search is completed.
iii. If not, keep looking for the next entry till the array is finished.
iv. Return note "x not found" if any suitable element is not found in the array (A).

To confirm the presence of a specific object, you must search the whole collection. Let's have a look at the following array:

i	I	II	III	IV	V	VI	VII	VIII
A	35	17	26	34	8	23	49	9

For example, if we require to look for the value x = 34 in this array (A). We require a comparison of x with (35, 17, 26, 34), with every element being compared just once each. Position 4 contains the required number (34) which is present. Thus, after four comparisons have been performed, we return 4.

If the search for the value x = 19 in this specific array is necessary. To complete this task, we must compare x with every one of the following elements: (35, 17, 26, 34, 8, 23, 49, 9), every element once. After going through all of the objects in this array, we are unable to locate number 19. Hence, we return "18 not found." In this particular situation, we have carried out a total of eight comparisons. Most of the time, it is necessary to do a determination (search) of x in an array of unordered objects that has n entries. It may be necessary to search through the entire array to find the appropriate response in some cases. It entails the implementation of a set of n contrasts. It is possible to create the following equation to express the number (n) of executed comparisons: T (n) = n (Brin, 1995; Bozkaya & Ozsoyoglu, 1999).

KEYWORD

Linear search algorithm is a sequential searching algorithm where we start from one end and check every element of the list until the desired element is found.

7.2. ORDERED LINEAR SEARCH

Assume that the array you're given is sorted. In these circumstances, a search across the entire list to identify a specific object or enquire about its existence in the collection of objects is not required. For example, if a collection of test results is sorted by name, it is not necessary to look beyond the "J"s to see if the exam score for "Jacob" is included in the collection or not included. The ordered linear search algorithms are the outcome of a simple modification of the algorithm (Brusoni et al., 1995; Console et al., 1995; Buneman et al., 1998). The following is an example of an Ordered Linear Search model:

Input: B-objects array; n-number of objects; determining the x-key value.

Output: return point "*i,*" if not, return note "x not found"

i. From the beginning of the array B, perform the comparison of x with the element B[i] in A to confirm their equality.

ii. If x = B[i], stop the search and return location i.

iii. If not, execute the comparison of x with that element once again too if the value of x is larger than B[i].

iv. If x > B[i], continue looking for the next object in array B.

v. If not (such as x is less than B[i]), stop the search and return a message “x not found.”

Take a look at the sorted version of the earlier utilized array:

i	I	II	III	IV	V	VI	VII	VIII
B	8	9	17	23	26	34	35	49

When looking for x = 34 in the earlier-mentioned array, the comparison of x with each element (8, 9, 17, 23, 26) is done twice (such as once for “=“ and again for “>“). The comparison of x with (34) is then performed just once for “=.” As a result, we’ll locate 34 in position 6 and it’ll return to position 6. 2*5 + 1 = 11 is the total number of comparisons.

When searching this array for x = 19, the comparison of x with each member (8, 9, 17, 23, 26) is done twice (such as once for “=“ and again for “>“). And in the last comparison (such as if x > 25), we receive a “NO” result, implying that all of the objects in this array after 26 are effectively bigger than x. As a result, the message “x not found” is returned. 2*4 = 8 is the total number of comparisons.

In general, determining (searching) for x in an array of ordered objects with n objects is necessary. When the value of x is larger than all of the array’s values, it’s often necessary to search the entire array for the required response. It entails executing n x 2 comparisons (such as n for “=“ and another n for “>“). T (n) = 2n is an equation that represents the number (n) of executed comparisons.

7.3. CHUNK SEARCH

There is no requirement to look through the entire collection chronologically in the scenario of an ordered list. Suppose identifying a name in a phone book or a specific exam in a sorted collection: one may immediately select forty or more pages from the phone book or twenty or more examinations from the collection to easily identify the forty-page (or 20 exams) chunk (pile) wherein the needed information is included. An organized linear search technique must be used to carefully sift through this pile (chunk). Suppose that c is the chunk size for forty pages or Twenty examinations. Furthermore, we might suppose that we have access to a much more generic method for ordered linear search. Such assumptions, when combined with the previously discussed notions, may lead to the development of the chunk search algorithm (Burns & Riseman, 1992). The following is an example of a common Chunk search algorithm:

Input: an A-ordered array of objects, c-chunk size, n-the number of elements, determining the x-key value.

Output: if found, return position "*i*," if not, return the message "x not found." Disintegrate array A into c-sized chunks.

i. Compare x with the last components of every chunk, except the last chunk.
ii. Check to see if the value of x is larger than that element.
iii. If affirmative, go to the next chunks.
iv. If no, it signifies that x is in that chunk.
v. Within the chunk, run the Ordered Linear Search algorithm.

Take a look at the following array:

i	I	II	III	IV	V	VI	VII	VIII
B	8	9	17	23	26	34	35	49

Let's say the chunk size is 2 and we're looking for x = 34. We begin by dividing the array into 4 chunks of size 2, then doing a one-time comparison of x with the final piece of every element (9, 23, 34). We compare the values of x and that element to check if the value of x is bigger. Whenever we ran the comparison for 34, we got the result "NO," implying that x must be in the 3rd chunk.

Ultimately, in the 3rd chunk, an ordered liner search is performed, followed by the location of 33 at position 6. In this instance, we run three comparisons to select the appropriate chunk, then three more comparisons within the chunk (such as 2 for 26 and 1 for 34). In total, 6 comparisons are made. In general, searching for x in an array of ordered objects with chunk sizes of c and n items is required (Chase, 1987).

In the worst-case situation, n/c – 1 comparison are performed to select the correct chunk, whereas 2c comparisons are performed to do the linear search. $T(n) = n/c + 2c - 1$ is an equation that may be used to describe the number (n) of executed comparisons. We usually ignore the constant number since it has no effect as n increases. Ultimately, $T(n) = n/c + 2c$ is obtained (Cai et al., 1992; Caouette et al., 1998).

KEYWORD

Constant is a value that should not be altered by the program during normal execution, i.e., the value is constant.

7.4. BINARY SEARCH

Consider the following notion for a search algorithm using the phone book as an instance. Assume we pick a page from the center of a phonebook at random. We've succeeded if the name we're looking for is listed on this page (Figure 7.3).

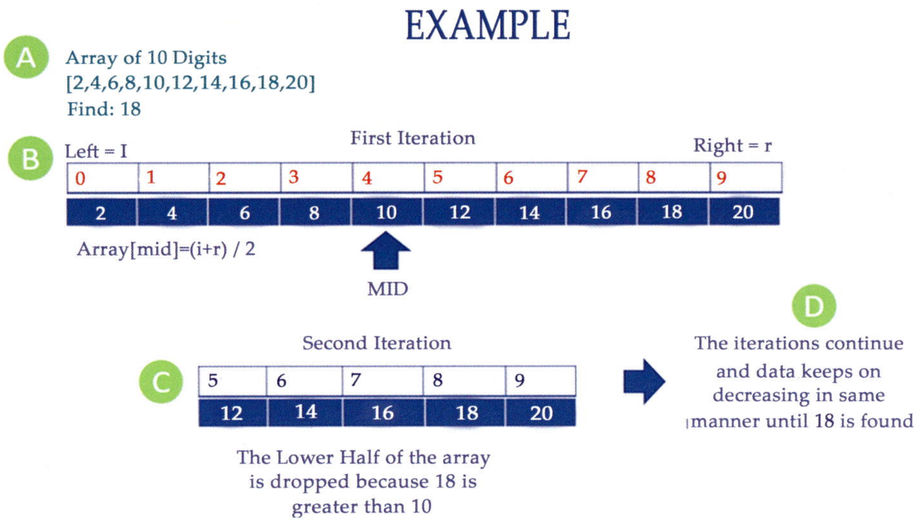

Figure 7.3. Illustration of binary search algorithm with an example (Source: Alyssa Walker, Creative Commons License).

The operations are repeated on the 1st half of the phonebook if the specific name being determined appears alphabetically before this page; alternatively, the processes are repeated on the 2nd half of the phonebook. It should be noted that every iteration entails splitting the remaining piece of the phonebook to be searched into 2 halves; this approach is referred to as binary search (Chiueh, 1994; Christmas et al., 1995; Ciaccia et al., 1997). Although this technique can not appear to be the best for scanning a phonebook (or an ordered list), it is likely the fastest. This is true for several computer algorithms; the most natural (appropriate) algorithm isn't always the best (Cole & Hariharan, 1997). The following is an example of a Binary Search algorithm model:

Input: determining the "x" key-value, n-the number of elements, an A-ordered array of objects.

Output: if found, return position "*i*," if not, return the message "x not found."

i. Split the array into 2 equal halves.
ii. Check equivalence of x with the 1st half's final element by comparing it to that element.
iii. If so, stop looking and return to your original location.

iv. If no, compare the value of x to the final element of the 1st half to check if the value of x is larger than that element.

v. If yes, x must be in the 2nd part of the equation. The 2nd half of the array should now be handled as a new array to run the Binary Search on it.

vi. If no, then x should be placed in the 1st half. The 1st half of the array should now be handled as a new array, and Binary Search should be run on it.

vii. If x isn't discovered, display a notice that says "x not found."

Consider the following depicted array once more:

i	I	II	III	IV	V	VI	VII	VIII
B	8	9	17	23	26	34	35	49

If we require to find x = 26. We shall compare x to every element (23, 34) two times (such as one for "=" and another for ">"), followed by a single comparison to element (26) for "=." Ultimately, at the fifth place, we discover x. There are a total number of comparisons: 2 x 2 + 1 = 5. T (n) = 2log2n in the worst-case situation (Cook & Holder, 1993; Cole, et al., 1999).

7.5. SEARCHING IN GRAPHS

Due to their broad, powerful, and flexible form, graphs are commonly employed to describe data in a variety of applications. A graph is made up of a collection of vertices and edges that connect the pairs of vertices. Generally, edges are utilized to depict the relationships between various data variables, and vertices are utilized to depict the data itself (such as anything which needs a description). Based upon the level of abstraction used to describe the information (data), a graph illustrates the data either semantically or syntactically (Figure 7.4).

Let's look at a biological database system (e.g., proteins). Commonly, proteins are described utilizing labeled graphs, in which the edges reflect the links between distinct atoms and the vertices show specific atoms. Proteins are often classified depending upon their shared structural characteristics. Estimating the functioning of a novel protein fragment is one of the uses of these classifications (such as synthesized or discovered). The functioning of the novel fragments may be deduced by looking for structural similarities between the novel fragments and known proteins. Furthermore,

KEYWORD

Biological database is a large, organized body of persistent data, usually associated with computerized software designed to update, query, and retrieve components of the data stored within the system.

wildcards can be present in searches that have matching properties with the data's vertices or pathways (Corneil & Gotlieb, 1970; Day et al., 1995).

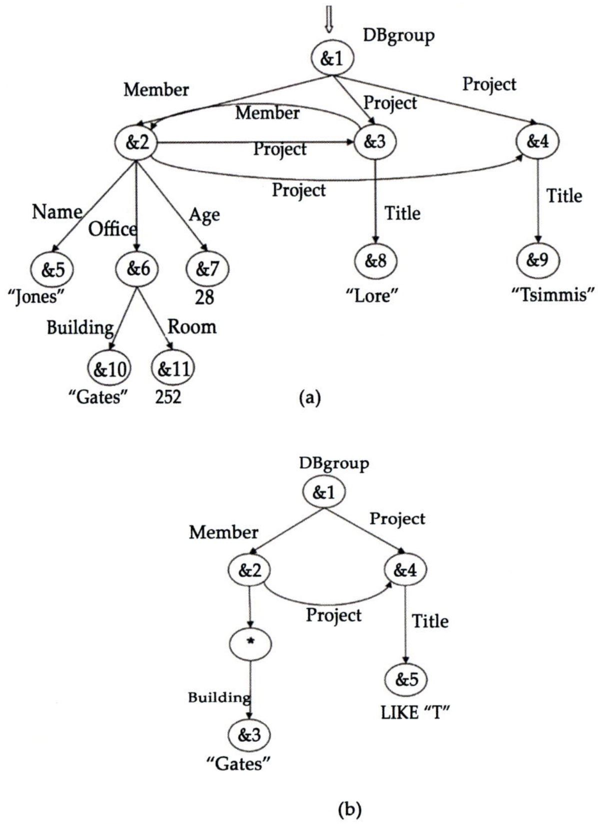

Figure 7.4. Illustration of (a)A structured database tree and (b)A query containing wildcards (Source: R.Giugno, Creative Commons License).

Did you Know?

The Monte Carlo tree search algorithm, which is commonly used in game AI, is named after the famous Monte Carlo casino in Monaco.

Graphs are used as the fundamental data structures in visual languages. Such languages are used in computer science and software engineering to design projects and tools for integrated environments, in CIM systems to display process modeling, and in visual database systems to describe query language semantics (Bancilhon et al., 1992; Dehaspe et al., 1998; Dekhtyar et al., 2001).

Computer vision graphs are utilized to depict a variety of pictures at various degrees of abstraction (DeWitt et al., 1994; Deutsch et al., 1999). The graph vertices relate to edges, and pixels to spatial relationships between pixels, in a depiction with the low-level description (Djoko et al., 1997; Dinitz et al., 1999). The picture depicted by a graph (that is, RAG) is carried out at higher description levels in a way that image breakdown in areas occur. The areas in this case reflect the graph vertices, while the edges reflect the geographical relationships between them (Dutta, 1989; Dubiner et al., 1994).

Graphs are commonly used to model data in semi-structured database systems, network directories, and the Web (Dyreson & Snodgrass, 1998). These database systems generally comprise directed labeled graphs with complicated items at the vertices and links between the objects represented by the edges. The huge size of these database systems necessitates the use of wildcards in query specification. Such a phenomenon enables the retrieval of sub-graphs using just a portion of the graph's data (Eshera & Fu, 1984; Engels et al., 1992; Cesarini et al., 2001).

KEYWORD

Database systems is software that caters to the collection of electronic and digital records to extract useful information and store that information.

Besides storing data in graphs, most of the applications listed above need the usage of tools for comparing graphs, identifying distinct sections of graphs, obtaining graphical data, and categorizing data. Recent search engines provide quick responses for keyword-based searches in the case of non-structured data (e.g., strings). Caching, inverted (smart) index structures and the utilization of parallel and distributed computing are only a few of the variables that contribute to the high speed (Ferro et al., 1999, 2001; Foggia et al., 2001).

The query graphs are compared against the core data graphs in key graph searching, identical to how words are matched in keyword searching. There have been considerable efforts to generalize keyword searches for key graph searching (Frakes & Baeza-Yates, 1992; Fortin, 1996). Furthermore, such generalizations are not entirely natural; for example, keyword searching has exponential complexity as a function of database size. Key graph searching, on either side, has exponential complexity, making it a different class of issues. The next sections cover the many sorts of issues connected with key graph searching (Gadia et al., 1992; Fernandez et al., 1998; Fernández &Valiente, 2001).

7.5.1. Exact Match or Isomorphisms

We can tell if two graphs are the same if we have a data graph G_b and a query graph G_a. The isomorphic nature of the graphs G_b and G_a are determined, as well as the mapping of G_b vertices and G_a vertices while keeping the conforming edges in G_b and G_a. This problem is known to be in NP (nondeterministic polynomial time), and whether it is in NP-complete or P (polynomial time) is uncertain (Garey & Johnson, 1979; Gold & Rangarajan, 1996; Goldman & Widom, 1997) (Figure 7.5).

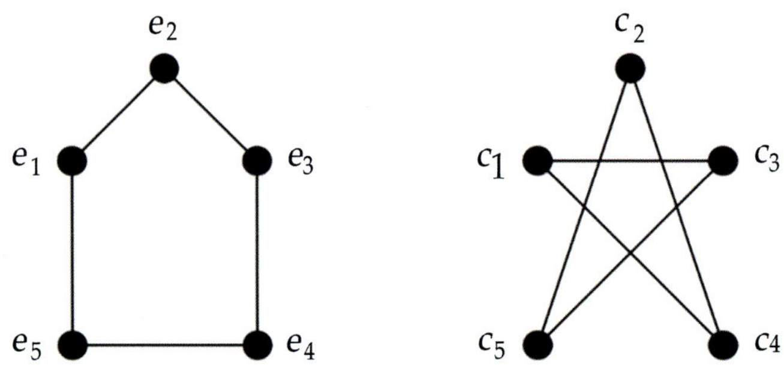

Figure 7.5. Instances of isomorphic graphs (Source: Bruce Schneier, Creative Commons License).

7.5.2. Subgraph Exact Matching or Subgraph Isomorphism

We may readily suppose that G_a is a subgraph isomorphic to G_b given a data graph G_b and a query graph G_a, assuming that G_a is also isomorphic to the subgraph of G_b. It's worth noting that G_a has the potential to be subgraph isomorphic for a variety of G_b subgraphs. That problem is thought to be NP-complete. Furthermore, instead of identifying a single instance of Gagraph in G_b, it is far more costly to locate all the subgraphs that demonstrate similarity with the query graph G_a (e.g., demonstrating the most occurrences of Gagraph in G_b) (Gonnet & Tompa, 1987; Grossi, 1991, 1993).

7.5.3. Matching of Subgraph in a Graphs' Database

We wish to find all the G_a occurrences in every graph of D given a data graph D and a query graph G_a. While graph-to-graph matching algorithms may be used, particular strategies have shown to be effective in reducing the time complexity and search space in database systems. This issue is also NP-complete (Hirata & Kato, 1992; Güting, 1994; Gupta & Nishimura, 1998).

The construction of all possible maps in-between vertices of the 2 graphs, accompanied by a verification of the map's matching attributes, is a basic listing method for discovering the existence of the query graph G_a in the data graph G_b. The algorithms with these networks had exponential complexity (Hirschberg & Wong, 1976; Kannan, 1980; Goodman & O'Rourke, 1997).

There have been several attempts to reduce the combinatorial costs of graph searching. The following 3 suggestions for research have been pursued in this domain:

i. The 1st effort is to investigate matching algorithms for particular graph structures, such as associated graphs, planar graphs, and bounded valence graphs (Umeyama, 1988; Cour et al., 2007);

ii. The 2nd effort is to investigate mechanisms for decreasing the number (quantity) of generated maps (Wilson & Hancock, 1997; Luo & Hancock, 2001).

iii. Ultimately, the 3rd research effort is to provide approximate polynomial-complexity methods; nevertheless, these algorithms don't guarantee a proper solution (Leordeanu & Hebert, 2005; Leordeanu et al., 2009).

For key graph searching, a variety of algorithms are developed to cope with situations in which accurate matches are hard to locate (Milo & Suciu, 1999; Conte et al., 2004). These kinds of algorithms are extremely effective in situations that include noisy graphs. Such algorithms generally make use of a cost function to forecast the similarity of two graphs and to accomplish the conversion of two graphs into each other, respectively (McHugh et al., 1997; Al-Khalifa et al., 2002; Chung et al., 2002). For example, *semantic transformations* may be utilized to construct a cost function that is primarily based upon the particular application domains and to allow the vertices to match with discordant values when the application domains are different. Additionally, syntactic changes (such as branch deletion and insertion) are required for matching structurally dissimilar regions of the graphs, and these changes are reliant on *semantic transformations* as well. In the case of noisy data graphs, approximation techniques can also be used as an alternative (Ciaccia et al., 1997; Cooper et al., 2001; Kaushik et al., 2002).

In the scenario of query graphs that are present in the database of graphs, the majority of modern approaches are designed for particular purposes in mind (Gyssens et al., 1989; Salminen & Tompa, 1992). Different researchers have suggested numerous querying techniques for semi-structured database systems. Furthermore, a large number of commercial products and research studies have been completed that use subgraph searching in various biochemicals database systems (Macleod, 1991; Kilpeläinen & Mannila, 1993). These 2 separate instances have underlying data models that are distinct from one another (such as initially the database is seen as a large graph in case of commercial products whereas the database is seen as a collection of graphs in case of academic projects). The strategies outlined above, on the other hand, demonstrate the following common approaches:

KEYWORD

Data model is an abstract model that organizes elements of data and standardizes how they relate to one another and to the properties of real-world entities.

1. regular path expressions;
2. regular indexing methods.

These approaches are utilized during query time to discover the database's substructures as well as avoid needless database traversals (Tague et al., 1991; Navarro & Baeza-Yates, 1995).

Just a few application-independent strategies exist for querying graph database systems, compared to application-specific alternatives. In most database systems, query graphs of the identical size are used; although, certain approaches allow the same-size limitation to be restricted (Dublish, 1990; Burkowski, 1992; Clark et al., 1995). The algorithms are based on the development of a similarity index between the database's subgraphs and graphs, accompanied by their arrangement of appropriate data structures. Bunke (2000) suggested a technique for indexing labeled database graphs in exponential time and computing the isomorphism of a subgraph in polynomial time. Matching and indexing are both dependent upon all possible permutations of the graphs' neighboring matrices. If only a set of plausible permutations is kept in mind, the aforementioned method may perform better (Verma & Reyner, 1989; Nishimura et al., 2000). Cook and Holder (1993) proposed an alternative way for looking for a subgraph in a database that was not reliant on any indexing mechanism. After applying traditional graph matching techniques to a single-graph database system, they discovered comparable recurring subgraphs (Luccio & Pagli, 1991; Fukagawa & Akutsu, 2004).

KEYWORD

Subgraph is a graph all of whose points and lines are contained in a larger graph.

7.6. GRAPH GREP

Here we will explain how to use a graph database system to execute precise subgraph queries utilizing an application-independent technique. GraphGrep is a tool that searches a graph database for all potential instances of a specific graph (Güting, 1994; Ganapathysaravanabavan & Warnow, 2001). The indexing techniques that categorize minor substructures of the graphs existing in a database are frequently used in search algorithms employing application-independent methods. The graph vertices of GraphGrep have a label (label-vertex) and an identification number (such as id-vertex). We may suppose that graph labeling occurs solely at the vertices in this case. An empath of length n is a series of n + 1 id-vertices with a binary relationship between any two consecutive vertices. A label route of length n, on the other hand, depicts a succession of n + 1 label vertices (Gupta & Nishimura, 1995; Kao et al., 1999 (Figure 7.6)). Database fingerprints are the names given to the indexes. They are often built during the database's preparation step and serve as an abstract representation of the graphs' structural properties. The fingerprints are implemented utilizing a hash table, whereby each row displays the number of id-paths that are associated with the label path hashed in that row (Consens & Mendelzon, 1990; Kato et al., 1992; Hlaoui & Wang, 2002). Label pathways are normally 0 in length and have a constant value, in other words, lp. The pre-processing feature of the graphs can be executed in polynomial time with the right lp value. The id-paths created during fingerprinting are normally maintained rather than discarded; nonetheless, they are kept in tables, with every table representing a different label path. The data provided in tables is used by algebra to discover a match for the query (Hoffmann & O'Donnell, 1982; Hong & Huang, 2001).

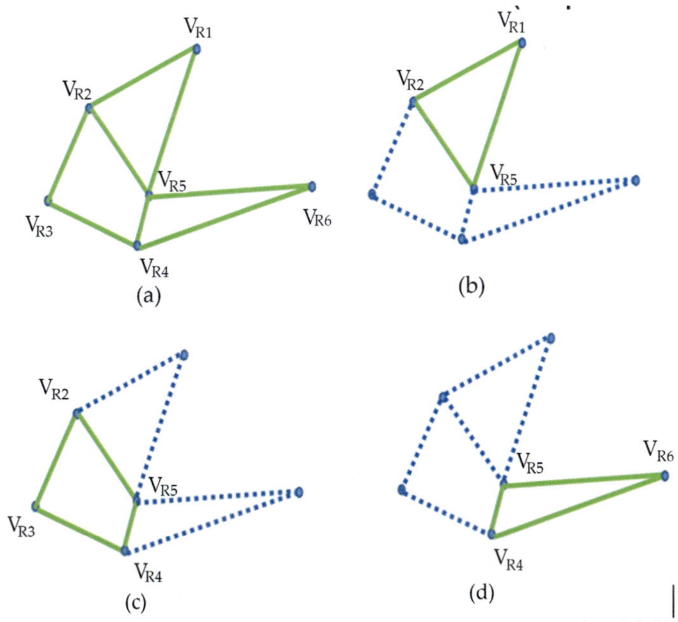

Figure 7.6. Representation of (a)graph (GRep) with 6 vertices and eight edges; (b, c, and d) possible cliques of GRep is D1={VR1, VR2, VR5}, D2={VR2, VR3, VR4,VR5}, and D3={VR6, VR5, VR4} (Source: Soft Computing, Creative Commons License).

Graph Linear Description language is a graph query language that we present for query formulation. XPath for XML documents and Smart-Smiles for molecules are 2 query languages that Glide is derived from (Hopcroft & Wong, 1974; James et al., 2000). Smart is a query language for identifying components in Smiles databases, while SMILES is a language meant for coding molecules. Glide takes Smiles' cycle notation and optimizes it for usage in any graph application. Complicated path expressions are utilized in XPath to represent queries that contain both the matching conditions and the filter in the vertex notation. Graph expressions are used instead of path expressions in Glide (Jensen & Snodgrass,

1999; Kanza & Sagiv, 2001). Scientists evaluated the algorithm's effectiveness on NCI datasets with up to 120,000 molecules and also random databases (Kilpeläinen, 1992; Kilpeläinen & Mannila, 1994). Furthermore, experts have compared GraphGrep to the most widely used tools (Frowns and Daylight) and have come up with really encouraging results. The website (www.cs.nyu.edu/shasha/papers/graphgrep) has a software version of GraphGrep and a demo.

7.7. SEARCHING IN TREES

KEYWORD

Rooted tree is a tree in which one vertex has been designated the root. The edges of a rooted tree can be assigned a natural orientation, either away from or towards the root, in which case the structure becomes a directed rooted tree.

Trees are specialized forms of graphs that are used in many applications to describe data. There are several tools for searching, storing, indexing, and retrieving sub-trees inside a set of trees. The phrase "key tree searching" refers to a set of rooted tree sub-graph and graph matching techniques (Hlaoui & Wang, 2002; 2004; Drira & Rodriguez, 2009).

Take, for example, a database of old coins. The traditional technique of exchanging information about antique coins or other valuable ancient artifacts between archeological institutes and museums is through photo collections. Generally, when a new coin is discovered, an expert applies his past knowledge and reviews all pertinent facts previously known about the object to determine the coin's origin and categorization (Pelegri-Llopart & Graham, 1988; Aho et al., 1989). Accessibility to coin databases, such as the one mentioned above, is a highly valuable tool for the confirmation or denial of any archeological hypotheses during working on this difficult endeavor. Nonetheless, the quantity and size of catalogs accessible for consultation are restricted (Aho & Ganapathi, 1985; Karray et al., 2007). Computers are now altering this traditional framework in a variety of ways. To begin with, quick and low-cost scanning technology has greatly increased the number of available images. Secondly, "intelligent" procedures give essential assistance. When the size of picture databases reaches a certain point, traditional image search approaches become virtually ineffective. Algorithms for effectively evaluating and comparing hundreds of thousands of images signal a breakthrough in this direction (Hong et al., 2000; Hong & Huang, 2004). A coin is a complex object with a specific structure and syntax from a semantic standpoint. Its structure and syntax are defined by an expert by defining its most important traits, which aid in determining its identification. Such characteristics may be grouped into a tree, and the distance between two trees may be used as a heuristic way for estimating the distance between related coins (Luks, 1982; Xu et al., 1999). Figure 7.7 depicts a partial features tree for a generic coin. The arrangement of a tree-like structure is mostly based upon a detailed examination performed by an information technologist in collaboration with an archeologist specialist. The more selective traits are associated with the higher-level nodes of a tree, according to a standard rule. This criterion, although, can be overridden if it will result in incompetence in dealing with the resulting tree structure (Filotti & Mayer, 1980; Babai et al., 1982).

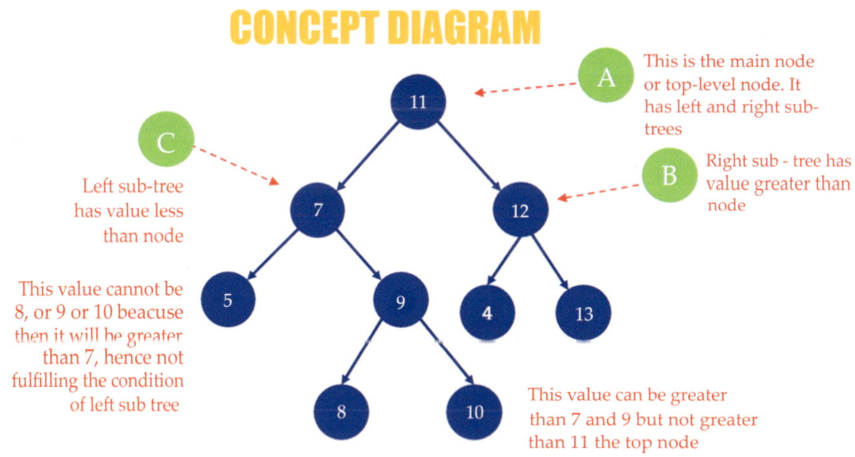

Figure 7.7. Attributes of binary search tree (Source: Alyssa Walker, Creative Commons License).

XML is a standard language for exchanging and describing information on the internet that is becoming popular. This is due to the unique technique of reference between the components of XML, which results in the natural data structure of a graph being used. By omitting these references, an XML document is transformed into an ordered tree. The bulk of XML database systems have selected trees as their fundamental data model, and this is a good thing.

For the presentation of statements or the architecture of the document, trees are used in many applications of natural language processing (for instance, looking for matches in example-based translation systems and retrieving material from digital libraries). Authors from a variety of fields have established the hierarchical patterns of trees that describe the syntactic principles that govern the creation of English sentences. Furthermore, trees may be used to depict the geometrical aspects of document pages, which can be used to answer questions such as "find all of the pages that have the title next to an image" and "find all of the pages that have the title next to an image" (Jensen et al., 1998; Schlieder, 2002). In this situation, the hierarchical structures of trees correlate to such a portion in regions of pages where that portion in a page is an image or text between columns and white spaces, and the hierarchical structures of trees correlate to such a portion in regions of pages (Lueker & Booth, 1979).

Certain properties of the apps listed above are shared by all of them. We may show the database as either a single tree or as a collection of trees in our diagram. The order of siblings in a tree may also be crucial (as in the XML data format), or a tree may be unordered (as in certain archeological databases and hereditary trees), depending on the situation. In the same way that graphs require searching, finding an "approximate" or precise tree and sub-tree matching may be required. When working with approximate values, one approach of being accurate on the low end is to count the total number of routes in the query tree that do not appear in the data tree (Dolog et al., 2009). The matching with query trees that contain wildcards is included in the approximate tree matching (Navarro & Baeza-yates, 1995).

Remember

Search algorithms have applications beyond computer science such as in medicine for searching through large databases of patient records.

The complexity of key-tree searching issues varies based upon the structure of the tree and ranges from linear (P) to exponential (NP-complete) based upon the size of the tree. More precisely, the time required to solve an accurate sub-tree or tree matching issue is polynomial in both sorted and unordered trees, depending on the complexity of the challenge (Sikora, 2012). Estimated tree searching issues fall into the P class for ordered trees and the NP-complete class for unordered trees.

Extensive research efforts are undertaken to integrate different complex data structures with different approximation tree matching algorithms which work across generic metric spaces to reduce the processing time of the query (that is, algorithms that are not based upon specific characteristics of the distance function considered).

Some tree-searching algorithms rely on the characteristics of the basic distance function between database items. Others merely consider the distance function to be a metric. The Fixed Query tree (FQ-tree) algorithm, the Vantage Point tree (VP-tree) method, its upgraded form (referred to as MVP-tree) algorithm, and the M-tree algorithm are all examples of this.

7.8. SEARCHING IN TEMPORAL PROBABILISTIC OBJECT DATA MODEL

After that, we will look at another component of next-generation databases: the specification of a temporal, probabilistic object database, which will be discussed in more detail later. In a wide range of applications, object data models have been used to model them. Examples include financial risk applications, multimedia applications, logistics and supply chain management systems and meteorological applications, amongst several others. Several of such applications are forced to express and handle both uncertainty and time as a matter of course.

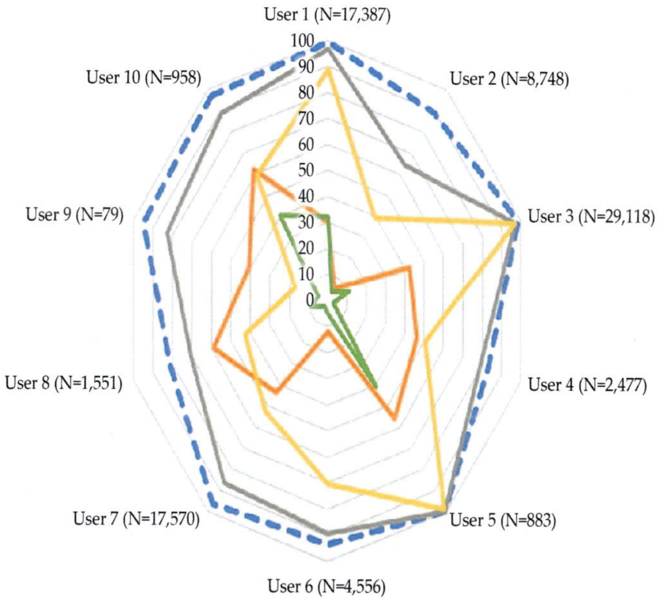

Figure 7.8. Illustration of temporal persistence modeling for object search (Source: Russel Toris, Creative Commons License).

Firstly, we'll look at a logistics application for transportation. A commercial package delivery business (like DHL, FedEx, UPS, and others) possesses precise statistical data on how long it takes packages to travel from one zip code to another, and frequently even more particular data (such as how long it takes for a package from the address of one street to another street address). A company anticipating deliveries will like data of the form "the package would be transported between 1 p.m. and 5 p.m. with a probability between 0.8 and 0.9 and between 9 a.m. and 1 p.m. with a probability between 0.1 and 0.2" (here, probabilities are levels of belief about a future event, which can be derived from statistical data about identical previous events). The answer "It would be supplied sometime today between 9 a.m. and 5 p.m." is considerably less beneficial to the company's decision-making procedures. For instance, it aids in the scheduling of workers, the preparation of receiving facilities (for toxic and other heavy products), the preparation of future production plans, and so on. Furthermore, object models have been normally utilized to store the various entities involved in an application, as various automobiles (trucks, airplanes, and so on.) have distinct characteristics and various packages (tube, letter, toxic material shipments for commercial clients, and so on.) have widely varying characteristics. The shipping firm itself has a high demand for this information. For instance, the corporation will need to query this information to build plans that best distribute and/or utilize current sources (staff, truck space, etc.) depending upon their estimates of future workload (Aho &Ganapathi, 1985; Karray et al., 2007).

ACTIVITY 7.1

Create a visual representation of different search algorithms using a graph or tree data structure to see how they traverse the data.

Object models are used to express weather data in weather database systems (like the US Department of Defense's total Atmospheric and Ocean System, or TAOS). In weather models, uncertainty and time are ubiquitous and most decision-making algorithms depend upon this information to make judgments.

Banks and institutional lenders employ a variety of financial models to try to anticipate when clients would default on borrowing. Complicated mathematical models incorporating probabilities and time are examples of these models (the predictions specify the probability with which a given customer would default in a given time). In addition, models for predicting loan defaults and bankruptcies differ significantly based upon the market, the kind of credit instrument (mortgage, construction loan, customer credit card, HUD loan, commercial real estate loan, so on.), the factors that impact the loan, different aspects about the consumer, and so on. Object models are simply used to express these models, and uncertainty and time are used to parameterize different aspects of the model (Filotti & Mayer, 1980; Babai et al., 1982).

SUMMARY

In data structures, search algorithms are used to locate an element within the structure. The choice of search algorithms depends on the type of data structure being and the properties of the data. The linear search algorithms are used to search elements in arrays and lists. It is easy and simple to implement but can be slow for large targets. The binary search algorithm is used for searching elements in sorted arrays or lists. It is faster than linear search but requires that the data structure be sorted. The hashing algorithm is used for searching elements in hash tables. Hashing can be very fast for large structures, but can also suffer from collisions that require additional processing. The search algorithms can be combined with other data structures, such as trees and hash tables, to provide efficient search capabilities. The choice of algorithm and data structure depends on the properties of the data being searched such as size, sparsity and access patterns.

REVIEW QUESTIONS

1. What are search algorithms and why are they important in computer science?
2. What are the different types of search algorithms and how do they differ from one another?
3. What is linear search and what types of data structures it is used for?
4. What factors should be considered when choosing a search algorithm for a particular data structure?
5. What are some real-world applications of search algorithms in computer science and other fields?

MULTIPLE CHOICE QUESTIONS

1. Which of the following search algorithms is used for traversing graphs or trees?

a. Linear search
b. Binary search
c. Depth-First search
d. Breadth-First search

2. Which of the following search algorithms is used for searching elements in sorted arrays or lists?

a. Linear search
b. Binary search
c. Depth-First search
d. Breadth-First search

3. Which of the following factors should be considered when choosing a search algorithm for a particular data structure?

a. Size of the data structure

b. Sparsity of the data

c. The access patterns for the data

d. All of the above

4. Which of the following search algorithms involves computing a hash value for the target element?

a. Linear search

b. Binary search

c. Depth-First search

d. Hashing

5. Which of the following algorithms formed the basis for the Quick search algorithm?

a. Boyer-Moore's algorithm

b. Parallel string matching algorithm

c. Binary Search algorithm

d. Linear Search algorithm

Answers to Multiple Choice Questions

1. (c) 2. (b) 3. (d) 4. (d) 5. (a)

REFERENCES

1. Abiteboul, S., & Vianu, V., (1999). Regular path queries with constraints. *Journal of Computer and System Sciences, 58*(3), 428–452.
2. Abiteboul, S., Hull, R., & Vianu, V., (1995). *Foundations of Databases: The Logical Level.* Addison-Wesley Longman Publishing Co., Inc.
3. Abiteboul, S., Quass, D., McHugh, J., Widom, J., & Wiener, J. L., (1997). The Lorel query language for semistructured data. *International Journal on Digital Libraries, 1*(1), 68–88.
4. Adalı, S., & Pigaty, L., (2003). The DARPA advanced logistics project. *Annals of Mathematics and Artificial Intelligence, 37*(4), 409–452.
5. Aho, A. V., & Ganapathi, M., (1985). Efficient tree pattern matching (extended abstract): An aid to code generation. In: *Proceedings of the 12th ACM SIGACT-SIGPLAN Symposium on Principles of Programming Languages* (pp. 334–340). ACM.
6. Aho, A. V., Ganapathi, M., & Tjiang, S. W., (1989). Code generation using tree

matching and dynamic programming. *ACM Transactions on Programming Languages and Systems (TOPLAS), 11*(4), 491–516.

7. Al-Khalifa, S., Jagadish, H. V., Koudas, N., Patel, J. M., Srivastava, D., & Wu, Y., (2002). Structural joins: A primitive for efficient XML query pattern matching. In: *Data Engineering, 2002; Proceedings 18th International Conference* (pp. 141–152). IEEE.
8. Almohamad, H. A., & Duffuaa, S. O., (1993). A linear programming approach for the weighted graph matching problem. *IEEE Transactions on Pattern Analysis and Machine Intelligence, 15*(5), 522–525.
9. Altınel, M., & Franklin, M. J., (2000). Efficient filtering of XML documents for selective dissemination of information. In: *Proc. of the 26th Int'l Conference on Very Large Data Bases (VLDB).* Cairo, Egypt.
10. Altman, E. I., (1968). Financial ratios, discriminant analysis and the prediction of corporate bankruptcy. *The Journal of Finance, 23*(4), 589–609.
11. Amer-Yahia, S., Cho, S., & Srivastava, D., (2002). Tree pattern relaxation. In: *International Conference on Extending Database Technology* (pp. 496–513). Springer, Berlin, Heidelberg.
12. Amer-Yahia, S., Cho, S., Lakshmanan, L. V., & Srivastava, D., (2001). Minimization of tree pattern queries. In: *ACM SIGMOD Record* (Vol. 30, No. 2, pp. 497–508). ACM.
13. Andries, M., & Engels, G., (1994). Syntax and semantics of hybrid database languages. In: *Graph Transformations in Computer Science* (pp. 19–36). Springer, Berlin, Heidelberg.
14. Atkinson, M., DeWitt, D., Maier, D., Bancilhon, F., Dittrich, K., & Zdonik, S., (1990). The object-oriented database system manifesto. In: *Deductive and Object-Oriented Databases* (pp. 223–240).
15. Babai, L., Grigoryev, D. Y., & Mount, D. M., (1982). Isomorphism of graphs with bounded eigenvalue multiplicity. In: *Proceedings of the Fourteenth Annual ACM Symposium on Theory of Computing* (pp. 310–324). ACM.
16. Baeza-Yates, R. A., & Gonnet, G. H., (1996). Fast text searching for regular expressions or automaton searching on tries. *Journal of the ACM (JACM), 43*(6), 915–936.
17. Baeza-Yates, R. A., (1989). Algorithms for string searching. In: *ACM SIGIR Forum* (Vol. 23, No. 3–4, pp. 34–58). ACM.
18. Baeza-Yates, R., & Ribeiro-Neto, B., (1999). *Modern Information Retrieval* (Vol. 463, pp. 1–20). New York: ACM press.
19. Baeza-Yates, R., Cunto, W., Manber, U., & Wu, S., (1994). Proximity matching using fixed-queries trees. In: *Annual Symposium on Combinatorial Pattern Matching* (Vol. 1, pp. 198–212). Springer, Berlin, Heidelberg.
20. Bancilhon, F., Delobel, C., & Kanellakis, P., (1992). *Building an Object-Oriented Database System: The Story of 0 2.* Morgan Kaufmann Publishers Inc.
21. Barbosa, D., Barta, A., Mendelzon, A. O., Mihaila, G. A., Rizzolo, F., & Rodriguez-Gianolli, P., (2001). ToX-the Toronto XML engine. In: *Workshop on Information Integration on the Web* (pp. 66–73).

22. Barrow, H. G., & Burstall, R. M., (1976). Subgraph isomorphism, matching relational structures and maximal cliques. *Information Processing Letters, 4*(4), 83–84.
23. Boag, S., Chamberlin, D., Fernández, M. F., Florescu, D., Robie, J., Siméon, J., & Stefanescu, M., (2002). *XQuery 1.0: An XML Query Language, 7, 4-18.*
24. Bomze, I. M., Budinich, M., Pardalos, P. M., & Pelillo, M., (1999). The maximum clique problem. In: *Handbook of Combinatorial Optimization* (pp. 1–74). Springer, Boston, MA.
25. Boncz, P., Wilshut, A. N., & Kersten, M. L., (1998). Flattening an object algebra to provide performance. In: *Data Engineering, 1998; Proceedings, 14th International Conference on* (pp. 568–577). IEEE.
26. Boole, G., (1916). *The Laws of Thought* (Vol. 2, pp. 1–20). Open Court Publishing Company.
27. Bowersox, D. J., Closs, D. J., & Cooper, M. B., (2002). *Supply Chain Logistics Management* (Vol. 2, pp. 5–16). New York, NY: McGraw-Hill.
28. Bozkaya, T., & Ozsoyoglu, M., (1999). Indexing large metric spaces for similarity search queries. *ACM Transactions on Database Systems (TODS), 24*(3), 361–404.
29. Brin, S., (1995). *Near Neighbor Search in Large Metric Spaces, 1*, 1–22.
30. Brusoni, V., Console, L., Terenziani, P., & Pernici, B., (1995). Extending temporal relational databases to deal with imprecise and qualitative temporal information. In: *Recent Advances in Temporal Databases* (Vol. 1, pp. 3–22). Springer, London.
31. Buneman, P., Fan, W., & Weinstein, S., (1998). Path constraints on semistructured and structured data. In: *Proceedings of the Seventeenth ACM SIGACT-SIGMOD-SIGART Symposium on Principles of Database Systems* (Vol. 7, pp. 129–138). ACM.
32. Burkowski, F. J., (1992). An algebra for hierarchically organized text-dominated databases. *Information Processing & Management, 28*(3), 333–348.
33. Burns, J. B., & Riseman, E. M., (1992). Matching complex images to multiple 3D objects using view description networks. In: *Computer Vision and Pattern Recognition, 1992; Proceedings CVPR'92, 1992 IEEE Computer Society Conference* (pp. 328–334). IEEE.
34. Cai, J., Paige, R., & Tarjan, R., (1992). More efficient bottom-up multi-pattern matching in trees. *Theoretical Computer Science, 106*(1), 21–60.
35. Caouette, J. B., Altman, E. I., & Narayanan, P., (1998). *Managing Credit Risk: The Next Great Financial Challenge* (Vol. 2, pp. 1–20). John Wiley & Sons.
36. Cesarini, F., Lastri, M., Marinai, S., & Soda, G., (2001). Page classification for meta-data extraction from digital collections. In: *International Conference on Database and Expert Systems Applications* (Vol. 1, pp. 82–91). Springer, Berlin, Heidelberg.
37. Chase, D. R., (1987). An improvement to bottom-up tree pattern matching. In: *Proceedings of the 14th ACM SIGACT-SIGPLAN Symposium on Principles of Programming Languages* (Vol. 14, pp. 168–177). ACM.
38. Chiueh, T. C., (1994). Content-based image indexing. In: *VLDB* (Vol. 94, pp. 582–593).

39. Christmas, W. J., Kittler, J., & Petrou, M., (1995). Structural matching in computer vision using probabilistic relaxation. *IEEE Transactions on Pattern Analysis and Machine Intelligence, 17*(8), 749–764.

40. Chung, C. W., Min, J. K., & Shim, K., (2002). APEX: An adaptive path index for XML data. In: *Proceedings of the 2002 ACM SIGMOD International Conference on Management of Data* (Vol. 1, pp. 121–132). ACM.

41. Ciaccia, P., Patella, M., & Zezula, P., (1997). DEIS-CSITE-CNR. In: *Proceedings of the International Conference on Very Large Data Bases* (Vol. 23, pp. 426–435).

42. Clarke, C. L., Cormack, G. V., & Burkowski, F. J., (1995). An algebra for structured text search and a framework for its implementation. *The Computer Journal, 38*(1), 43–56.

43. Cole, R., & Hariharan, R., (1997). Tree pattern matching and subset matching in randomized O ($n\log^3 m$) time. In: *Proceedings of the Twenty-Ninth Annual ACM Symposium on Theory of Computing* (Vol. 1, pp. 66–75). ACM.

44. Cole, R., Hariharan, R., & Indyk, P., (1999). Tree pattern matching and subset matching in deterministic O (n log super (3) n)-time. In: *The 1999 10th Annual ACM-SIAM Symposium on Discrete Algorithms* (Vol. 10, pp. 245–254).

45. Consens, M. P., & Mendelzon, A. O., (1990). GraphLog: A visual formalism for real life recursion. In: *Proceedings of the Ninth ACM SIGACT-SIGMOD-SIGART Symposium on Principles of Database Systems* (Vol. 1, pp. 404–416). ACM.

46. Console, L., Brusoni, V., Pernici, B., & Terenziani, P., (1995). *Extending Temporal Relational Databases to Deal with Imprecise and Qualitative Temporal Information, 1*, 1–20.

47. Conte, D., Foggia, P., Sansone, C., & Vento, M., (2004). Thirty years of graph matching in pattern recognition. *International Journal of Pattern Recognition and Artificial Intelligence, 18*(03), 265–298.

48. Cook, D. J., & Holder, L. B., (1993). Substructure discovery using minimum description length and background knowledge. *Journal of Artificial Intelligence Research, 1*, 231–255.

49. Cooper, B. F., Sample, N., Franklin, M. J., Hjaltason, G. R., & Shadmon, M., (2001). A fast index for semistructured data. In: *VLDB* (Vol. 1, pp. 341–350).

50. Corneil, D. G., & Gotlieb, C. C., (1970). An efficient algorithm for graph isomorphism. *Journal of the ACM (JACM), 17*(1), 51–64.

51. Cour, T., Srinivasan, P., & Shi, J., (2007). Balanced graph matching. In: *Advances in Neural Information Processing Systems* (Vol. 1, pp. 313–320).

52. Day, Y. F., Dagtas, S., Iino, M., Khokhar, A., & Ghafoor, A., (1995). Object-oriented conceptual modeling of video data. In: *Data Engineering, 1995; Proceedings of the Eleventh International Conference* (Vol. 1, pp. 401–408). IEEE.

53. Dehaspe, L., Toivonen, H., & King, R. D., (1998). Finding frequent substructures in chemical compounds. In: *KDD* (Vol. 98, p. 1998).

54. Dekhtyar, A., Ross, R., & Subrahmanian, V. S., (2001). Probabilistic temporal databases, I: Algebra. *ACM Transactions on Database Systems (TODS), 26*(1), 41–95.
55. Deutsch, A., Fernandez, M., Florescu, D., Levy, A., & Suciu, D., (1999). A query language for XML. *Computer Networks, 31*(11–16), 1155–1169.
56. DeWitt, D. J., Kabra, N., & Luo, J., (1994). Client-server paradise. In: Patel, J. M., & Yu, J., (eds.), *Proceedings of the International Conference on Very Large Databases (VLDB), 1*, 1–22.
57. Dinitz, Y., Itai, A., & Rodeh, M., (1999). On an algorithm of zemlyachenko for subtree isomorphism. *Information Processing Letters, 70*(3), 141–146.
58. Djoko, S., Cook, D. J., & Holder, L. B., (1997). An empirical study of domain knowledge and its benefits to substructure discovery. *IEEE Transactions on Knowledge and Data Engineering, 9*(4), 575–586.
59. Dolog, P., Stuckenschmidt, H., Wache, H., & Diederich, J., (2009). Relaxing RDF queries based on user and domain preferences. *Journal of Intelligent Information Systems, 33*(3), 239.
60. Drira, K., & Rodriguez, I. B., (2009). *A Demonstration of an Efficient Tool for Graph Matching and Transformation, 1*, 1–20.
61. Dubiner, M., Galil, Z., & Magen, E., (1994). Faster tree pattern matching. *Journal of the ACM (JACM), 41*(2), 205–213.
62. Dublish, P., (1990). Some comments on the subtree isomorphism problem for ordered trees. *Information Processing Letters, 36*(5), 273–275.
63. Dubois, D., & Prade, H., (1989). Processing fuzzy temporal knowledge. *IEEE Transactions on Systems, Man, and Cybernetics, 19*(4), 729–744.
64. Dutta, S., (1989). Generalized events in temporal databases. In: *Data Engineering, 1989; Proceedings Fifth International Conference on* (Vol. 5, pp. 118–125). IEEE.
65. Dyreson, C. E., & Snodgrass, R. T., (1998). Supporting valid-time indeterminacy. *ACM Transactions on Database Systems (TODS), 23*(1), 1–57.
66. Eiter, T., Lukasiewicz, T., & Walter, M., (2001). A data model and algebra for probabilistic complex values. *Annals of Mathematics and Artificial Intelligence, 33*(2–4), 205–252.
67. Engels, G., Lewerentz, C., Nagl, M., Schäfer, W., & Schürr, A., (1992). Building integrated software development environments. Part I: Tool specification. *ACM Transactions on Software Engineering and Methodology (TOSEM), 1*(2), 135–167.
68. Eshera, M. A., & Fu, K. S., (1984). A graph distance measure for image analysis. *IEEE Transactions on Systems, man, and Cybernetics*, (3), 398–408.
69. Fernández, M. L., & Valiente, G., (2001). A graph distance metric combining maximum common subgraph and minimum common supergraph. *Pattern Recognition Letters, 22*(6, 7), 753–758.
70. Fernandez, M., Florescu, D., Kang, J., Levy, A., & Suciu, D., (1998). Catching the boat with strudel: Experiences with a web-site management system. In: *ACM*

SIGMOD Record (Vol. 27, No. 2, pp. 414–425). ACM.

71. Ferro, A., Gallo, G., & Giugno, R., (1999). Error-tolerant database for structured images. In: *International Conference on Advances in Visual Information Systems* (pp. 51–59). Springer, Berlin, Heidelberg.
72. Ferro, A., Gallo, G., Giugno, R., & Pulvirenti, A., (2001). Best-match retrieval for structured images. *IEEE Transactions on Pattern Analysis and Machine Intelligence, 23*(7), 707–718.
73. Filotti, I. S., & Mayer, J. N., (1980). A polynomial-time algorithm for determining the isomorphism of graphs of fixed genus. In: *Proceedings of the Twelfth Annual ACM Symposium on Theory of Computing* (pp. 236–243). ACM.
74. Foggia, P., Sansone, C., & Vento, M., (2001). A database of graphs for isomorphism and sub-graph isomorphism benchmarking. In: *Proc. of the 3rd IAPR TC-15 International Workshop on Graph-based Representations* (Vol. 3, pp. 176–187).
75. Fortin, S., (1996). Technical report 96-20, University of Alberta, Edomonton, Alberta, Canada. *The Graph Isomorphism Problem, 1*, 1–22.
76. Frakes, W. B., & Baeza-Yates, R., (1992). *Information Retrieval: Data Structures & Algorithms* (Vol. 331, pp. 1–30). Englewood Cliffs, New Jersey: Prentice Hall.
77. Fukagawa, D., & Akutsu, T., (2004). Fast algorithms for comparison of similar unordered trees. In: *International Symposium on Algorithms and Computation* (Vol. 1, pp. 452–463). Springer, Berlin, Heidelberg.
78. Gadia, S. K., Nair, S. S., & Poon, Y. C., (1992). Incomplete information in relational temporal databases. In: *VLDB* (Vol. 1992, pp. 395–406).
79. Ganapathysaravanabavan, G., & Warnow, T., (2001). Finding a maximum compatible tree for a bounded number of trees with bounded degree is solvable in polynomial time. In: *International Workshop on Algorithms in Bioinformatics* (pp. 156–163). Springer, Berlin, Heidelberg.
80. Garey, M. R., & Johnson, D. S., (1979). Computers and intractability: A guide to NP-completeness.
81. Gold, S., & Rangarajan, A., (1996). A graduated assignment algorithm for graph matching. *IEEE Transactions on Pattern Analysis and Machine Intelligence, 18*(4), 377–388.
82. Goldman, R., & Widom, J., (1997). *Dataguides: Enabling Query Formulation and Optimization in Semistructured Databases* (Vol. 1, pp. 1–22).
83. Gonnet, G. H., & Tompa, F. W., (1987). *Mind Your Grammar: A New Approach to Modeling Text*. UW Centre for the New Oxford English Dictionary.
84. Goodman, J. E., & O'Rourke, J., (1997). *Handbook of Discrete and Computational Geometry: Series on Discrete Mathematics and its Applications* (Vol. 6, pp. 1–20). CRC Press.
85. Grossi, R., (1991). A note on the subtree isomorphism for ordered trees and related problems. *Information Processing Letters, 39*, 81–84.

86. Grossi, R., (1993). On finding common subtrees. *Theoretical Computer Science, 108*(2), 345–356.

87. Gupta, A., & Nishimura, N., (1995). Finding smallest supertrees. In: *International Symposium on Algorithms and Computation* (pp. 112–121). Springer, Berlin, Heidelberg.

88. Gupta, A., & Nishimura, N., (1998). Finding largest subtrees and smallest supertrees. *Algorithmica, 21*(2), 183–210.

89. Güting, R. H., (1994). GraphDB: Modeling and querying graphs in databases. In: *VLDB* (Vol. 94, pp. 12–15).

90. Gyssens, M., Paredaens, J., & Van, G. D., (1989). *A Grammar-Based Approach Towards Unifying Hierarchical Data Models* (Vol. 18, No. 2, pp. 263–272). ACM.

91. Hirata, K., & Kato, T., (1992). Query by visual example. In: *International Conference on Extending Database Technology* (Vol. 1, pp. 56–71). Springer, Berlin, Heidelberg.

92. Hirschberg, D. S., & Wong, C. K., (1976). A polynomial-time algorithm for the knapsack problem with two variables. *Journal of the ACM (JACM), 23*(1), 147–154.

93. Hlaoui, A., & Wang, S., (2002). A new algorithm for inexact graph matching. In: *Pattern Recognition, 2002; Proceedings 16th International Conference* (Vol. 4, pp. 180–183). IEEE.

94. Hlaoui, A., & Wang, S., (2004). A node-mapping-based algorithm for graph matching. *J. Discrete Algorithms, 1*, 1–22.

95. Hoffmann, C. M., & O'Donnell, M. J., (1982). Pattern matching in trees. *Journal of the ACM (JACM), 29*(1), 68–95.

96. Hong, P., & Huang, T. S., (2001). Spatial pattern discovering by learning the isomorphic subgraph from multiple attributed relational graphs. *Electronic Notes in Theoretical Computer Science, 46*, 113–132.

97. Hong, P., & Huang, T. S., (2004). Spatial pattern discovery by learning a probabilistic parametric model from multiple attributed relational graphs. *Discrete Applied Mathematics, 139*(1–3), 113–135.

98. Hong, P., Wang, R., & Huang, T., (2000). Learning patterns from images by combining soft decisions and hard decisions. In: *Computer Vision and Pattern Recognition, 2000; Proceedings IEEE Conference* (Vol. 1, pp. 78–83). IEEE.

99. Hopcroft, J. E., & Wong, J. K., (1974). Linear time algorithm for isomorphism of planar graphs (preliminary report). In: *Proceedings of the Sixth Annual ACM Symposium on Theory of Computing* (Vol. 1, pp. 172–184). ACM.

100. James, C. A., Weininger, D., & Delany, J., (2000). *Daylight Theory Manual 4.71, Daylight Chemical Information Systems.* Inc., Irvine, CA.

101. Jensen, C. S., & Snodgrass, R. T., (1999). Temporal data management. *IEEE Transactions on Knowledge and Data Engineering, 11*(1), 36–44.

102. Jensen, C. S., Dyreson, C. E., Böhlen, M., Clifford, J., Elmasri, R., Gadia, S. K., & Kline, N., (1998). The consensus glossary of temporal database concepts—February

1998 version. In: *Temporal Databases: Research and Practice* (pp. 367–405). Springer, Berlin, Heidelberg.

103. Kannan, R., (1980). A polynomial algorithm for the two-variable integer programming problem. *Journal of the ACM (JACM), 27*(1), 118–122.
104. Kanza, Y., & Sagiv, Y., (2001). Flexible queries over semistructured data. In: *Proceedings of the Twentieth ACM SIGMOD-SIGACT-SIGART Symposium on Principles of Database Systems* (Vol. 1, pp. 40–51). ACM.
105. Kao, M. Y., Lam, T. W., Sung, W. K., & Ting, H. F., (1999). A decomposition theorem for maximum weight bipartite matchings with applications to evolutionary trees. In: *European Symposium on Algorithms* (Vol. 1, pp. 438–449). Springer, Berlin, Heidelberg.
106. Karray, A., Ogier, J. M., Kanoun, S., & Alimi, M. A., (2007). An ancient graphic documents indexing method based on spatial similarity. In: *International Workshop on Graphics Recognition* (Vol. 1, pp. 126–134). Springer, Berlin, Heidelberg.
107. Kato, T., Kurita, T., Otsu, N., & Hirata, K., (1992). A sketch retrieval method for full color image database-query by visual example. In: *Pattern Recognition, 1992; Conference A: Computer Vision and Applications, Proceedings., 11th IAPR International Conference* (Vol. 1, pp. 530–533). IEEE.
108. Kaushik, R., Bohannon, P., Naughton, J. F., & Korth, H. F., (2002). Covering indexes for branching path queries. In: *Proceedings of the 2002 ACM SIGMOD International Conference on Management of Data* (pp. 133–144). ACM.
109. Kilpeläinen, P., & Mannila, H., (1993). Retrieval from hierarchical texts by partial patterns. In: *Proceedings of the 16th Annual International ACM SIGIR Conference on Research and Development in Information Retrieval* (Vol. 1, pp. 214–222). ACM.
110. Kilpeläinen, P., & Mannila, H., (1994). Query primitives for tree-structured data. In: *Annual Symposium on Combinatorial Pattern Matching* (Vol. 1, pp. 213–225). Springer, Berlin, Heidelberg.
111. Kilpeläinen, P., (1992). *Tree Matching Problems with Applications to Structured Text Databases, 1*, 1–20.
112. Leordeanu, M., & Hebert, M., (2005). A spectral technique for correspondence problems using pairwise constraints. In: *Computer Vision, 2005. ICCV 2005; Tenth IEEE International Conference* (Vol. 2, pp. 1482–1489). IEEE.
113. Leordeanu, M., Hebert, M., & Sukthankar, R., (2009). An integer projected fixed point method for graph matching and map inference. In: *Advances in Neural Information Processing Systems* (pp. 1114–1122).
114. Luccio, F., & Pagli, L., (1991). Simple solutions for approximate tree matching problems. In: *Colloquium on Trees in Algebra and Programming* (pp. 193–201). Springer, Berlin, Heidelberg.
115. Lueker, G. S., & Booth, K. S., (1979). A linear time algorithm for deciding interval graph isomorphism. *Journal of the ACM (JACM), 26*(2), 183–195.
116. Luks, E. M., (1982). Isomorphism of graphs of bounded valence can be tested in polynomial time. *Journal of Computer and System Sciences, 25*(1), 42–65.

117. Luo, B., & Hancock, E. R., (2001). Structural graph matching using the EM algorithm and singular value decomposition. *IEEE Transactions on Pattern Analysis and Machine Intelligence, 23*(10), 1120–1136.
118. Macleod, I. A., (1991). A query language for retrieving information from hierarchic text structures. *The Computer Journal, 34*(3), 254–264.
119. McHugh, J., Abiteboul, S., Goldman, R., Quass, D., & Widom, J., (1997). Lore: A database management system for semistructured data. *SIGMOD Record, 26*(3), 54–66.
120. Milo, T., & Suciu, D., (1999). Index structures for path expressions. In: *International Conference on Database Theory* (pp. 277–295). Springer, Berlin, Heidelberg.
121. Navarro, G., & Baeza-yates, R., (1995). Expressive power of a new model for structured text databases. In: *In Proc. PANEL'95* (pp. 1–20).
122. Nishimura, N., Ragde, P., & Thilikos, D. M., (2000). Finding smallest supertrees under minor containment. *International Journal of Foundations of Computer Science, 11*(03), 445–465.
123. Pelegri-Llopart, E., & Graham, S. L., (1988). Optimal code generation for expression trees: An application BURS theory. In: *Proceedings of the 15th ACM SIGPLAN-SIGACT Symposium on Principles of Programming Languages* (pp. 294–308). ACM.
124. Salminen, A., & Tompa, F. W., (1992). PAT expressions: An algebra for text search. *Acta Linguistica Hungarica, 41*(1, 4), 277–306.
125. Schlieder, T., (2002). Schema-driven evaluation of approximate tree-pattern queries. In: *International Conference on Extending Database Technology* (Vol. 1, pp. 514–532). Springer, Berlin, Heidelberg.
126. Shaw, S., Vermeulen, A. F., Gupta, A., & Kjerrumgaard, D., (2016). Querying semi-structured data. In: *Practical Hive* (pp. 115–131). A Press, Berkeley, CA.
127. Sikora, F., (2012). *An (Almost Complete) State of the Art Around the Graph Motif Problem* (Vol. 1, pp. 1–22). Université Paris-Est Technical reports.
128. Tague, J., Salminen, A., & McClellan, C., (1991). Complete formal model for information retrieval systems. In: *Proceedings of the 14th Annual International ACM SIGIR Conference on Research and Development in Information Retrieval* (pp. 14–20). ACM.
129. Umeyama, S., (1988). An eigen decomposition approach to weighted graph matching problems. *IEEE Transactions on Pattern Analysis and Machine Intelligence, 10*(5), 695–703.
130. Verma, R. M., & Reyner, S. W., (1989). An analysis of a good algorithm for the subtree problem, corrected. *SIAM Journal on Computing, 18*(5), 906–908.
131. Wilson, R. C., & Hancock, E. R., (1997). Structural matching by discrete relaxation. *IEEE Transactions on Pattern Analysis and Machine Intelligence, 19*(6), 634–648.
132. Xu, Y., Saber, E., & Tekalp, A. M., (1999). Hierarchical content description and object formation by learning. In: *Content-Based Access of Image and Video Libraries, 1999 (CBAIVL'99) Proceedings IEEE Workshop* (pp. 84–88). IEEE.

CHAPTER 8

GOVERNANCE OF ALGORITHMS IN DATA STRUCTURES

UNIT INTRODUCTION

The purpose of this chapter is to provide a contribution to the development of a greater grasp of governance choice in the context of algorithm selection. Algorithms on the Internet have a role in the creation of our realities and the conduct of our everyday lives. It is their job to first choose the material, then mechanically assign significance to it, saving individuals from drowning in a sea of knowledge. Nonetheless, the benefits of algorithms come with a number of hazards as well as governance difficulties to consider.

According to assessments of actual case studies and a literature study, we shall outline a risk-based approach to corporate governance. This technique analyzes and then categorizes the applications of algorithmic choice, as well as the dangers associated with them. Following that, it investigates the wide range of institutional governance alternatives available and briefly analyzes the many governance measures that have been implemented and recommended for algorithmic selection, as well as the constraints of governance options. According to the findings of the study, there are no one-size-fits-all methods for regulating algorithms.

A growing number of algorithms have been implemented into the Internet-based apps that we use in our everyday lives. These software intermediaries operate in the background and have an impact on a wide range of operations. The ingestion of video and music entertainment through recommender systems, the selection of online news through various news and aggregators search engines, the display of status messages on various online social networks, the selection of products and services in online shops, and algorithmic trading in stock exchange markets worldwide are some of the most visible examples of this pervasive trend. While their purpose and operation modes greatly differ in detail, Latzer et al. (2015) identified nine groups of different Internet services that are dependent on algorithmic selection applications because while their purpose and operation modes greatly differ in feature, all of these applications are categorized by a mutual basic functionality; they all automatically select information elements (Senecal & Nantel, 2004; Hinz & Eckert, 2010).

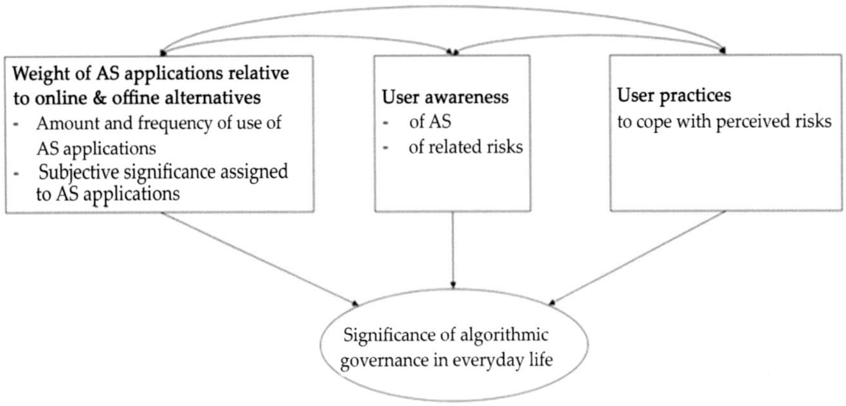

Figure 8.1. Theoretical model of variables measuring the significance of algorithmic governance in everyday life (Source: Beau Cranes, Creative Commons License).

The widespread proliferation of algorithms in an increasing number of fields is one of the key explanations for the rising discussion on the "power of algorithms." The influence of recommendation systems on customer choice in electronic commerce, the effect of Google rankings (Epstein & Robertson, 2013; Döpfner, 2014), and the impact of Facebook's News Feed on the news industry are all examples of this power (Bucher, 2012; Somaiya, 2014) (Table 8.1).

Table 8.1. Illustration of Different Algorithm Types and Their Examples

Types	Examples
Search	General search engines Metasearch engines Special search engines Question and answer services Semantic search engines
Allocation	Computational advertising (e.g., Google AdSense, Yahoo! *Bing* Network) Algorithmic trading (e.g., Quantopian)

Scoring	Reputation systems: music, film, etc. (e.g., eBay's reputation system) News scoring (e.g., Reddit, Digg) Credit scoring (e.g., Kreditech) Social scoring (e.g., Klout)
Content production	Algorithmic journalism (e.g., Quill; Quakebot)
Recommendation	Recommender systems (e.g., Spotify; Netflix)
Filtering	Spam filter (e.g., Norton) Child protection filter (e.g., Net Nanny)
Prognosis/forecast	Predictive policing (e.g., PredPol), Predicting developments: success, diffusion, etc. (e.g., Google Flu Trends, scoreAhit)
Observation/ surveillance	Surveillance Employee monitoring General monitoring software
Aggregation	News aggregators

Source: David Restrepo, Creative Commons License.

The dominance of Facebook's and Google's algorithms stands out in a broader discussion over the economic and social consequences of software in common and algorithms in specific and serves as a notable example. Software, as per Manovich (2013), "takes command" by substituting a diverse array of mechanical, physical, and electrical technologies that are responsible for the creation, allocation, supply, and interaction with cultural objects, among other things (Musiani, 2013; Gillespie, 2014; Pasquale, 2015). In the same way that laws and regulations have controlling powers, algorithms and codes have as well (Lessig, 1999; Mager, 2012).

"The power of technology" and "Increasing automation" have been extensively discussed by a number of journalists and researchers whose primary focus is the role of algorithms and code as agents, ideologues, institutions, gatekeepers, as well as modes of intermediation and modes of mediation (Machill & Beiler, 2007; Steiner, 2012). From the standpoint of intermediation, their role as receptionists and their effect on the development of public opinion, the establishment of public circles, and the building of realities are particularly highlighted. In information societies, algorithmic selection automates a profit-driven reality-construction and reality-mining process (Jürgens et al., 2011; Katzenbach, 2011; Napoli, 2013; Wallace & Dörr, 2015).

Learning Objectives

At the chapter's end, students will get the ability to comprehend the following:

- The basic concept of algorithm governance in data structures
- Understanding risk associated with algorithmic selection
- Learn about governance mechanisms to address the risks associated with algorithmic selection
- Limitations of algorithmic governance options

Key Terms

1. Accountability
2. Algorithm
3. Bias
4. Best Practices
5. Data
6. Decision-making
7. Discrimination
8. Framework
9. Governance
10. Heteronomy

8.1. ANALYTICAL FRAMEWORK

Dangers give grounds for algorithm control; these risks originate from the distribution of algorithmic selection. Governance should reinforce benefits while reducing dangers from a public-interest standpoint (Van Dalen, 2012). Advantages and risks are inextricably linked since hazards jeopardize advantage exploitation. As a result, a "risk-based strategy" (Black, 2010) analyzes and analyzes the risks, as well as the possibilities and constraints for reducing them.

Latzer et al. (2007) have identified nine classes of risk which be associated with algorithmic selection:

i. Manipulation (Rietjens, 2006; Bar-Ilan, 2007; Schormann, 2012);
ii. Restrictions on the freedom of expression and communication, for instance, censorship through intelligent filtering (Zittrain & Palfrey, 2008);
iii. Weakening variety, the formation of echo chambers (Bozdag, 2013) and filter bubbles (Pariser, 2011), biases and distortions of reality;
iv. Surveillance and threats to data protection and privacy
v. Social discrimination;
vi. Violation of intellectual property rights;
vii. Abuse of market power;
viii. Effects on cognitive capabilities and the human brain
ix. Growing heteronomy and loss of human sovereignty and controllability of technology.

There are a variety of governance methods available for algorithmic selection that may help to reduce risks while also enhancing profitability (Figure 8.2). As a result of having various types of resources at their disposal, different actors take different techniques and, as a result, have varying levels of skill. A "governance viewpoint," as it is often understood by scientists, is a valuable lens through which to analyze, assess and improve regulatory policies (Grasser & Schulz, 2015). If we look at governance from an institutional standpoint, there is a continuum that runs from market contrivances on one end of the spectrum to control and command regulation via state authorities on the other end of the spectrum. The middle ground is occupied by a variety of alternate governance modes, which fall into the categories of (2) self-help through single companies; (3) collective self-regulation

Did you Know?

The use of algorithms in hiring and employment has been a controversial topic in recent years, with concerns about potential bias and discrimination in algorithmic decision-making.

with the assistance of industry branches; and (4) co-regulation, which is a regulatory collaboration between industry state and authorities, among others.

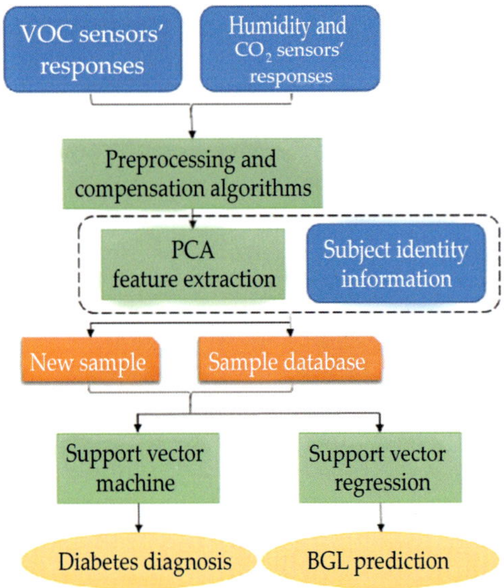

Figure 8.2. Framework of the data analysis algorithms (Source: Ke Yan, Creative Commons License).

For some years now, researchers have been paying close attention to alternate methods to governance (Gunningham & Rees, 1997; Sinclair, 1997), and their findings have been widely published. In particular, their applicability, application, as well as performance in the communications industries are all being investigated. The majority of the time, in a market economy, market solutions are favored over government involvement. However, only when issues cannot be resolved by private activity (subsidiarity) is it necessary for the state to intervene. Nevertheless, it must be justified by the alleged restrictions or failures of market solutions, as well as by the self-regulation of the industry in question. In order to do so, we must make a comparison between the advantages and disadvantages of alternative governance models.

There are two significant pillars that form the basis of this assessment:

1. It is informed by proof of risk-specific measures of governance, comprising previously established and hitherto only proposed interventions. Overall, this exhibits an extensive range of governance options.
2. The evaluation, moreover, rests on a structure for choice of governance (Saurwein, 2011).

For algorithmic selection, there is a range of governance mechanisms that can assist decrease risks while simultaneously increasing profitability. Different actors use different tactics as a consequence of having different sorts of materials at their disposal, and as a result, they have differing degrees of expertise. A "governance viewpoint," as it is commonly referred to by scientists, is a useful lens for analyzing, evaluating, and improving regulatory systems (Grasser & Schulz, 2015). When it comes to institutional governance, there is a continuum that goes from (1) market manipulations on one end of the spectrum to (5) control and command regulation by state authorities on the other. Various different governance systems occupy the middle ground, including (2) self-help through single firms; (3) collective self-regulation with the support of industry sections; and (4) co-regulation, which is a regulatory partnership between state and industry authorities, among others (Bartle & Vass, 2005).

Researchers have been studying alternative governance techniques for some years (Gunningham & Rees, 1997; Sinclair, 1997), and their findings have been extensively disseminated. Their adaptability, use, and performance in the communications sectors, in particular, are all being researched. In a market economy, market solutions are usually preferred above government intervention. However, the state must interfere only when difficulties cannot be remedied through private action. However, it must be explained by the apparent failures or limitations of market solutions, as well as by the industry's self-regulation. To do so, we must compare the benefits and drawbacks of various governance structures.

Did you Know?

Algorithmic decision-making can have intended consequences as demonstrated by the "flash crash" of 2010, when an algorithmic trading program caused a sudden and dramatic drop in the stock market.

8.2. GOVERNANCE OPTIONS BY RISKS

We investigate the governance of algorithms by doing a positive analysis of the mechanisms that have been created or those that have been proposed for managing the hazards associated with algorithmic selection. As a result of the investigation, we have a summary of patterns in the governance of algorithms, which reveals distinct disparities in the selection and grouping of different governance techniques in response to certain hazards.

Some hazards have previously been handled by various ways to governance (data protection), whilst others have yet to be addressed through any means (heteronomy). Certain risks are often left entirely to market solutions (bias). However, for a few others, governance is institutionalized equally by both state and private regulatory mechanisms, resulting in a hybrid governance structure. Though several arrangements and proposals for measures in the form of self-organization through corporations exist, there are only a small number of co-regulatory arrangements in place. Overall, there does not appear to be any overarching institutional framework for managing the hazards associated with algorithmic selection. In spite of this, there is a wide range of currently implemented governance measures, in addition to proposals by policymakers and scholars for more governance measures.

8.2.1. Potential of Market Solutions and Governance by Design

KEYWORD

Virtual private network is a service that creates a safe, encrypted online connection.

For all of the dangers connected with algorithmic selection, specific governance mechanisms are not required. We may also lower risks by changing the market behavior of content providers, consumers, and algorithmic service providers voluntarily. Consumers, for example, might avoid utilizing problematic services by transferring to another supplier or relying on knowledge to protect themselves against hazards. Consumers can benefit from technological self-help solutions, for example. Bias, censorship, and privacy infringement are reduced as a result of such solutions. Clients can use a variety of anonymization techniques, like Virtual Private Networks (VPNs), Tor, or Open DNS, to avoid censorship and protect their privacy. Cookie management, encryption, and do-not-track technologies are examples of privacy-enhancing technologies (PETs) that may be used to secure data (browser). As a result, using chances for de-personalization of services can help to eliminate prejudice. In general, these examples show several choices for user self-protection, although several of these "demand-side solutions" are reliant on and reduced by the availability of sufficient supply (Cavoukia, 2012).

Providers of such services, which are based on algorithmic selection, might mitigate risks by employing commercial tactics. This can be accomplished through introducing product innovations, such as updates to existing services or the introduction of new services. There are various instances of such services that have been developed to avoid copyright and privacy infringement and prejudice. Few news aggregators' business models include content suppliers who are compensated (for example. nachrichten.de). It is possible to minimize privacy problems by using algorithmic services that do not gather user data (Resnick et al., 2013; Krishnan et al., 2014). If these product developments are successful, they may contribute to market variety as well as a decrease in market concentration (Schaar, 2010).

Other examples focus on the technology layout of services for mitigating risks, such as prejudice, privacy violations, and manipulation. "Privacy by design" and "Privacy by default" are two technological methods to enhance privacy. By including serendipity components, services like Reflect, ConsiderIt, and OpinionSpace aim to eliminate prejudice and filter bubbles (Munson & Resnick, 2010; Schedl et al., 2012). Machine learning can significantly minimize bias in recommender systems. Strong self-protection is, therefore, for the suppliers of algorithmic services' own good in order to avoid manipulation. They frequently employ technical safeguards to counteract third-party exploitation. We can see a digital arms race in areas such as filtering, recommendation, and search, where content producers are putting out the effort to prevent problems by applying content-optimization tactics (Jansen, 2007; Wittel & Wu, 2004). Copyright infractions are also avoided through technical self-help (robots.txt files) by content producers.

KEYWORD

Machine learning is a branch of artificial intelligence (AI) and computer science which focuses on the use of data and algorithms to imitate the way that humans learn, gradually improving its accuracy.

8.2.2. Options for the Industry: Self-regulation and Self-organization

Individual enterprises can minimize costs through "self-organization" in addition to technical self-protection and product improvements. Company norms and principles that represent internal quality evaluation in respect to specified hazards, the public interest, and ombudsman programs for dealing with complaints are typical instances of self-organization (Langheinrich, 2001; Cavoukia, 2009). The dedication to self-organization is usually part of a company's overall CSR (corporate social responsibility) strategy. From an economic standpoint, the goal of self-organization is to improve or avoid losing reputation. Service providers whose services are based on algorithmic selection may give to certain "values," like the "minimal principle" of data acquisition. There are also different recommendations for ethical boards at the corporate level to deal with involvement in user experiences or software development concerns (Lin & Selinger, 2014). Companies can create principles as well as observe internal quality control for various hazards such as discrimination, prejudice, and manipulation. Google, for instance, announced the formation of an ethics board. In the context of big data, in-house algorithms have been proposed as a way to oversee big-data operations and as the first point of contact for individuals who feel misled by an organization's big-data activities (Mayer-Schönberger & Cukier, 2013). Unlike individual company self-organization, self-regulation refers to a group of companies/branches working together to achieve public-interest goals through self-restriction. Technical and organizational industry standards, codes of conduct, arbitration and ombudsmen boards, quality seals and certification agencies, and ethics committees/commissions are only some examples of industry self-regulation instruments. There are sectoral self-regulation projects in the marketing business (Europe, USA), online social networks, the search engine market, and algorithmic trading in an extended field of algorithmic selection. These initiatives address issues like copyright and privacy infringement, controllability, and algorithmic transaction manipulation. The stock exchange has implemented warning and monitoring systems to identify manipulation and circumstances when automated trading runs out of hand. Similarly, in the field of online behavioral advertising, there are a number of attempts in the advertising business to improve data privacy (OBA). The Digital Advertising Alliances in the United States and Europe are in charge of this. Various tools, including codes of conduct, general online opt-out boundaries for customers, and certification systems, are part of the projects. In addition, the advertising industry is active in the technological standards for do-not-track, alongside Web browser providers (DNT). Furthermore, industry efforts such as digital rights management systems (DRM) and the creative commons licensing system exist to preserve copyrights on a technological and organizational level. In this instance, "self-regulation" through shared standards tailored to the interests of the business would be appropriate. Furthermore, ombudsmen, ethics commissions, and certification systems appear to be appropriate tools for dealing with the specific hazards of algorithmic selections. Nonetheless, the sector has yet to implement these choices, and it appears that there is a significant amount of untapped potential for self-regulatory governance solutions.

KEYWORD

Data privacy means the ability of a person to determine for themselves when, how, and to what extent personal information about them is shared with or communicated to others.

8.2.3. Examples and Possibilities of State Intervention

The algorithmic selection also poses issues to the state and to political institutions, as previously stated. The limits of market systems, as well as the effectiveness of self-regulation in reducing risks, can serve as explanations and arguments for government involvement. Command-and-control regulation, the provision of public services, enticements in the form of taxes/fees and subsidies/funding, co-regulation, information measures, and soft law are all examples of typical state intervention instruments (Lewandowski, 2014). These instruments are used to increase people's knowledge and awareness of risks in order to encourage appropriate behavior. It is possible to find multiple examples of governmental action in the sphere of algorithmic selection; furthermore, the restrictions are linked to specific hazards rather than a specific technology or a specific industry (Schulz et al., 2005). Individuals in Europe, for example, are protected against automated choices on some personal elements such as work performance, reliability, creditworthiness, and conduct under the European Union's privacy legislation (Argenton & Prüfer, 2012). Another area of ongoing regulatory dispute is the use of search engines on the internet. Google is being investigated by European and American competition authorities due to worries about fair competition. Contestants allege that a search on Google offers an unwarranted advantage to the company's other services, prompting the authorities to launch an inquiry. The majority of proposals for governing activities in the search-engine market call for increased controllability and transparency on the part of public authorities, while only a minority of proposals seek to reduce market entry barriers or establish the principle of neutral search. In order to promote market contestability, aid market entrance, and support healthy competition, it is advocated that the public fund an "index of the web" or user data sets as shared resources (Lao, 2013).

KEYWORD

Quality assurance is any systematic process used to determine if a product or service meets quality standards.

In addition to control-and-command regulation, state actors can employ different modes of interference, like taxes, soft law, subsidies, co-regulation, and information, in addition to control-and-command regulation. The implementation of a machine tax to offset financial losses caused by automation, as well as the introduction of a data tax/fee to reduce the economic incentives for data collecting, have been advocated by a few. In most cases, the state intervenes through the use of monetary incentives. For example, there are a number of initiatives aimed at maximizing the potential of automation in the manufacturing business by encouraging reorganization in the sector. However, financing can also be utilized to assist in the reduction of risk. For instance, the European Union (EU) funds the growth of PETs through its Research and Development initiatives. In the realm of data protection, co-regulation and soft law have also become established practices. Renowned instruments include certification schemes for data protection and quality assurance seals, as well as the Safe Harbor Principles and the Fair Information Practice Principles in the United States, which control data transfers for commercial purposes between the European Union and the United States (Collin & Colin, 2013).

8.3. LIMITATIONS OF ALGORITHMIC GOVERNANCE OPTIONS

The discovery of algorithms' powerful influence ("government by algorithms") has sparked a debate about how to properly control these capabilities ("governance of algorithms"). Google's dominating and influential position, in particular, is regularly challenged (Zuboff, 2014). The administration of internet search is gaining public and regulatory attention (Lewandowski, 2014; König & Rasch, 2014). Disagreements over some search and news aggregation tactics and outcomes have been caused in regulatory legislation addressing privacy and copyright infringement. The German auxiliary copyright is one example (Moffat, 2009) (Figure 8.3).

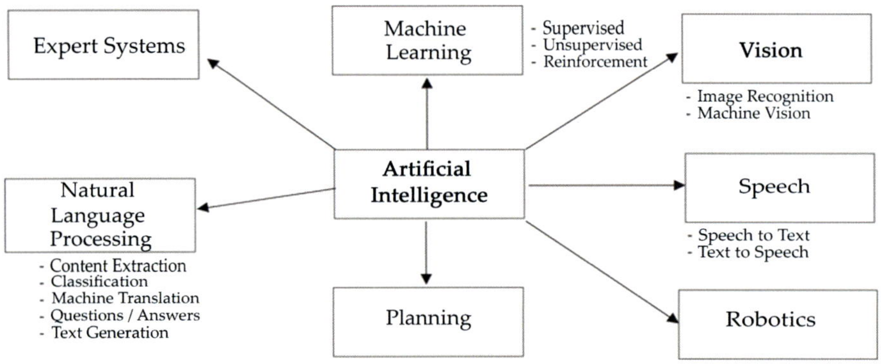

Figure 8.3. Illustration of algorithmic decision systems (Source: David Restrepo, Creative Commons License).

Nonetheless, algorithmic selection's uses and related concerns extend far beyond internet search and Google. As a result, it is critical to broadening the area of study in order to appreciate the broad range of applications, their function, related features, and repercussions for societies and markets, as well as their numerous problematic implications and governance prospects (Latzer, 2007, 2014). This chapter briefly examines algorithmic governance by offering the rationales for algorithmic governance as well as an outline and classification of the hazards associated with algorithmic selection. There are various institutional governance choices accessible, each with its own set of restrictions. We may make a conclusion for our choice of governance based on our tastes and requirements by considering the limits of governance alternatives (Latzer et al., 2015).

In addition to the range of governance measures, the choice of governance must take into account the institutional governance alternatives' boundaries. Contextual variables for governance help to describe the possibility of implementing specific governance systems as well as their suitability in respect to certain hazards

(Saurwein, 2011). Options are implicated by the consideration of enabling contextual elements following the boundaries/limitations of institutional governance.

8.3.1. Limitations of Market Solutions and Self-help Strategies

Consumer self-help measures (switch, opt-out, technological self-protection) can assist in mitigating some of the hazards of algorithmic selection; nonetheless, there are a number of roadblocks to successful self-help; additionally, we must not overstate the capability of user self-protection. Consumers have the option of discontinuing troublesome services or switching to different goods. Algorithmic applications, on the other hand, frequently operate without express agreement. For example, there is no way to opt out of a government monitoring program. Switching service providers need the availability of replacement services; yet, many markets are highly consolidated, and hence switching chances are restricted (Lao, 2013). Due to information asymmetries, the hazards of algorithmic selection are frequently overlooked by customers, resulting in poor-risk awareness. A typical Internet user, for example, is unlikely to notice censorship, manipulation, or bias. As a result, if hazards are not obvious, there is no incentive to seek self-protection techniques (Langheinrich, 2001). Free services, on the other hand, reduce transparency and provide consumers with fewer incentives to switch to lower-risk alternatives. If there are technological instruments for self-defense accessible, they almost often require abilities that the majority of users lack. For example, in the realm of data protection, anonymization necessitates technological expertise and may be challenged by succeeding re-identification. Ultimately, using self-protection or switching tactics needs the availability of alternative services and protective technology. As a result, in terms of access to tools and services, customer options are decided by the supply side of the market (Ohm, 2010).

Remember

Algorithms are not infallible and can make mistakes as demonstrated by the "Siri fails" trends on social media which higlights humorous and absurd errors made by Apple's voice assistant algorithm.

Another way to mitigate the risks of algorithmic selection is to implement supply-side measures (e.g., product improvements), but suppliers, too, suffer constraints when it comes to risk-reduction business strategies. First and foremost, certain market categories have substantial entry barriers, making circumstances tough for newcomers and product improvements. Furthermore, risk minimization might lead to a drop in service quality, resulting in competitive drawbacks. For instance, while services devoid of personalization decrease the potential of privacy violations, they may also reduce the value of the service for users. As a result, "alternative goods" are frequently specialized services with a small customer base. Reduced quality and a small number of consumers reinforce each other, lowering the attraction of specialized services even further.

8.3.2. Limitations of Self-Regulation and Self-Organization

For self-organization, the examination of governance measures at the firm level reveals several choices; however, impediments obstruct voluntary approaches. Implementation is frequently based on incentives, which are the cost and benefits to the firm (London Economics, 2010; Hustinx, 2010). For example, there may be no incentive for robust voluntary standards in the domain of data privacy. Data has been referred to as the "new oil" in the twenty-first century. As a result, it is a necessary source for both service innovation and economic success. As a result, it's improbable that businesses will readily stop collecting data. Several governance solutions aim to improve algorithmic process transparency (Elgesem, 2008). Companies, on the other hand, have little incentive to freely publish algorithms because doing so increases the risk of copying and manipulation. As a result, a "transparency challenge" has arisen (Rieder, 2005; Bracha & Pasquale, 2008; Granka, 2010). Furthermore, a company's willingness to self-organize is influenced by its reputation sensitivity (Latzer et al., 2007). Increased focus on firms in the B2C (business-to-consumer) market, like Amazon, may encourage self-restriction in the public interest. On the other side, reduced public emphasis on B2B enterprises like data brokers reduces reputation sensitivity and, as a result, the reasons for voluntary self-organization (Krishnan et al., 2014).

KEYWORD

Customer base is the group of clients to whom a business markets and sells their goods or services.

The examination of current governance methods reveals a few examples of industrial branches cooperating to regulate themselves (for instance, advertising). In actuality, the activities are limited to specific hazards in well-established and narrowly defined industries, but the overall background requirements for self-regulation are complicated. Self-regulation is hindered most notably by the variety and fragmentation of the sectors concerned. Advertising, news, entertainment, social interaction, commerce, health, and traffic are just a few of the industries where algorithmic selection is used (Lessig, 1999; Jürgens et al., 2011; Katzenbach, 2011). A broad self-regulatory initiative is unlikely due to the great number and variability of the branches. Furthermore, due to the diversity of the businesses involved, self-regulatory solutions for the lowest of standards are not likely. As a result, statutory regulation must be used to establish basic standards that apply to all market participants (Jansen, 2007). Aside from heterogeneity, there are a few other variables that make self-regulation difficult. Self-regulation, for instance, is more expected to occur in established sectors with like-minded market participants. However, the markets for services that depend on the algorithmic selection are frequently experimental and new (e.g., algorithmic content generation), and the algorithmic solution developers are typically novices looking to disrupt established business models and market structures. Newcomers are often on the lookout for fresh opportunities and, as a result, do not always comply with existing industry strategies (Hinz & Eckert, 2010).

8.3.3. Limitations of State Intervention

Ultimately, the study of governance possibilities points to a broad spectrum of prospects for state action in order to mitigate the dangers associated with algorithmic selection, which is encouraging. However, when it comes to the governance of algorithms, the state is not exempt from these constraints. In general, neither every form of risk is well-suited to state intervention, nor is control in particular (Gunningham & Rees, 1997; Grasser & Schulz, 2015). It is difficult for legislative instructions to address risks like cognitive impacts, prejudice, and heteronomy of algorithmic selection since they are so complex. Several examples testify to a lack of practicability and legitimacy in the case of government involvement. For example, in the event of bias issues, the goal of enhancing "objectivity" can be pursued in order to mitigate the problem (Epstein & Robertson, 2013). Aside from that, because several markets are still in their early stages, there is only a limited amount of knowledge available about the future growth of markets, as well as the dangers that may be associated with them. The uncertainty is exacerbated by the fact that threats like "uncontrollability" are unique and that there is little prior experience with issues of a similar kind to those being faced. In addition, because of the complex interdependencies that exist within the socio-technical system, the impact of possible state regulatory measures is usually difficult to foresee. Because of persistent ambiguities surrounding the growth of a market or the impact of regulatory policy, the control of algorithmic selection has been hampered, and as a result, the role of the state has not been decided yet (Gillespie, 2014).

ACTIVITY 8.1

Conduct research on the current state of algorithm governance, including best practices, challenges and emerging trends.

SUMMARY

With the increasing use of algorithms and data structures in decision-making processes, there is a growing concern about how these technologies are governed. The governance of algorithms in data structures refers to the ways in which these technologies are managed, regulated and held accountable. This includes issues such as transparency, accountability, and fairness in algorithmic decision-making processes. The algorithms should be explainable so that users can understand how they work and the criteria they use to make decisions. Algorithms should be designed to avoid bias and discrimination, and to ensure that all individuals are treated equally. Algorithm governance also involves issues such as data privacy, security and accountability. The governance of algorithms in data structures is a complex and evolving field that requires ongoing attention and regulation.

REVIEW QUESTIONS

1. What is algorithm governance and why is it important in the context of data structures?
2. What are some of the key challenges associated with algorithm governance?
3. How can transparency and accountability be ensured in algorithm decision-making process?
4. How can algorithm governance be effectively implemented across different industries and sectors?
5. What are some of the current trends and developments in algorithm governance and what do they mean for the future of this field?

MULTIPLE CHOICE QUESTIONS

1. Why is algorithm governance important in the context of data structures?

a. To ensure that algorithms are used ethically and fairly
b. To increase the speed and efficiency of data processing
c. To reduce the cost of implementing algorithm
d. None of the above

2. What are some of the key challenges associated with algorithm governance?

a. Ensuring transparency and accountability
b. Addressing bias and discrimination
c. Protecting data privacy and security
d. All of the above

3. How can transparency and accountability be ensured in algorithmic decision-making processes?

a. By using open-source algorithms
b. By requiring algorithm developers to disclose their methods
c. By establishing third-party oversight and auditing
d. All of the above

4. What are some of the potential risks associated with algorithm governance?

a. The perpetuation of bias and discrimination
b. The infringement of individuals privacy and rights
c. The misinterpretation of data and flawed decision-making
d. All of the above

5. What is the disadvantage of selection sort?

a. It requires auxiliary memory
b. It is not scalable
c. It can be used for small keys
d. It takes linear time to sort the elements

Answers to Multiple Choice Questions

1. (a) 2. (d) 3. (d) 4. (d) 5. (b)

REFERENCES

1. Argenton, C., & Prüfer, J., (2012). Search engine competition with network externalities. *Journal of Competition Law & Economics, 8*(1), 73–105.
2. Bar-Ilan, J., (2007). Google bombing from a time perspective. *Journal of Computer-Mediated Communication, 12*(3), 910–938.
3. Bartle, I., & Vass, P., (2005). *Self-Regulation and the Regulatory State: A Survey of Policy and Practice* (Vol. 1, pp. 1–22). University of Bath School of Management.
4. Black, J., (2010). Risk-based regulation: Choices, practices and lessons learnt. In: OECD, (ed.), *Risk and Regulatory Policy: Improving the Governance of Risk* (pp. 185–224). OECD Publishing, Paris.
5. Bozdag, E., (2013). Bias in algorithmic filtering and personalization. *Ethics and Information Technology, 15*(3), 209–227.
6. Bracha, O., & Pasquale, F., (2008). Federal search commission? Access, fairness and accountability in the law of search. *Cornell Law Review, 93*(6), 1149–1210.
7. Bucher, T., (2012). Want to be on top? Algorithmic power and the threat of invisibility on Facebook. *New Media & Society, 14*(7), 1164–1180.
8. Cavoukia, A., (2012). *Privacy by Design: Origins, Meaning, and Prospects for Ensuring Privacy and Trust in the Information Era* (Vol. 1, pp. 1–20).

9. Collin, P., & Colin, N., (2013). *Mission D'expertise Sur la Fiscalité de L'économie Numérique* (Vol. 1, pp. 1–20). Available at: www.redressement-productif.gouv.fr/files/rapport-fiscalite-du-numerique_2013.pdf (accessed on 25 April 2023).
10. Döpfner, M., (2014). *Warum wir Google Fürchten: Offener Brief an Eric Schmidt* (Vol. 1, pp. 1–19). Frankfurter Allgemeine Zeitung. Available at: www.faz.net/aktuell/feuilleton/medien/mathias-doepfnerwarum-wir-google-fuerchten-12897463.html (accessed on 25 April 2023).
11. Elgesem, D., (2008). Search engines and the public use of reason. *Ethics and Information Technology, 10*(4), 233–242.
12. Epstein, R., & Robertson, R. E., (2013). *Democracy at Risk: Manipulating Search Rankings Can Shift Voters' Preferences Substantially Without Their Awareness* (Vol. 1, pp. 1–20). Available at: http://aibrt.org/downloads/EPSTEIN_and_Robertson_2013-Democracy_at_Risk-APS-summary-5-13.pdf (accessed on 25 April 2023).
13. Gillespie, T., (2014). The relevance of algorithms. In: Gillespie, T., Boczkowski, P., & Foot, K., (eds.), *Media Technologies: Essays on Communication, Materiality, and Society* (pp. 167–194). MIT Press, Cambridge, MA.
14. Granka, L. A., (2010). The politics of search: A decade retrospective. *The Information Society, 26*(5), 364–374.
15. Grasser, U., & Schulz, W., (2015). *Governance of Online Intermediaries Observations from a Series of National Case Studies* (Vol. 1, pp. 1–23).
16. Gunningham, N., & Rees, J., (1997). Industry self-regulation: An institutional perspective. *Law & Policy, 19*(4), 363–414.
17. Hinz, O., & Eckert, J., (2010). The impact of search and recommendation systems on sales in electronic commerce. *Business & Information Systems Engineering, 2*(2), 67–77.
18. Hustinx, P., (2010). Privacy by design: Delivering the promises. *Identity in the Information Society, 3*(2), 253–255.
19. Jansen, B. J., (2007). Click fraud. *Computer, 40*(7), 85, 86.
20. Jürgens, P., Jungherr, A., & Schoen, H., (2011). *Small Worlds with a Difference: New Gatekeepers and the Filtering of Political Information on Twitter* (Vol. 1, pp. 1–20). Association for Computing Machinery (ACM).
21. Katzenbach, C., (2011). Technologies as institutions: Rethinking the role of technology in media governance constellations. In: Puppis, M., & Just, N., (eds.), *Trends in Communication Policy Research* (pp. 117–138). Intellect, Bristol.
22. König, R., & Rasch, M., (2014). *Society of the Query Reader: Reflections on Web Search* (Vol. 1, pp. 1–23). Institute of Network Cultures, Amsterdam.
23. Krishnan, S., Patel, J., Franklin, M. J., & Goldberg, K., (2014). *Social Influence Bias in Recommender Systems: A Methodology for Learning, Analyzing, and Mitigating Bias in Ratings* (Vol. 1, pp. 1–28). Available at: http://goldberg.berkeley.edu/pubs/sanjay-recsys-v10.pdf (accessed on 25 April 2023).

24. Langheinrich, M., (2001). Privacy by design – principles of privacy-aware ubiquitous systems. In: Abowd, G. D., Brumitt, B., & Shafer, S. A., (eds.), *Proceedings of the Third International Conference on Ubiquitous Computing (UbiComp 2001), Lecture Notes in Computer Science (LNCS)* (Vol. 1(2), pp. 273–291). Atlanta, Georgia.
25. Lao, M., (2013). 'Neutral' search as a basis for antitrust action? *Harvard Journal of Law & Technology, 26*(2), 1–12.
26. Latzer, M., (2007). Regulatory choice in communications governance. *Communications – The European Journal of Communication Research, 32*(3), 399–405.
27. Latzer, M., (2014). *Algorithmische Selektion im Internet: Ökonomie und Politik Automatisierter Relevanzzuweisung in der Informationsgesellschaft* (Vol. 1, pp. 1–19). Forschungsbericht, Universität Zürich, IPMZ, Abteilung für Medienwandel & Innovation.
28. Latzer, M., Hollnbuchner, K., Just, N., & Saurwein, F., (2015). The economics of algorithmic selection on the Internet. In: Bauer, J., & Latzer, M., (eds.), *Handbook on the Economics of the Internet, Edward Elgar, Cheltenham, Northampton* (Vol. 1, pp. 1–25).
29. Latzer, M., Price, M. E., Saurwein, F., Verhulst, S. G., Hollnbuchner, K., & Ranca, L., (2007). *Comparative Analysis of International co- and Self-regulation in Communications Markets* (Vol. 1, pp. 1–20). Research report commissioned by Ofcom, ITA, Vienna.
30. Lessig, L., (1999). *Code and Other Laws of Cyberspace, Basic Books* (Vol. 1, pp. 1–25). New York, NY.
31. Lewandowski, D., (2014). Why we need an independent index of the web. In: König, R., & Rasch, M., (eds.), *Society of the Query Reader: Reflections on Web Search* (pp. 50–58). Institute of Network Cultures, Amsterdam.
32. Lin, P., & Selinger, E., (2014). *Inside Google's Mysterious Ethics Board* (Vol. 1, pp. 1–19), Forbes. Available at: www.forbes.com/sites/privacynotice/2014/02/03/inside-googles-mysterious-ethics-board/ (accessed on 25 April 2023).
33. London Economics, (2010). *Study on the Economic Benefits of Privacy Enhancing Technologies (PETs)* (Vol. 1, pp. 1–20). Final Report to the European Commission DG Justice, Freedom and Security. Available at: http://ec.europa.eu/justice/policies/privacy/docs/studies/final_report_pets_16_07_10_en.pdf (accessed on 25 April 2023).
34. Machill, M., & Beiler, M., (2007). *Die Macht der Suchmaschinen – The Power of Search Engines* (Vol. 1, pp. 1–20). Herbert von Halem Verlag, Cologne.
35. Mager, A., (2012). Algorithmic ideology: How capitalist society shapes search engines. *Information, Communication & Society, 15*(5), 769–787.
36. Manovich, L., (2013). *Software Takes Command* (Vol. 1, pp. 1–30). Bloomsbury, New York, NY.
37. Mayer-Schönberger, V., & Cukier, K., (2013). *Big Data: Die Revolution, die Unser Leben Verändern Wird* (Vol. 1, pp. 1–30). Redline Verlag, Munich.
38. Moffat, V. R., (2009). Regulating search. *Harvard Journal of Law & Technology, 22*(2), 475–513.

39. Munson, S. A., & Resnick, P., (2010). Presenting diverse political opinions: How and how much. *Proceedings of ACM CHI 2010 Conference on Human Factors in Computing Systems 2010* (pp. 1457–1466). Atlanta, Georgia.
40. Musiani, F., (2013). Governance by algorithms. *Internet Policy Review, 2*(3), available at: http://policyreview.info/articles/analysis/governance-algorithms (accessed on 25 April 2023).
41. Napoli, P. M., (2013). *The Algorithm as Institution: Toward a Theoretical Framework for Automated Media Production and Consumption* (Vol. 1, pp. 1–10). Paper presented at the Media in Transition Conference, MIT Cambridge.
42. Ohm, P., (2010). Broken promises of privacy: Responding to the surprising failure of anonymization. *UCLA Law Review, 57*, 1701–1777.
43. Pariser, E., (2011). *The Filter Bubble: What the Internet is Hiding from You* (Vol. 1, pp. 1–20). Penguin Books, London.
44. Pasquale, F., (2015). *The Black Box Society. The Secret Algorithms That Control Money and Information* (Vol. 1, pp. 1–20). Harvard University Press.
45. Resnick, P., Kelly, G. R., Kriplean, T., Munson, S. A., & Stroud, N. J., (2013). Bursting your (filter) bubble: Strategies for promoting diverse exposure. *Proceedings of the 2013 Conference on Computer-Supported Cooperative Work Companion* (pp. 95–100). San Antonio, Texas.
46. Rieder, B., (2005). Networked control: Search engines and the symmetry of confidence. *International Review of Information Ethics, 3*, 26–32.
47. Rietjens, B., (2006). Trust and reputation on eBay: Towards a legal framework for feedback intermediaries. *Information & Communications Technology Law, 15*(1), 55–78.
48. Saurwein, F., (2011). Regulatory choice for alternative modes of regulation: How context matters. *Law & Policy, 33*(3), 334–366.
49. Schaar, P., (2010). Privacy by design. *Identity in the Information Society, 3*(2), 267–274.
50. Schedl, M., Hauger, D., & Schnitzer, D., (2012). A model for serendipitous music retrieval. *Proceedings of the 2nd Workshop on Context-awareness in Retrieval and Recommendation* (pp. 10–13). Lisbon.
51. Schormann, T., (2012). *Online-Portale: Großer Teil der Hotelbewertungen ist Manipuliert* (Vol. 1, pp. 1–10). Spiegel Online. Available at: www.spiegel.de/reise/aktuell/online-portale-grosser-teil-der-hotelbewertungenist-manipuliert-a-820383.html (accessed on 25 April 2023).
52. Schulz, W., Held, T., & Laudien, A., (2005). Search engines as gatekeepers of public communication: Analysis of the German framework applicable to internet search engines including media law and anti-trust law. *German Law Journal, 6*(10), 1418–1433.
53. Senecal, S., & Nantel, J., (2004). The influence of online product recommendation on consumers' online choice. *Journal of Retailing, 80*(2), 159–169.

54. Sinclair, D., (1997). Self-regulation versus command and control? Beyond false dichotomies. *Law & Policy, 19*(4), 529–559.
55. Somaiya, R., (2014). *How Facebook is Changing the Way its Users Consume Journalism* (Vol. 1, pp. 1–10). New York Times.
56. Steiner, C., (2012). *Automate This: How Algorithms Came to Rule Our World* (Vol. 1, pp. 1–10). Penguin Books, New York, NY.
57. Van, D. A., (2012). The algorithms behind the headlines. *Journalism Practice, 6*(5, 6), 648–658.
58. *Wallace, J., & Dörr, K. (2015). Beyond traditional gatekeeping. How algorithms and users restructure the online gatekeeping process. In Conference Paper, Digital Disruption to Journalism and Mass Communication Theory, 1, 33-45.*
59. Wittel, G. L., & Wu, S. F., (2004). On attacking statistical spam filters. *Proceedings of the First Conference on Email and Anti-Spam (CEAS)*. Available at: http://pdf.aminer.org/000/085/123/on_attacking_statistical_spam_filters.pdf (accessed on 25 April 2023).
60. Zittrain, J., & Palfrey, J., (2008). Internet filtering: The politics and mechanisms of control. In: Deibert, R., Palfrey, J., Rohozinski, R., & Zittrain, J., (eds.), *Access Denied: The Practice and Policy of Global Internet Filtering* (pp. 29–56). MIT Press, Cambridge.

INDEX

N

O

P

Q

R